THE BECKONING LAND

BY THE SAME AUTHOR:

SEAL MORNING
GYPSY IDYLL

THE BECKONING LAND

by

ROWENA FARRE

THE VANGUARD PRESS, INC.
NEW YORK, N.Y.

Copyright, ©, 1969, by Rowena Farre.
Library of Congress Catalogue Card Number: 74-134668
SBN: 8149-0685-0

All rights reserved. No part of this publication may be reproduced or transmitted in any form or by any means, electronic or mechanical, including photocopy, recording, or any information or retrieval system, or otherwise, without the written permission of the publisher, except by a reviewer, who may wish to quote brief passages in connection with a review for a newspaper, magazine, radio, or television.

For the purposes of this book, the story of *The Peach Blossom Fountain* on page 48 has been adapted from a translation by Yang Yeh-tzu which appeared in *The White Pony* published by the New American Library, edited by Robert Payne and used here by his permission.

Manufactured in the United States of America.

Find a way or make one
SENECA

CONTENTS

Chapter		Page
1	A Flat in Hong Kong	11
2	A Bowl of Flowers	19
3	A Storm	35
4	The Chinese New Year	45
5	A Room in Lantao	53
6	Birds of Passage	64
7	Walk to a Mountain	72
8	Mountaintop	81
9	Hermits	87
10	Return to Hong Kong	105
11	Mauritius	113
12	Ceylon	121
13	Rooftop	143
14	My Gotra	157
15	The Door is Open	177
16	Two Eagles	183
17	Pilgrim Special	199
18	City of Temples	214
19	A Forest Sage	222
20	Towns along the Way	233
21	Abode of Snow	247
22	An Unknown Land	269

CHAPTER ONE

A FLAT IN HONG KONG

THE LINER MOVED slowly forwards and the foghorn sounded like a blast from a huge conch-shell. Tugs hooted. I leaned against the rail and peered into the mist. In less than an hour I would be disembarking in the Crown Colony all these years later. As the foghorn boomed, I asked myself why it was I had returned.

Superficially, at least, I could answer my own question easily enough; the Orient was in my blood and I simply wanted to live again for a while in some of the places I had known and loved as a child. But that was only part of the reason for my return and the less important part. I did not just want to stay in Hong Kong and, later, on the sub-continent; there would be little point in that. I had returned because of a promise I had made to myself long ago, and I hoped that I was at the start of a voyage of discovery. But what did I hope to discover? I could give no clear answer to this question but only adumbrate it faintly to myself. No matter. Sufficient for the present was the fact that very soon I would be setting foot in the Colony once more on the first lap of a long-planned eastern journey.

When I had left Hong Kong as a child I had said to myself, 'One day I'll come back.' I had said this again on leaving Wei-hai-wei and India. But it would be almost as easy now to take a trip to the moon as to return to Wei-hai-wei.

A lot of water had flowed past the Colony's shores since those faraway days of my early childhood when I had lived with my parents up on the Peak. And a good deal had flowed under my own small bridge.

There came another long reverberating boom.

We passengers leaning against the rail were unable to see anything of our destination. A large junk with batswing sails loomed suddenly out of the mist and almost dashed itself against the prows of the liner. It managed to sheer off just in time and disappeared as suddenly as it had appeared.

Then a patch of fog dissolved to reveal the top of the Peak. The summit was clearly visible against a strip of blue sky and from it streamed a plume of white mist, like a scarf. Moments later, a veil of fog swept it from sight again.

A long 'Ah!' went up from the passengers as they caught this brief glimpse of the island. I thought: Still a siren island in spite of being something of a cheap and vulgar harpy too, trailing your scarf to entice unwary mortals to your shores. The woman standing next to me exclaimed to her husband, "Wasn't that lovely, Eric? The travel agent did tell me before we left England that Hong Kong is called the Fairyland of the Far East. I must say, that was just how it looked to me then!"

I pulled myself together after hearing those remarks. I would indulge in no more romantic imagery about a siren trailing her scarf. Fairyland of the Far East! I did know that whatever else Hong Kong might be it was certainly no fairyland today, if it ever had been. The thought came to me then that when the Peak had made its brief appearance it had looked just like an active volcano—no scarf, but a plume of smoke blowing from its summit giving warning of possible eruptions.

The ship slowed down almost to a stop. Just visible through the fog were the dark shapes of buildings ahead. We were docking at Kowloon. A voice came over the tannoy system telling us that in a few minutes we could disembark. I took my passport from my handbag and began to shuffle along with the rest of the crowd towards the gangway. We were all of us eager to be off and away to our various destinations. I was leaving my luggage on the boat to be delivered to my hotel later.

Down the gangway and through a quick and courteous customs. The first passengers out of the customs' shed had taken all the taxis. A long line of people were waiting patiently for other cabs to come in.

I caught sight of a rickshaw and waved to the coolie, hoping he would see me through the mist. He did, and came over to where I was standing. I told him the name of the hotel where I had a room booked and we set off. "Damn!" someone said in an exasperated voice; "never thought of taking a rickshaw. Seem to have missed the only one going."

The coolie ran at a brisk pace down Nathan Road, the main road of Kowloon. A sudden explosion of crackers almost blasted me from my seat. A new shop had just been declared open and this was the Chinese way of celebrating the event. The coolie was quite unperturbed by the explosion and continued to run at the same even pace, swinging off the main road and into a side-street where the hotel was located. I had booked a room at this hotel for a week prior to leaving England and I hoped that before the week was out I would have found myself a flat, either in Kowloon or over in Hong Kong. I had decided to stay in the Colony for about a year.

I stepped down from the rickshaw and handed the coolie his fare. He asked, "You Old China Hand, missie?"

"Yes," I said, "I suppose in a way I am."

On the day after my arrival in the Colony I went by Star Ferry to Hong Kong. Unlike the previous day, the weather was now sunny and bright.

I looked with delight once again at the animated harbour scene with its moving craft of all kinds. As the ferry progressed over the mile-long strip of water that separates Kowloon from Hong Kong, I remembered some prophetic lines of verse. In the year 1100 A.D., when Hong Kong was a barren island, a Chinese scholar visited it and found a large stone embedded in the earth on which were inscribed these words:—

Across these waters when it's dark a million lights will glow,
And in their paths ten thousand ships will sail to and fro.

The composer of those lines, if not in the front rank of poets, was surely the father and mother of all prophets.

The big skyscraper buildings of the banks loomed ahead. The ferry steered a straight course to the wharf.

I bought an English daily and walked to a cafe that was

situated in the central shopping area. As I sipped a fresh lime squash and ate a sandwich, I read through the section of the paper in which flats for renting were advertised. There appeared to be plenty of flats going, for a price, of course. Living is expensive in the Colony even though it is a free port.

Having read through the advertisements, I went to have a look at the town. I peered into shop windows filled with enticing displays of goods from both the Orient and Occident. Everywhere, in the wide range of locally produced goods and in the milling crowds, I sensed a creative talent and a pulsating vitality, together with a feeling of freedom combined with a lightly imposed order. This was not surprising, as British rule at its best has always combined the quality of freedom with a flexible form of order, together with the British peace. The British peace has gone from the world now but a few scattered remnants of it remained at that time in some faraway places still under British rule, one of them being Hong Kong.

As I was wending my way through the crowds, the words of a Chinese proverb came to mind: If you have two loaves, sell one and buy a flower.

How could I have forgotten! Besides making inquiries about a suitable flat, I had also intended on reaching Hong Kong to buy myself a bowl of flowers, flowers which for me would always have a special significance.

So I set off for Flower Street, that narrow congested thoroughfare on either side of which are stalls crammed with bunches and bowls of flowers. Further up the street, which gets steeper at every yard, there are vegetables for sale; at least, that was how things were in the past, and, so I found, were they still. Throngs of people moved up and down the street. Dogs barked, vendors shouted, and toddlers fed themselves expertly with chopsticks amid all the hurly burly. Yes, Flower Street was just as I remembered it.

I paused at each stall. There were bunches of sweet-smelling frangipani, pots of dwarf rhododendrons, hydrangeas, and expensive displays of flower-heads of various species which had been wired to thin bamboo sticks. People bought these flowering sticks for special dinner parties or banquets. They only lasted a single evening and cost a dollar or so apiece. A Chinese stallholder sprayed some carefully and asked me what I wanted. I told him the flowers I wished for but he had none.

"Plenty of other flowers," he said—"carnation, lily, violet."

I shook my head and moved on to the next stall, but again, the flowers I was looking for were not to be had. And so it was with the rest of the stalls. On the last stall of all was a large earthenware bowl filled with big red peonies, and I decided to buy one or two of these flowers instead.

"Kay taw?" I asked—how much?—using two of the approximate twelve words I knew of Cantonese. I thought the vendor might lower the price a little if he suspected I was an experienced Old China Hand.

"One and a half dollars each peony," he replied in good English, evidently not taken in by my Cantonese. Sixteen Hong Kong dollars equal one pound sterling.

I gasped at the price but I did not feel like bargaining.

"Just one peony, please."

"These velly lucky flowers," he told me, wrapping some paper round the bloom and handing it to me.

Red is held to be the colour of good fortune among the Chinese. I am no great believer in luck myself. I had bought the peony because, the flowers I wanted not being available, I thought it would make a bright splash of colour in my room. If it should bring me luck by way of a suitable flat, so much the better.

Whether it was the peony or my own exertions or a combination of both, I do not know, but I managed to find a flat over in Hong Kong before the week was out. It was situated at mid-level and was in a newly erected block. The paint was still damp on the walls when I inspected it with the landlady, a wealthy Eurasian woman.

"It will be dry before you move in," she assured me.

I took her at her word and agreed to rent the flat for a year.

There are three levels in Hong Kong. Low level consists of the major area of Victoria—the main town on the island—and the harbour and waterfront areas. Mid-level is a kind of in-between area. It includes a part of Victoria which ascends steeply up the a travel agent smiling benignly and saying, 'Well, weren't we right after all?'

There was a distant explosion of firecrackers. I could just make out whirling circles of Catherine Wheels on the taipan's rooftop where the fireworks were being set off. The display culminated in a final flight of rockets whose falling sprays of shimmering sparks changed colour as they fell from gold to emerald, from emerald to mauve, and from mauve to scarlet. It is the custom among wealthy Chinese to give these firework displays to celebrate some auspicious personal event. They can be enjoyed by their own guests as well as by numerous other people in the vicinity.

I stood for a long time gazing down at the scene below me and up at the star-filled sky. It was well past midnight when I reluctantly left the veranda and went to bed.

CHAPTER TWO

A BOWL OF FLOWERS

THERE WAS PLENTY to be done in the flat but I made slow headway. My thoughts kept returning to those years when I had lived on the Peak. I would sit, a half unpacked suitcase in front of me, and drift into a reverie as distant events renewed themselves in my mind.

A Chinese vendor used to live in a small Peak shop. If I had ever known his name I had long since forgotten it. But his name did not matter. I remembered him clearly enough, and I remembered a lesson he had once taught me, a lesson in life. It had stood me in good stead in later years.

He would be gone now, surely, and his little shop too. Death would have taken him or he would have moved away and be living elsewhere, an old man whom I would not recognise even if I did chance to meet him. I wanted, yet did not want, to see the Peak again. Mount Austin Barracks had been pulled down, so I had heard, and new buildings erected in its place. Everything up there had changed. Where there had been trees and gardens and clumps of wild bamboo there were now acres of concrete. Yet I foolishly persisted in hoping that time might have left the vendor and his shop by the road which curled around the Peak, just where they had been when I was living as a child on the Peak's summit in Mount Austin Barracks.

My travels had started early. I was two when I sailed with my parents to Hong Kong where my father, a junior army officer, had been posted with his regiment.

Like most of the other English children, I had an amah, a Chinese nurse. She dressed, like the other amahs, in a white high-collared jacket, white cotton trousers, and her black hair was always neatly done up in a bun.

The electric tram went as far as the lower levels of the Peak, but it did not go right up to the summit on which the barracks was situated. To get there, one either had to walk or one could hire a sedan chair and be carried up by two coolies. Chairs have since been abolished in Hong Kong and rickshaws are on the way out.

Amah and I, after a walk around the Peak, would sometimes hire a chair and be carried up that long steep mile. But, more often than not, we slogged up the hill on foot.

In the mornings we often joined other amahs and their charges at a favourite meeting place on one of the Peak roads. The amahs would chatter together in Cantonese while they minded the babies. Their older charges would play together and run wild, for the amahs were able to exert little discipline. We older children had a marvellous time doing just what we liked, but we seldom went to extremes of misbehaviour. One of our favourite pastimes was trying to catch the brilliant blue butterflies whose wings used to be made into brooches. These beauties have virtually disappeared from the island now.

Not far from where the amahs used to sit was a chalk cliff composed of several colours. We used to pull out bits of this chalk and use it to make drawings on the roadway. A rail edged this road and we would crawl underneath it, jump down and explore the jungly bush country which covered this part of the hillside. There was a narrow pathway, almost hidden by bushes, which led down to the farms and paddy fields at low level.

I would often leave the other children and slip under the rail. I would push my way through the bushes until I reached a clearing encircled by tall bamboos. This was my secret hiding place. Here I would sit alone, often for hours at a time, until I heard amah calling me in the distance. There was a streak of the solitary in me and even then I was something of a hermit by nature.

The ground of the clearing would be patterned by sunshine and the shadows of leaves. I would sit very still listening for the sound of pipes. Sometimes I would hear them and even catch a glimpse of the player in his plumed hat, patched cloak of two colours, tunic and thonged sandals, as he stood there in the dappled glade. The piping would be soft at first, hardly distinguishable from birdsong, but gradually it would increase in volume until the whole glade would be filled with music. I knew who the player was; none other than the Pied Piper of Hamelin.

Robert Browning had written a poem about this strange individual for a member of my family. I happened to know that the well-known poem had been based largely on facts, with a certain amount of poetic licence here and there. It had made a deep impression on me when I had first heard it and, like my forbear for whom it had been written, I learnt it off by heart. It never seemed odd to me that the Piper should visit this eastern glade with its rustling bamboos and that I should hear the sounds of his piping.

The Pied Piper was believed to have been a gypsy. Like many Romanies, he had been able to attract creatures to him by the music he played on his pipes. If the creatures were vermin they would be destroyed.

The town of Hamelin had been infested with rats and the citizens had hired the Piper to get rid of them, promising him a thousand guilders if he did so. A promise is a sacred oath in the gypsies' code of honour and there are few worse crimes in their eyes than to break one.

The Pied Piper duly rid the town of its rats and then asked for his fee, but the mean citizens refused to pay him.

'If that is the case,' he said, 'I shall play a different tune.' And he did. All the children left their homes and followed him out of the town and along a road leading to a mountain. When they reached the mountain a cavern opened up in the side of it into which they walked. It closed behind them and they were gone forever. Only a little lame boy who had not been able to keep up with the rest was left behind. He returned to the town weeping bitterly because he had not been able to follow his companions and the Piper into the mountain. Where had they gone to—down to the bowels of the earth? No, the little boy said to the anguished citizens. The Piper had told them as they marched along that they would walk through a fissure in the mountain and they would step out of the darkness into a beautiful and radiant land which lay beyond. 'Follow me and the sounds of my piping and I'll reveal this land to you, so much brighter than the one you know, and free of all cares and sadness.' The children had followed him and disappeared for good.

Whenever I caught the sounds of his mysterious piping it was as though I myself were transported for a brief while to another sphere, brighter than the one in which my body was sitting. After the music had died away, I would get up and walk out of the wood. The natural world around me would appear less lovely than it usually did and seem peculiarly restricting. This feeling of restriction would lessen as the hours passed, but I would still remember with longing and a sense of loss that radiant and intangible realm which I had briefly visited.

Social life was a gay whirl in the Colony. If there was no party for me to go to in the afternoon and no dancing class, amah and I, after the usual mid-day rest, would take another walk. But on these afternoon walks we did not join any of the other amahs and children.

I had a favourite walk. The preliminary stages of it started off near the rickshaw and chair stand where the coolies waited for customers. Then the road went past a cluster of stalls and shops, after which it began to curl its way right round the Peak and back to the rickshaw stand.

Many areas of the Peak in those days were wild with dense copses of trees and thickets of bamboos, almost impenetrable in places. Cicadas whirred and butterflies in scores of different shades hovered singly and in clouds over bushes and grassy patches.

Quite often when amah and I set off on this walk we did not get any further than the 'shopping centre'. We would spend all afternoon gossiping with the vendors and inspecting their wares. Should amah buy anything, then I might be lucky and get a kumshaw, a free gift; perhaps a tiny paper parasol or little painted figurines, or, best of all, a packet filled with bits of tightly compressed paper. When the snippets of paper were dropped into water they miraculously opened out and became ducks, dragons, boats and lilies. Sometimes the vendors treated us to cups of pale Chinese tea served without milk or sugar.

There was one shop in particular at whose fascinating assortment of goods I never tired of looking. This shop, like the rest, was little bigger than a large-sized cupboard. It was owned by a middle-aged Chinaman who always dressed in the traditional style in a long grey one-piece gown.

In this herbal store was sold all manner of strange things. Hanging from the ceiling were bunches of herbs whose aroma mingled pleasantly with that of the scented joss-sticks, always kept burning somewhere at the back of the shop. Displayed in boxes were tigers' teeth, dried cuttlefish and sea horses, to name but a few of the items. There were bottles containing a glutinous yellow liquid in which floated portions of innards, both human and animal. In one jar was a two-headed mouse, its coat dyed almost black from the liquid preservative, while all four of its beady, malign little eyes were wide open. The sight of this monstrosity used to make me shudder, yet I could never stop myself from taking a quick look at it. On a nearby shelf were sticks of coral and fluted shells, infinitely more pleasant to look at than the mouse. If I pressed a shell to my ear I could hear the murmur of the ocean itself.

One hot and humid summer's afternoon amah and I walked down to the shops. As we rounded the bend of the road I caught sight of my favourite vendor. He was sitting outside his herbal store and fanning himself with a paper fan. Beside him in a bowl were some flowers which I could not remember having seen before. They immediately captured my attention because of their intense blue colour. I ran forward to get a closer look at them and squatted down on my heels beside the Chinaman.

"What are the flowers called?" I asked him.

"Blue poppies," he replied. "They grow wild in the western states of China and in Tibet."

There came the faintest of breezes and the poppy-heads bent and swayed at the light invisible touch.

"They're beautiful!" I exclaimed, enchanted by their delicacy and the almost transparent blue of the petals.

"Watch!" said the storekeeper.

He picked up a twig which was lying on the road and, placing it between thumb and forefinger, pressed it slightly at either end. Immediately, the twig snapped in two.

"Now, watch again," he said.

This time, with a finger, he touched one of the flower stems, bending it right over and down until the head brushed the road. But the stem did not snap and when he removed his finger the poppy swung back to its former upright position.

"Tell me, why did the twig snap but not the stem of the poppy?" he asked.

I muttered something to the effect that it was because the twig was a twig and the poppy a poppy.

"But why did one break and not the other?" he persisted.

Suddenly I knew the answer. "Because the twig was dry and stiff and the stem is supple!"

"That's right. Always bow before the winds of life and swim with the waves, then they will never break you. The ignorant think it's good to be hard and tough, to swim against the tide. Like the twig, they get broken. The wise are sensitive and they bend—like these flowers. They do not break and they reach the farther shore. Remember that."

And I did.

The days of my Hong Kong childhood passed slowly and happily. By all normal dictates I had small cause for happiness, for there were few ties of affection between my parents and myself. They were parents to me in name only. There was always an unease and lack of communication between us. From my earliest years my affections and interests were to lie outside the family circle. But I was happy in those early years; no clouds had yet gathered on my horizon.

One summer my mother and I, along with other army wives and their children, sailed up to Wei-hai-wei for a holiday. It was cooler up there in mid-summer. Husbands and fathers were to follow on later after manoeuvres were over.

Wei-hai-wei (pronounced—Way-hi-way) was a small island

off the northern coast of China, not far from the town of Chefoo, and was situated in the Yellow Sea. It had been turned into a holiday resort by the British. There was an excellent bungalow-style hotel, pleasant bathing beaches, and green downlands studded with twisted Chinese pines. The sparkling sea was never far away.

We children loved Wei-hai-wei. There was a quality about this little island which made it seem not quite of this world. The best of East and West had been blended together to form something unique and rare. There were Chinese houses with upturned roofs, English gardens, old Buddhist temples and, in the distance, other islands set like jewels in the ocean and the great landmass of China itself. I used to tell myself with the certainty of the very young that when I was older I would return to Wei-hai-wei, stay for a while and then cross over to China and journey to the far western states where the blue poppies grow wild. I might even get as far as Tibet itself, the legendary Land of Snows.

We children bathed in quiet inlets and picnicked on other nearby islands, played hide-and-seek in the large hotel garden and crossed over to the mainland with our parents and visited the town of Chefoo. But inevitably and all too soon, the day came when we had to leave this flowery islet and board the ship for home.

We had not been sailing long when we ran into one of the worst typhoons in the history of the China Seas. It sprang suddenly, like a tiger, without warning. I and another small girl were the only two passengers who did not take to our bunks. I was to discover during those perilous days that I was a good sailor.

We two peered wide-eyed at the monster waves through a porthole in the deserted lounge, clinging to a curtain as the ship made its shivering ascent as though straining every fibre to reach the top of a wave, and then started to slide down those menacing watery slopes, a greyish-green under the leaden skies.

We limped into Hong Kong harbour. We had made landfall—just. There was a crowd waiting to greet us on the quay, anxious relatives and harbour officials who had thought we would never get through the storm.

In the East it is believed that all civilised countries have a predominant colour. China's is blue, the deep blue that the peasants used to wear as they worked in the fields and drove the slow-footed buffaloes along the roads. The blue of hydrangeas; the blue of Chinese pottery; the blue of the China Seas. Some shades of blue are warm and dazzlingly beautiful. But there are some which are cold, cruel, even.

Several memories of my early years in the Colony and elsewhere within China's orbit are concerned in some way or other with the colour blue. Some are happy memories and have been personally fruitful; I have gleaned a little wisdom from them. But others are negative or imbued with cruelty or tragedy.

One of the latter kind is connected with my father. The few memories I have of him are nearly all negative ones. I have great difficulty now in conjuring up his face, perhaps because I have no real wish to remember him. He was often in the centre of a crowd and much in demand for social occasions and amateur dramatics. But I did not seek out his company and when he was not around I seldom thought about him.

One evening he and I were sitting on the veranda with its wire baskets of maidenhair fern hanging from the ceiling and its bamboo furniture. He had come in from work and was drinking a cocktail. He put down the glass, opened his briefcase and took out some white sheets of paper and some flimsy blue ones.

"Come over here," he said; "I'll show you something."

He inserted the blue sheets between the white ones and drew a cat, backview. Not being anything of an artist, he found faces difficult to execute. The cat was sitting on a wall, whiskers sticking out, tail hanging down.

"Not a bad effort," said my father, giving his drawing an appraising glance.

He spread the white sheets out on the table. There was nothing on the blue sheets and he put these away again in his briefcase. But on each of the white sheets was a cat sitting on a wall. The only difference in the drawings was that the cat on the top sheet was in pencil while the rest were in blue. I was amazed.

"Well, how do you think I did that?" asked my father, enjoying my evident astonishment.

I had no idea. "Tell me," I begged.

Then a teasing look appeared on his face. This look invariably meant that he was going to proffer nothing by way of an explanation after he had aroused my curiosity in some way. He continued to sit there smiling, not saying a word.

"Oh, please, Father? I'll not be able to sleep tonight if you don't tell me how you did it," I pleaded.

"I'll tell you when you are twelve," he said.

He might just as well have said, 'When you are a hundred,' or 'Never.' I was years and years away from twelve and, anyway, I wanted to know right then.

In bed that night I racked my brains for hours over the enigma of how my father had managed to get a plethora of felines although, as I had seen for myself, he had only drawn one cat. The secret, I felt sure, lay in those flimsy blue sheets. Although I stayed awake for hours pondering the question and staring up at the mosquito netting, I was unable to solve the mystery. Moreover, I sensed deep down that even if I were able to do so by some unlikely chance, the answer to the enigma would not prove revealing but be virtually useless to me, like a handful of ashes.

Years later, when I came to learn how my father had accomplished those drawings by means of the blue carbon sheets—though I did not learn how from him—the knowledge proved to be, as I had previously suspected it would, of no account; just a superficial bit of information which held no inner meaning or value beyond the purely practical.

Amah went on holiday to her relatives in Canton, leaving me in the charge of my mother.

One afternoon she decided to take me for a walk and asked me which way I would like to go. I made a point of never choosing my favourite anything when I was with my mother, for she had a way of spoiling it if I did. So I picked a road I used to take when I went by rickshaw to my weekly dancing class. I neither particularly liked nor disliked this road. My mother thought for a moment after I had made my choice. "No, I don't think we'll go that way," she said. "It's not a very interesting walk."

And she started off in the direction of my favourite walk.

"Come on, hurry up!" she called. "We won't go far—it's too hot. And we'll take a chair back up the hill."

Reluctantly, I followed her. We reached the shops. At the herbal store I stopped, unable to resist showing her the mouse, although I ought to have known better.

"Look, Mother, there's a mouse with two heads in that jar. And in those bottles are pieces of inside—*human* pieces!"

I had a foot in the shop and the vendor was already stepping forward to greet me. Then he caught sight of my mother and his face became as impassive as the face of the meditating god's by the burning joss-sticks.

My mother gave a shriek. "Oh, how horrid! Why did you show it to me? Come out at once. And don't you dare go into this nasty dirty little shop again."

But I often went into the shop again, though I kept my visits a secret from my mother.

I used to ask myself as a child why I had been born to this particular couple with whom I always felt myself to be a stranger. This was always puzzling to me because I believed, as people believe in the East, that birth is no matter of chance and that one picks one's own parents, and vice versa, as well as one's race, country and era. Perhaps it was partly because of this that I I found it easy years later to make a complete break from them and lead my own kind of life.

But although there was never any affinity between my parents and myself, I felt a sense of kinship with certain of my ancestors when I came to learn about them as I grew older.

In the flat next to ours lived a lieutenant and his invalid wife, their two small children and a nurse they had brought out with them from Britain.

Little Mrs. O'Brien, as she was always called by the other wives, had had three children in quick succession. The last one had died soon after birth and little Mrs. O'Brien had nearly died too. Now she lay in bed all day attended to partly by an amah and partly by the children's nurse.

Sometimes I used to go into the O'Briens' flat with my mother, but I used to dread these visits. There was a claustrophobic atmosphere about the place and the smell of the sickroom. The curtains in the bedroom were kept half-drawn and it took one's eyes some seconds to adjust themselves to the twilight.

Little Mrs. O'Brien would be propped up in bed against the pillows and probably working on a piece of embroidery, her pale Irish face framed by a thick black plait like a heavy chain. Religious knick-knacks and paintings were everywhere. She was very devout. From her neck hung a gold medallion and a rosary was often twisted round her thin wrist. Over the bed was a painting of a large carmine heart from which blood dripped realistically against a dark background. Further along the wall was a painting of Christ, his head encircled by a crown of thorns. His eyes gazed upwards in untold agony and rivulets of blood ran down his forehead. There were other paintings of a like kind; tortured martyrs, their bodies wracked and twisted . . . bloodshed, thorns, torture, darkness and agonising deaths in whichever direction one turned. To me, this room was a veritable chamber of horrors and once, unable to stand the atmosphere a moment longer, I turned and fled, much to my mother's embarrassment.

The wives said that Mrs. O'Brien looked just like a little lost angel. They were all very fond of the pale, listless young invalid and used to take it in turns to sit with her and do her shopping down in Victoria. It was whispered among them that she might never recover her health and was doomed to spend the rest of her life in bed.

They were not nearly so fond of her husband Patrick.

"Pat ought to have been shot for getting her pregnant again so soon after the other two," was a remark they often made about him.

So it was his fault, we children concluded, that his wife was so ill and might have to spend the rest of her life as a bedridden invalid. Although our mothers might think her angelic, we children knew that she was certainly no angel. Ill though she undoubtedly was, she should never have allowed the nurse to ill-treat her two small children in the way this woman did.

Nurse Hewlett had the palest, iciest blue eyes I have ever seen. She was a woman who should not have been left in charge of a cat for ten minutes, let alone a child. She used to brutally beat these children, pinch them, terrify them with threats, and generally torment them in a variety of ways which only a sadist could have thought of, and all this more or less openly. Everyone was aware of what was going on under their noses, yet not one of those bemedalled officers or the well-educated wives made any protest at the way the children were being treated, and the terrible nurse stayed on. The officers and their wives used to discuss her over cocktails and refer to her as 'that awful woman'.

Only once, when Nurse Hewlett was smacking the little girl with an almost insane fury in Mrs. O'Brien's bedroom, did I hear the mother utter a mild protest, "Oh, Nanny, that's enough".

Nurse Hewlett administered a few more wicked slaps, then went and pushed a bunch of flowers a visitor had brought into a vase and Mrs. O'Brien carried on serenely with her embroidery. The child, meanwhile, was sobbing hysterically on the floor.

Towards the end of my father's four years posting to the Colony the atmosphere seemed to darken imperceptibly. The skies were still blue; the dark clouds were intangible ones but none the less real for that. They cast a shadow over Hong Kong. When I look back, this shadow seems to presage the darkness that was soon to engulf my own life. The invisible shadows were cast by a tragedy that made world news for a few days. This tragedy did not take place in the Colony itself but on a homeward-bound ship.

One of the difficult decisions married couples with children had to make before leaving the Colony was whether or not to take their amahs with them, if the amah in question was willing to go. If she did go, she would look after the children during the voyage and help get the family settled into their new home before returning to the Colony. In many ways it was better not to take an amah with one but to say good-bye to her in Hong Kong where she was among her own people. The partings between amahs and their charges were often painful affairs and the agony was only postponed if she were taken to Britain or elsewhere.

A young naval couple, due to be posted home, had decided to take their amah with them, mainly because she had requested this herself. They had two older children and a baby boy. We knew them quite well. They were popular in the Colony.

"Amah is wonderful with the children and utterly devoted to baby. She doesn't trust anyone but herself to look after him—not even me! She even calls him 'my baby'," the young wife told friends laughingly when she called on them to say good-bye.

These friends were to recall her words later, but no one at the time, least of all the young wife, seemed aware of their ominous portent.

The couple boarded the ship for home. A few days before the vessel was due to reach Southampton a big fancy-dress party was held on board. The young couple went to say goodnight to their children in the cabin which they shared with the amah, and then went up to the party. That night, as the parents were dancing and the two older children were lying fast asleep, the amah opened the porthole and, with the baby clasped tightly to her breast, worked her way out of it to fall several hundred feet into the sea below, taking with her the child whom she had come to regard as her own and from whom she refused to be parted.

News of the tragedy hit the Colony like a bombshell, and it cast a shadow over the European and Chinese communities alike.

This was my first experience of death coming to persons I had actually known. Whenever I thought about the amah and baby plunging down from the liner at night to disappear without a trace into the waves, I was overcome with a feeling of horror. She and the three children had often been among our group on the Peak road. She had seemed no different from the other amahs, yet she had deliberately committed this terrible act.

Shortly after this tragedy had occurred, my father was given a posting to Singapore. There was a flurry of packing; wooden crates on the veranda and coolies wrapping the glass and china-ware in straw and then nonchalantly tossing the pieces into the crates. Not a single piece was broken during the voyage. The Chinese, whether poor coolies or educated scholars, handle 'things' better than any other race.

There were rounds of farewell parties and endless good-byes.

One morning, a week or so before we were due to sail, I watched my mother and Ah Kum, our Number One Boy, deliberating over the day's menu. Then, when he had returned to the kitchen, I asked my mother whether amah would be coming with us to Singapore.

"No, she won't be coming," my mother replied. "She wouldn't be happy there, so far from all her relatives."

"Who'll be looking after me, then?"

My mother paused a moment before answering, then said, "The O'Briens have decided not to keep on Nurse Hewlett, so I've engaged her to look after you."

I felt stunned.

"You've got very out of hand lately," my mother went on, continuing to jot down items on her shopping list, "Nurse Hewlett will be good for you. She's strict, of course, but you'll have to get used to that."

The day before we were due to sail, Nurse Hewlett took over charge of me from amah. She was quite a young woman, not more than twenty-three or four, and had received her training at one of the leading child-care training schools in Britain where she had gained a diploma. She was ruthlessly efficient and an out-and-out sadist. Her eyes were of such a pale shade of blue, a mere wash of colour, that in certain lights they appeared to be white. In the space of a few days she turned my life into an all too real nightmare.

She was my nurse for over a year and during that time not a day went by when I did not receive some form of brutal maltreatment from her. I used to pray for death to come and release me from the daily tortures, but death stayed away. Then I remembered a small incident of a poppy that bent under pressure and swung upright again when the pressure was released. And I taught myself to bend low, my face to the earth, and I survived. A hundred years later—or so it seemed to me—when this nurse eventually left and went on to another post 'caring' for children, I stood upright again.

Hong Kong, Singapore, Penang, and India. Bugles blowing

from the summit of the Peak and over the torrid plains of Mhow. Then 'home' to England. But if England was home, so too was the Orient. As the liner sailed from Bombay, taking me away from the East and back to the West, I stood by the rail and watched the sub-continent recede into the distance, and I said silently to myself words I had said when leaving Hong Kong, "One day I'll come back..."

And now, years later, I had come back to Hong Kong.
That afternoon I finished unpacking the last suitcase, then took the tram up to the Peak.
There was a smart new terminal, big new buildings everywhere. The rickshaw and chair stand had gone, of course. I walked past modern shops and then along what had been my favourite road as a child. The row of little shops and stalls were gone, vanished into the limbo of time, and in their place were tall modern buildings. Although I had known before coming up that this would almost certainly be the case, I was unable to restrain a pang of deep disappointment when I saw with my own eyes that they had indeed gone.
I walked on in brilliant sunshine but I had been seized by a mood of dark depression.
Presently, to my surprise, the road began to look much as I remembered it; the buildings gave place to spinneys of trees and bamboos. I came to the spot where we children and our amahs used to congregate. A little further along was the chalk cliff, bits of which we used to pull out and use as crayons.
I leaned against the rail bordering the road and gazed down at the cultivated land miles below, the bright green paddy fields and the farms, and beyond them the road leading into Victoria with traffic speeding along it.
On an impulse, I climbed under the rail and jumped down. Then I began to hunt about the bushes for the track. At last I found it, a narrow pathway overhung with branches. After a winding start, the path began to lead steadily downhill and in an hour or so I emerged from the forest and found myself in the open with a paddy field and a farm just ahead.

A fierce pi-dog came racing towards me. Two peasant women standing knee-deep in mud with rice-shoots in their hands looked up and called the dog off.

I walked past the farmhouse, a low white building with a slate roof, small but solidly built. A buffalo was roped to an old gnarled tree and there were several ugly slump-backed pigs rooting in the ground nearby. In the vegetable garden were neat rows of chokoes, tomatoes, kale, and bok-shaw (Chinese cabbage). How secure the lives of these farming folk seemed in comparison to those of the refugees in their hillside shacks and on the crowded rooftops of Wanchai.

This brief glimpse of pastoral life was quite refreshing. There is little enough of it in Hong Kong today, where the majority of the populace work in shops and factories.

I took a taxi back to the flat.

My mood of depression had lifted. Although time had swept away the row of little shops, I had at least managed to find the hidden track again and make my way down it. This small discovery had buoyed up my spirits and dispersed the cloud of gloom. It had given me the renewed hope that, because I had found this hidden pathway, I might—though goodness knows how—come across the Chinese herbalist again amongst the milling crowds of the Colony and, somehow recognising him, renew my acquaintance with this man. I had sensed there was something unique about him when I was a child, and the lesson he had taught me long ago, seemingly so trivial, had enabled me to survive one of the darkest periods of my life and to live more simply and naturally during the everyday and bright periods than I would otherwise have done.

CHAPTER THREE

A STORM

ONE EVENING I went to a lecture given by a Chinese artist. He talked about a subject familiar to most persons who have spent some time in the Orient, the 'spirit of the bamboo'.

"The prime object of the Eastern artist," said Mr. Chan, "when painting a spray of bamboo leaves or any other object—a rock, a man, a bird—is to try to capture the elusive essence of that thing. If the artist does so, then he has succeeded in his aim. If not, then no matter how beautiful or technically good the painting may be, he has failed. To discover the essence of things—the spirit of the bamboo—and make that potent yet elusive quality manifest in the painting should be each artist's constant endeavour."

I talked to him after the lecture and some days later he came to my flat and looked at a few of my paintings.

"This one," he said, holding up a seascape, "is not quite balanced from the Chinese point of view. As well as trying to capture the 'spirit of the bamboo', the Oriental artist has another aim; it is to make every object in his painting a part of the whole. Nothing in the painting must stick out like a sore thumb or be under or over estimated. You have given undue prominence to the human figure and made the ship and the sky appear relatively unimportant."

He unrolled some paintings he had brought. Most of them were reproductions of works by famous Chinese artists. He spread one out. It depicted a vast plain across which rode the tiny figure of a man on a buffalo. In the sky was a vee of geese and in the distance a range of mountains.

"Here you can see for yourself what I mean. Everything falls into place; every object is in balance and harmony with the rest. The man on the buffalo is not given undue prominence and neither are the geese or the mountains. The uniqueness of each object is clearly revealed, yet one does not overshadow all the rest. Do you like the painting?"

"I think it's superb," I said.

"Then I'll give it to you. It shows the Sage Lao Tzu riding off into wild border country. When he saw the confusion and disintegration that was taking place in his state, he left it and never returned. It is not known where or when he died."

"If Lao Tzu had been living today in the turmoil of our modern world, I wonder where he would have gone in order to find peace and quiet?" I said. "There are not many places left where these qualities exist."

"You are right. Disorder and upheaval seem to be everywhere. But I'm sure that Lao Tzu would have discovered some place where a spirit of harmony still prevails."

I cellotaped the reproduction on to the living-room wall. Whenever the noise in the street threatened to set my nerves on edge I had only to look at it to become more serene; wild untamed country, a wise old man on his buffalo, and in the sky, geese winging their way to some unknown destination, like the man below them who was riding off into nameless territory.

I had forgotten how cold it could be in Hong Kong during the winter months. The temperature kept dropping and the wind, which often blew for days on end, felt as though it had come straight from the icy steppes of Mongolia. On many of these winter days there was a lashing rain as well which was swept horizontally along the streets by the relentless wind.

This spell of cold weather was particularly grim for the homeless. They would creep into any cranny they could find. At nights volunteers belonging to various Christian organisations would be out and about looking for the homeless and distributing blankets and cups of hot soup to them.

On a 'ladder step' near my flat an elderly refugee was camped for some time on one of the stone platforms which are built at intervals on these steps. Here people can rest a while before continuing their upward or downward journeys. This man's 'home' was a large black umbrella, the handle of which he had stuck through a crack in one of the flagstones. He would hold out a tin begging-bowl to people as they passed. He was there for about a week during one of the coldest and wettest periods of that winter. Then he was gone, perhaps moved on by the police. Later, I saw him again. He had found a hole in a wall into which he and his half-opened umbrella just fitted. His bowl and few belongings were spread on the pavement below.

In spite of the hardships which many refugees undergo, particularly during periods of cold and drought, one sees or hears of few cases of actual starvation or death from exposure.

The cold spell continued into late January when, to add to life's difficulties, there was a storm of titanic proportions. It lasted a week and began with a howling wind, so fierce that I wondered whether a typhoon was on the way. Then came the rain. There is an English saying to the effect that wind and rain do not come together. This does not apply in Hong Kong, where wind and rain nearly always do come together, often with calamitous effects.

The rain started to fall from the sky as though a floodgate had been opened. The streets were soon deserted, not only of pedestrians but traffic too. Before long they were several inches deep in swirling water. Announcements came regularly over the radio warning people not to go out unless on some errand of dire necessity; not to take their cars out; that a certain street was now impassable due to flooding, another blocked by fallen debris; a house had collapsed and three people been killed; that the storm was continuing unabated—keep in!

I inspected my storecupboard and found it nearly empty; the weather had caught me unprepared. As the storm looked as though it would be raging for days to come, I would be going hungry unless I could get some food in. But it was next to impossible to go out and buy any. I picked up the phone and rang a store in Victoria.

"Could you send me—" I began.

"Whereabouts are you, madam?"

I gave my address.

"Sorry, madam. We are sending no delivery van to your area; many streets are impassable there."

So that was that. Then I remembered that I had thrown a lump of stale bread into the pig-bucket. I took it out, wiped it and put it on a plate. In the cupboard was an almost full packet of tea, plenty of sugar, and a tin of powdered milk, so at least I would be able to make myself cups of tea for some days yet. Tea and rationed slices of stale bread would have to keep me going until the storm abated.

I left the radio on so as to make sure of hearing any further announcements regarding the 'inclement weather', as one announcer had tactfully described the storm.

"It may interest listeners to know," came a voice, "that water rationing has now ended and the water will be on throughout the day and night until further notice."

Well, count your blessings! I hoped everyone would appreciate their good fortune.

There came the first flash of lightning, followed by a rumble of thunder. The lightning flickered out like a damp firecracker. But before long both thunder and lightning were continuous; never more than a few seconds elapsed between the flash and reverberating crash and then came a prolonged ripping sound as though some giant were tearing the heavens apart. Behind the explosions of thunder, like a backdrop of sound, was the continual roar of the torrential rain.

That first night after the thunder and lightning had started I closed the bedroom windows and drew the curtains right across them, then lay down and buried my head in the pillows. But the lightning flashes were so brilliant that even with the curtains drawn the room was lit up by a continuous vivid flickering. The thunder sounded louder than ever. It was quite impossible to sleep. When I got up in the morning, dog-eyed and weary, the storm, if anything, had increased in fury.

I turned on the wireless, but the crackling sounds made me turn it off quickly. Likewise, when I picked up the phone, crackles and sparks seemed to jump out of the handpiece. From then on it rang unanswered.

There I was in the flat, virtually marooned and cut off from the outside world. I did not need any radio announcement to tell me that the street below was impassable—a glance from the window was all that was necessary to tell me that. The street itself was not visible, it lay under several feet of dirty swirling water on which various objects—an orange box, dead hens, and a frantically paddling dog—made their appearance as I looked at the storm-swept landscape and blinked as lightning zig-zagged across a darkened sky. The force of the rain was so strong that as it lashed against the panes I was afraid some of them might break. I moved away from the window and went and sat on the far side of the room.

Presently, my brain dully registered that someone was hammering on the door.

Standing outside were two policemen and the young Englishwoman who lived in the flat below mine, a Mrs. Judy Vogel, whose husband Derek worked in one of the big Hong Kong trading firms.

"May we come in?" she shouted.

"Please do," I shouted back.

"We may have to move out."

"What?"

One of the policemen steered me to the window and pointed to a white block of flats situated directly above ours about half a mile up the hillside. It was a pale blur but still discernible through the driving rain.

"That block has been declared unsafe," he told me. "The occupants are having to leave straightaway. The foundations of the block have been undermined by a landslip and it may collapse. If it does, it will come crashing down the hill in your direction, as you can see. But there is no need for people here to move out yet. We'll warn you later if that becomes necessary. But get a suitcase packed."

The police left and Judy and I stood looking at each other.

"Isn't this ghastly?"

"Perfectly frightful!"

"Are you alright for food?" she asked.

"I've hardly got a thing," I said.

"I'm just dying for a cup of tea but I'm right out of milk powder."

I beckoned her into the kitchen. To keep trying to make oneself heard above the noise of the thunder was too much of a strain on one's vocal cords and sign language was less exhausting. I handed her a bowl into which I had emptied some milk powder.

"Wonderful!" she cried. "I think I'll be able to survive, now I can make myself a cup of tea. Come on down. I can give you a little food. Not much, I'm afraid."

She gave me some flour, a bit of margerine and a few vegetables.

"Don't forget to pack a suitcase," she reminded me. "I'll let you know at once if there's any more news from the police."

I turned on the cooker and started to sing—things were looking up. I began to rub some fat into the flour as a start to making a batch of scones. Lunch: some piping hot scones, vegetable stew and a pot of tea, a heart-warming prospect. I cut the scones out neatly and placed them on a baking tray, then opened the oven door. The oven was stone cold. . . . I rushed to the electric light switch and clicked it on—no light! The electricity had been cut off. My morale started to rapidly evaporate and tears welled in my eyes.

There came a wail from outside my front door and when I opened it, there was Judy again.

"I've just found out that the—"

"And so have I!"

She sank on to the sofa, a figure of stark despair. We commiserated a while with one another, then she went downstairs again. It was not possible now to even have a reviving cup of tea because, with the electricity off, I could not boil up a kettle of water. Lunch: a cup of cold water and a few mouthfuls of bread which had by now reached the consistency of granite.

Word came later from the police that we could stay in our flats for the night, but they advised us to go to bed fully clothed just in case it became necessary to make a quick getaway. They would come and tell us if they considered this to be necessary.

So that night I lay on my bed fully dressed in slacks and a blouse, with a packed suitcase close at hand. My nerves were strung taut by the thought that at any minute it might be necessary to make a dash from the building out into the darkness of the flooded street. But the night passed uneventfully and when I looked out of the window next morning the block of flats high up on the hillside was still standing.

The advice from the police that day was the same as for the previous one; go to bed dressed for a possible emergency.

So again I stretched out on the bed fully clothed. The storm seemed to have reached a pitch of unprecedented fury. The room was a-dazzle with lightning flashes, thunder rolled back and forth across the sky and exploded overhead, while rain continued to fall like a Niagara. I was exhausted but I could not sleep. Halfway through the night I got up, thinking that perhaps I might feel better moving about instead of lying sleepless on the bed.

As I was looking through the kitchen window at Victoria down below, the town lit up in the unearthly glare of lightning and swept by cascades of rain like huge waterfalls, I thought I discerned something a little different about the noise of the thunder. *Was* it thunder? The roar, growing louder every moment, struck me as being more like the sound of an erupting volcano than the crash of thunder.

The stupendous volume of noise was coming from the other side of the building. Then I remembered—the flats above ours must have collapsed and were hurtling down the hill! No time to put on a mackintosh or seize the suitcase. I dashed from the flat and almost into the arms of Judy's husband, Derek.

"Quick—for God's sake!" he gasped, pushing me downstairs in front of him.

Judy was just ahead of us. We stumbled and leapt down the darkened stairway. The noise was cataclysmic. I could feel the passageway vibrate under my feet. Perhaps it would be wiser to stay under cover. But Derek pushed me and Judy out into the street. In less than seconds, water rose almost to my thighs. I plunged forward amongst a crowd of frightened people. Noise was all around us, almost on top of us it seemed, as we struggled to make headway through the black, swirling waters.

I thought, 'We've left it too late.' But I plunged on instinctively with the rest. I saw Judy's blonde head for a moment, then lost sight of her in the chaos of the night.

There came a crash which seemed to knock all the teeth from my head. A huge volley of water shot up into the air, lit by lightning, and it was followed by the sound of falling rocks and earth.

The floodwaters made progress difficult but we eventually reached a part of the road which had been lined with trees and a grass verge, below which was a steep drop. Parts of the road here had disappeared along with many of the trees. One tree was lying half submerged, blocking our path. Water poured in a dangerous flood over the side of the damaged road. I clutched a branch, my feet groping for a foothold, as I struggled to climb over the trunk. There came an agonised shriek a short way ahead. I glanced up to see a figure vanish over the side of the road.

From then on everything assumed a nightmare quality. There were moments when objects around me took on an extreme vividness under the flare of lightning. And there were moments of blankness when I waded on through confusion and terror in a curiously dreamlike way.

The next thing I clearly remember was reaching the main road which winds up from low level to the Peak. Over to my right, then, must be the Botanical Gardens. With this knowledge of my whereabouts came the realisation that I could only walk a short way further. I had reached the limits of my physical endurance. I found the steps which led upwards into the gardens and I pulled my way along with the aid of overhanging branches.

The gardens did not appear to be so badly flooded as the roadway below. I found a bench under some dripping foliage and sat down, completely exhausted.

Dawn broke slowly and the flashes of lightning became less vivid. Everything about me was in varying shades of grey; the sky, the trees, the sweeping rain. Just ahead of me was the lily-pond on which floated rare blue waterlilies, their blue turned to grey now like everything else. This pond was enclosed by a low stone parapet. If grey was the colour of everything, then wetness was the state of everything, including myself. Water poured in rivulets from the top of my head down to my bare and muddied feet. My clothes gripped me in a wet and cold embrace. I sat there, my eyes closed, feeling the water trickle down my cheeks. When I opened my eyes and looked at the pond the lilies had turned to blue and the sky was a light pearly grey, the colour of an oyster shell, strangely beautiful, whereas a few minutes ago it had appeared ugly and glowering.

The lilies rested on the water like points of blue flame. I stared at them, every thought knocked out of my head by the events of the last few hours.

An old man approached the pond from out of the concealing grey bushes and sat down on the parapet. He was grey too; grey hair, a grey beard, and he was dressed in a long grey gown with flowing sleeves. He sat there, still and serene, looking at the lilies. Then he bent forward and touched one of them gently. At the sight of this graceful gesture I felt a sense of shock, as though I had been struck by a tongue of lightning. My mind started working again and I asked myself where had I seen this old man before, and blue waterlilies, blue? . . . I closed my eyes in an effort to concentrate. When I opened them again the old man had gone. But the lilies were still there and bluer than ever in the early morning light. I struggled to remember some connection between them and an earlier experience, but it was no good; my mind was unable to make the long jump backwards in time.

I set off home to what I hoped would still be a flat and I breathed a sigh of relief when I saw that our block was still standing. In the middle of the road, a short way beyond it, was a rock about the size of a two-story house. It was this rock which had come thundering down the mountainside, not the block of flats above ours, and it had flattened everything which had lain in its path, including a house, fortunately empty at the time.

The floodwater was subsiding. The storm had finally run its course.

I wearily climbed the stairs. By a fluke, I had left my front door open as I had raced from the flat and so was able to get in. I took a quick look round, but no one had entered during my absence, apparently, and made off with any of my belongings.

The thunder was now only an occasional distant rumble. I heard Derek and Judy returning.

When I stepped out on to the veranda to see if there was any nearby damage, the sky above me was so clear it appeared as though no rain had fallen from it for weeks.

And my mind had cleared, too. I suddenly remembered the connection between the old man who had touched the waterlily and the herbalist of years ago who had bent the stem of the blue poppy. Were they one and the same man? Surely! The graceful gesture, the traditional style grey gown, the blue flowers all hinted that this must be one and the same person. He was still alive! I knew some minutes of intense happiness. But what a fool I had been not to have stepped forward and greeted him. Now he was gone. Yet I felt confident that I would meet him again later somewhere.

The minutes of elation passed and doubts began to cloud my mind. I could not help but recall my state of battered exhaustion as I had sat in the gardens, and I began to wonder whether the old man by the pond had been just a figment of my imagination—an unreal mirage projected on to the grey screen of the atmosphere by my own mind. Yet I was loath to dismiss the old Chinaman I had seen as some unreal ghost. Whether the scene in the Botanical Gardens had been real or unreal, it had been altogether too vivid to be meaningless. I felt I had received an important message.

I went inside and took my passport from a drawer and looked at the date stamped in it by the customs official, the date of my arrival in the Colony. I saw from it that I had been in Hong Kong now for over three months. Three months had slipped by and I had hardly heard them go.

I took stock of my situation. I had enjoyed my return visit to the Colony but my life here had seldom risen above the mundane. Was it for this kind of life that I had returned?

No. That being the case, what should I do and where should I look? I asked myself. I had no more idea now than when I had arrived three months ago.

CHAPTER FOUR

THE CHINESE NEW YEAR

THE LAW OF averages ought to work better than it does. After that storm the Colony deserved at least a few months of calm during which the inhabitants could recover their equilibrium. But hardly had mopping-up operations been completed than the unfortunate residents had to brace themselves to meet four shattering days and nights of continuous explosions—the non-Chinese residents, I should say. The storm had been a natural disaster. What lay ahead of us was in the nature of a man-made din, a yearly orgy of noise: the Chinese New Year.

In the Chinese shops were displays of fireworks ranging from the usual crackers to varieties with ominous names such as atomic rocket, red butterfly bomb, super-charged squib, and ten-thousand dragons blast bomb. I viewed these displays with trepidation.

In the Western shops were displays of a different order. Notices in chemists read: Have you bought your ear-plugs and tranquillisers yet? On the counters were bottles of aspirin and tranquillisers as well as soothing medicine for the family pets. Undosed cats and dogs are liable to go beserk during this trying period.

Red and gold became the predominant colours everywhere. Tradesmen handed one red and gold envelopes in which one was expected to put some money. Scarlet lanterns hung from shop doorways. Red paper dragons, some of them fifty feet long, were being completed by craftsmen for the forthcoming dragon dances.

As New Year's Day drew close people in the streets started greeting one another with "Kung Hei Fat Choy," 'the season's greetings to you'.

I got in a supply of provender, aspirins, and reading material. The non-Chinese section of the populace, all those who can manage to do so, stay in, and I had every intention of doing the same. They swallow tranquillisers by the bottleful and plug their ears. For myself, I intended to live like a hermit during this time and catch up on some reading.

The reason for letting off a barrage of fireworks at the New Year is to scare away any devils lurking in the vicinity and so start the year free of their evil presence, not that many people take devils seriously these days. The festival now is just an excuse for a lot of noise, fun and frolic. Most of the non-Chinese residents fervently wish that they could emulate the devils and flee for quieter climes during this four-day period, but there is nowhere quiet within a reasonable distance to go to.

Late February drew near. On the day before blast-off the market stalls and Flower Street were full of peach blossom, the flowers with which all Chinese homes and shops are decorated during the New Year celebrations.

I bought a few sprays and arranged them in a tall vase. Then I closed the door of my flat firmly, determined not to open it again until the celebrations had ended. Before long, someone was knocking on it and ringing the bell. I took no notice. A red envelope was pushed under the door. Whoever had pushed it through would doubtless return in due course to collect it.

At the stroke of midnight a cannon was fired and the start of the New Year was announced with the first explosion of fireworks. The cannon-fire was like the bark of a sickly dog in comparison to the blasts of exploding rockets and strings of crackers. From midnight on there was not to be a second's respite from the barrage of noise until the celebrations ended. It was like the storm all over again, only this time my nerves were not in such a good state for withstanding the din. I started swallowing aspirins soon after the bangs, whooshes, crashes, and rat-a-tat-tats of exploding firecrackers had commenced. In the street below, on the rooftops, up in the sky, down in the city, the explosions formed a continuous eruption of non-stop and nerve-racking sound. As during the storm, sleep once again became an impossibility, and I found it difficult to concentrate on the most trivial task.

The books and magazines, bought to occupy my mind during this period, remained unopened.

On the third day of the festivities I stretched out on the sofa determined to read at least one chapter of a book, and I opened a volume about some Chinese poets. It says much for these poets that in spite of the ear-splitting din I did manage to become absorbed in their lives and verse for several hours. They were strange yet human persons. Although most of them had lived centuries ago, I felt a bond with many of them. The ones who interested me most had all lived during periods of wars and upheavals such as our own epoch, and many had been wanderers like myself.

There was the extraordinary Li Po, whose birthplace, date of birth and parentage are unknown and who was named after the white star Venus. He called himself a phoenix, and like the English poet and visionary Blake, he would talk in a matter-of-fact way of his meetings with angels and fairies. His was a spirit of freedom walking in a war-torn land. For long periods he would disappear and even his close friends would not know where he was. His poetry is like the flash of lightning. One evening while boating on a lake he was summoned by angelic hosts. His soul was carried to its celestial home on the back of a dolphin and his body was buried near a river. There is nothing to mark his grave except a small mound in an endless sea of grass.

> If you ask me—he wrote—why I live among green mountains,
> I should laugh silently; my soul is serene.
> The peach blossom follows the moving water;
> There is another heaven and earth beyond the world of men.

A friend of Li Po's was Tu Fu, A.D. 713–770, considered to be the greatest of all Chinese poets. The two were completely different characters. Whereas Li Po was flamboyant and sociable, Tu Fu was quiet and retiring.

Tu Fu, like his brilliant friend, knew wars and famine, poverty and corruption. Yet his poems are as calm and free from bitterness as though a god had written them, and he was able to extract the essence, the 'spirit of the bamboo', from everything about which he wrote. In early manhood he started to travel and from then on he seldom ceased from wandering. He died at the age of fifty-nine. The world had never tamed him.

Li Po described himself as a phoenix but Tu Fu liked to imagine himself as:

> The seagull who plays on the white waves,
> And flies to heaven, superb and tameless.

Both these poets were strongly influenced by a much earlier poet whose name was Tao Yuan-Ming. He was born about A.D. 373 and died in 427.

This poet spent most of his days living on a remote farm. He had the soul of a hermit and many of his poems are painted in quiet colours and speak of silence. But underneath the poems' rather colourless exterior runs a deep vein of passion.

This nightingale lived in times of change and confusion. The barbarians had over-run the northwest; civilisation was threatened. But unlike many Taoists, he did not seek refuge in a remote mountain fastness. He remained on his farm, tilling the soil and writing verse.

Tao Yuan-Ming's most famous piece is not a poem but a short tale, little more than a page in length; a brief, enigmatic story which, though prose, could only have been written by a poet. The theme, one much loved by Taoists, is that of the 'return to the source.'

In view of the story's title, I felt that it was an appropriate piece of reading for the Chinese New Year, symbolised as it is by the peach flower, some sprays of which were in front of me.

Here is the story:

The Peach Blossom Fountain

During the reign of T'ai Yuan of the Tsin dynasty, a fisherman of Wu-ling was pushing his boat up a stream, forgetting to notice how far he was going. Presently he came upon a forest of peach trees that lay on either side of the riverbank. The petals were continuously falling from the branches into the water like some floral fountain. Wondering at the place he had come to, the fisherman went on to find out where the forest ended, and he found that it ended at the source of the river. There he saw a mountain in which was a small cave with a crack of light gleaming beyond.

He left his boat and went through the opening of the cave. It was so narrow that he had difficulty in squeezing through, but after a struggle, he found himself in broad daylight.

Ahead of him lay open plains and farmsteads, paddy fields and enchanting lakes, mulberry trees and other countrylike things. Paths threaded across fields. He heard cocks crowing and dogs barking and he saw men and women walking about. They wore clothes exactly like those worn by people outside. The old men had white hair and the young men wore their hair in loops. All the people appeared joyous and contented.

But when these men and women saw the fisherman, they became alarmed and asked him where he had come from. He answered all their questions as best he could. They invited him into their homes, brought him wine and killed chickens for his supper. Soon other villagers heard about his arrival and came to enquire about him.

When the fisherman in his turn questioned these people, they replied that in ancient times their forefathers, in order to avoid the disasters that fell on the Ch'in dynasty, had fled with their children and neighbours to this secluded land. They never came out again, and so they became separated from the outside world. They asked him who was reigning; they had never heard of the Han dynasty, still less had they heard of Wei and Tsin. The fisherman told them all he knew. They sighed to hear it, deeply moved.

Each in turn invited the fisherman into his home and served him a meal. After staying several days, he bade them a reluctant farewell. The people said to him before he left, "There is no point in speaking of us to outsiders."

When he came out of the cave, he found his boat where he had left it and returned along the way he had come, all the while attempting to remember landmarks.

When he reached the city, he went to the governor and related his story. The governor sent some men to go with him. They searched for landmarks, lost their bearings, and never found the way to the place.

As time went by, the fisherman came to realise that although the people in that secluded land had seemed much the same as the Wu-ling folk, there was a difference between them, a difference that was not only in the people. It was as though everything in that unknown land had undergone some subtle transformation. And he often regretted having ever left the place.

Many years later, a high-minded scholar called Liu Tse-chi heard the story and hopefully made plans for the journey. But he too failed in his quest and died soon afterwards.

Since that time no one has sought to find the forest of peach trees and the hidden land lying beyond the cave.

I put down the book. Immediately, the cacophony of sound from outside intruded into my consciousness.

The tale I had just read had struck some chord within me. I wondered just where the difference lay between the Wu-ling people and those in the land the fisherman had discovered, a land looking little different from the world outside yet in some way transformed.

The word 'transformed' has gripped my imagination for years, and I can remember the first time I ever heard it, when I was living on the Peak. My father spoke to me one day about my great grandfather, an actor, who had transformed the stage of his time. The word transform, he had explained, meant that someone or something has undergone a deep change for the better. From that day to this, the word has continued to fascinate me.

For the rest of the evening I sat wondering about that far-off 'Peach Blossom Country'. Did it once actually exist or had it—and far more probably—simply been a place conjured up by the poet's imagination? Anyway, I concluded, there was little likelihood of any such place being able to exist today in this rackety modern world.

The explosions continued to reach crescendos of noise that I would not have believed possible had I not heard them myself.

When the fourth day dawned I got up feeling a wreck. This was the day the celebrations were due to end and by late afternoon there was only an occasional splutter from a string of exploding crackers.

There came a knock on the door. I hesitated about opening it, but the celebrations were virtually over and so I decided that I might as well emerge from my hermit-like existence now as later. The caller was probably only some tradesman come to collect his red envelope. But to my embarrassment, when I opened the door I saw Mr. Chan standing outside.

"Good afternoon!" he said, cheerfully, "I've just called round to wish you Kung Hei Fat Choy."

"Thank you and my greetings to you. Please come in and please excuse the untidy state of the room. I'm afraid I haven't done much housework these past few days."

He brushed aside my apology. I caught a glimpse of my face in the mirror as we sat down. My hair was unkempt, the skin around my eyes was a deep mauve due to lack of sleep and my cheeks an unhealthy white.

Mr. Chan looked at me intently, then asked, "Are you ill?"

In spite of feeling close to death's door, I replied with bravado, "Not ill exactly, but I do feel exhausted from all the noise."

He gave me a sympathetic glance. "I'm afraid our celebrations are rather upsetting for the nerves of non-Chinese residents."

I smiled wanly.

"You need a break," he said, "a respite from the noise and bustle of Hong Kong. Of course, the place has been exceptionally noisy lately, but at any time of the year the island is not exactly a haven of peace and quiet."

"You are right; I do need a break. But there's nowhere to go to for a week or so of quiet."

Mr. Chan looked mysterious. "You are wrong," he assured me. "I know a place not far from here which is excellent for restoring frayed nerves, a place where you can listen to the silence."

I looked at him in amazement. "Chengtau?" I asked, hazarding a guess.

"No, not Chengtau. That fisherman's island is almost as noisy as Hong Kong. The island I am going to suggest you visit is eight miles from here and can be reached by ferry. It is twice the size of Hong Kong and hardly developed at all. There is only a short strip of surfaced road in the whole of the island and only a tiny population, mostly farmers and fishermen, monks and hermits. The countryside is wild and unspoilt. Outside the few coastal villages and the farmlands, the only sounds you are likely to hear are the cries of birds, the wind, and the waves beating on the shore."

"What is the name of this island?"

"Lantao," he answered. "To me it is the most beautiful island in the whole group. But then, I am a Taoist at heart and enjoy silence and solitude, unlike the gregarious Confucians. What might seem heaven to me might very well seem hell to them. But I don't think you would find Lantao a hell. Would you like me to try and find you some simple accommodation there, a room in a farmhouse, say?"

"Oh, please! I'd be most grateful if you would."

"Then I'll do my best."

"Tell me, why are there so few people living in Lantao when Hong Kong is so overcrowded?" I asked him.

"Because there are no reservoirs on the island yet and so it can only support a negligible population."

He left me feeling a hundred times better than I had felt prior to his visit. The very thought of being able to leave the teeming, noisy island of Hong Kong for a quiet underpopulated one, if only for a few days, had the effect of banishing much of my exhaustion. Even so, after four days and nights of nerve-shattering explosions and being shut up in the flat throughout that time, my general health left a good deal to be desired.

The following day I went down to Victoria and met some friends for lunch. They inquired as to how things had gone for me during the celebrations. I answered their query with the words of the elderly Frenchman who, when asked at the end of the Revolution how he had fared during the Terror, had replied simply, "I survived."

CHAPTER FIVE

A ROOM IN LANTAO

TWO WEEKS AFTER Mr. Chan's visit, I set off with him by early ferry to Lantao. He had warned me that when we got out at Tung Chung we would have to walk over rough hilly country for nearly two hours before we reached the farm where I was to stay. He had managed to book me a room at this farm for a week and I would have the option of being able to rent it for the duration of my stay in the Colony if I wished. He would be staying at a neighbouring farm about a mile away.

The island of Lantao (pronounced Lantaw) is eight miles from Hong Kong. It is double the size of the parent island and receives twice the amount of rainfall, due, perhaps, to its high mountain ranges. But as there are no reservoirs on the island most of this rainfall runs to waste. A huge reservoir had been started at Shek Pik, but when completed the whole of its water supply will be for the benefit of Hong Kong residents, to be piped there by undersea pipes. There are no modern amenities on the island and the countryside is almost untouched by the hand of man. The few villages are mainly situated along the coast. The inland area is almost unpopulated except for a few farming folk living on isolated holdings, and monks, nuns and hermits. There are several Buddhist monasteries and nunneries on the island and because of the peaceful atmosphere and the unfrequented hills and valleys, it has attracted a number of Taoist recluses to its shores. The Chinese name for Lantao is Tai Yu Shan, the island of big mountains. From many of the peaks one can get a clear view of all the other islands in the group, the Pearl River Estuary and the coastline of China and a large area of inland China itself.

Lantao gets few visitors. Those who go there are mostly persons in search of a week or so of quiet. At weekends parties of hikers and climbers arrive. They camp out or spend the nights at monastery guest-houses. The peaks which rise to some 2,000 feet offer a real challenge to them. Men who have climbed in the Hebridean Island of Skye as well as in Lantao often comment on a certain similarity between the two islands: the barren hills rising sheer from the sea and the high, isolated mountains, many of them hidden behind ranges of hills. But the vegetation is much more luxuriant in the Lantao valleys than in those of Skye and the weather, on the whole, much warmer and sunnier.

We got off at the Tung Chung pier. There was a small crowd waiting for the ferry's arrival. Some crates were unloaded and baskets of produce were taken on before the ferry sailed away again.

The Tung Chung valley is a farming area. Mr. Chan had told me that most of the scenery in Lantao is stark and barren, with a wild beauty, and so the lushness of the wide valley with its terraced rice fields, mango, lychee, and banana trees came as a surprise to me. High up the valley were small villages and groups of houses all surrounded by deep groves of trees.

Mr. Chan and I shouldered our rucksacks and started off. We followed an ancient footpath that wound over the hills. These footpaths, some of which scale the mountain ranges while others follow the coastline, are often the only way of getting from one part of the island to another.

The track veered off in another direction and we walked over pathless hills covered by wiry grass.

"Lantao is rugged in more ways than one," said Mr. Chan, as we stopped to rest a minute. "In the farmhouse where I stay, the farmer keeps a gun loaded. The gun is to fire at possible marauders; pirates, bandits, or just common thieves. Families who live in isolated parts of the island are allowed by law to keep a gun and ammunition because Lantao is hardly policed at all."

"Pirates?" I queried.

"Yes. The occasional pirate vessel still puts into lonely creeks from time to time. The crew may attack one of the coastal villages or an isolated farm. When we get to the top of the next hill you'll be able to see one of these villages. It has a fort, like most of them, and if the villagers think they are in danger of being attacked, then they all get into the fort and barricade the door. I must warn you not to wander about by yourself," he went on. "Don't go lengthy distances from the farm just in case you meet an undesirable character. And don't approach a village alone or without a stick. The dogs in them, as well as on the farms, are very fierce and are trained to attack strangers."

We stopped on a hilltop and Mr. Chan pointed to a distant settlement which was centred around one of the square 'cannon towers' which are a feature of Lantao.

After another hour's walk we came to the farm where I was to stay. It lay in a valley with high hills at the rear.

Mr. Chan introduced me to the farmer and his wife, a Mr. and Mrs. Soong. The old man could speak a little English, his wife, none. Mr. Soong told me that his wife would cook my meals and bring them up to my room. I was to ask him for anything I wanted.

Mr. Chan said good-bye and told me he would come round next morning and take me for a walk.

The old wife, with smiles and gestures, led me through a large white-washed living-room and up a short flight of wooden steps. My room was at the bottom of a narrow passage. It was very small. The only furniture it contained was a bed, a low table, a stool and a cupboard. But this was sufficient for my needs. With more signs, Mrs. Soong indicated that she was going to bring me up lunch.

I looked out of the window. Between the peaks of the hills I caught a glimpse of the sea. A green sward stretched out from the farm and merged with the wiry grass of the surrounding hills. A flock of white ducks walked over the emerald grass, snapping at succulent stalks. Near the farm was a stone well, shaded by a banyan tree, and just below my window grew some bamboos whose topmost leaves reached the ledge.

My lunch consisted of a bowl of mushroom soup, noodles and mixed vegetables, bean cakes and a pot of tea. Chinese food, whether restaurant fare or home cooked, is nearly always excellent, as was this simple meal.

In the afternoon I walked over the hills at the rear of the farm, taking care to keep the buildings within view. After I had eaten supper, I sat outside on the well, enjoying the cool evening air. Mr. Soong came and joined me.

"Have you been to Hong Kong lately?" I asked him, speaking slowly.

"Five, six years ago I used to catch ferry for Hong Kong once a month. Now I no go at all; I no leave Lantao. Too much work for me here," he laughed.

"Have you no children to help you?"

"One son. He is clerk in Hong Kong. He no like Lantao—too quiet, nothing to do, no cinemas or dancing." And the old farmer extended his hands in a gesture of helplessness, as though to say, 'And what can I do about that?'

"It's the same in England," I said. "The young people are moving away from the countryside and into the towns where there are plenty of amusements. So you do all the farmwork by yourself?"

"My wife, she helps, and once a week my nephew who lives on other side of these hills, he comes over to work here. Hong Kong, you like?" he asked.

"I like Lantao better," I said.

He smiled widely. "You been here one day, yet you say you like Lantao better. How is that?"

"Too many people in Hong Kong and too much noise."

"I no like to live over there."

He pointed to a distant ridge of hills beyond which was the faint outline of a mountain.

"On that mountain lives old Hong Kong man. He had shop for many years over there. Now he lives on top of mountain."

"Why?" I asked.

"He is hermit now. Very peaceful up there. Lantao good place for hermits. Hong Kong not so good. This nephew I tell you about, he go once a week—long walk—to take food to this old man who gives him some money."

"I see."

The light was fading fast. I could just make out the mountain-top on which lived the old hermit. The idea of a person living up there alone stirred my imagination and I decided that I would try and visit him.

Before going to bed, I sat by the window staring at the dark shapes of the hills and the silvery shimmer of the sea. The bamboos rustled. A pig grunted. The rest was silence.

Mr. Chan was carrying a wooden staff when he called for me in the morning, and he advised me to get one too as an aid to walking over rough country and as a weapon against any fierce canines I might chance to meet.

We walked up the hills at the back of the farm and presently plunged down a ravine, following a tiny track edged by dense thickets of rhododendrons and bamboos. Several rhesus monkeys swung through the tree-tops, shrieking as they went, no doubt in protest at this sudden appearance of two human beings. Down we went until we reached the valley floor through which ran a clear stream. A white crane flew away slowly as we approached. Then came a coughing sound from somewhere in the bushes.

"Barking deer," said Mr. Chan. "They are quite numerous in Lantao and the New Territories."

It was a pleasant walk through the leafy ravine. We climbed out at the far end and found ourselves on the hills again. No sheep wandered these hills which were bereft of all pastoral life.

"Tomorrow I have to return to Hong Kong," said Mr. Chan. "I hope you enjoy the remainder of your stay here. Make sure you get someone to accompany you back to the ferry when you leave."

Some days later I walked up to the ravine again. The weather continued fine but the humidity was increasing daily, which made walking something of an effort. I had a sketching-block with me as I wanted to draw some of the flora in the valley and perhaps a monkey swinging from a branch.

I stood on a knoll with the valleys splayed out below me. After some minutes' hesitation, I started off down a track on either side of which were dense spinneys of bush. My progress was slow. When I reached the bottom of the ravine I was surprised to find no stream. A cliff-like rockface reared skywards and down it trickled small rivulets of water. Wild rose bushes grew thickly beside it.

I walked on, still expecting to come upon the stream at any moment. Shallow pools of water lay under the cliff and the rocks were covered with a thick velvety moss. I realised after a while that I must have entered the wrong valley; nevertheless, I thought I would go on a bit further.

I came to a rock pool. Moss grew over the stone like a green quilt and from the cliff-face hung strands of maidenhair fern. I paused to admire this wild green garden. The birds kept up a constant chattering and whistling. They flew out of the bamboos and splashed noisily in the pool a few yards from me. I felt that I must have intruded into a birds' causerie.

A sudden feeling, a sense that I was not alone, made me glance around. I got a shock. A black-gowned figure was standing watching me intently. His appearance was so wild and strange that instinct told me to take to my heels. But I had my back, literally, to the wall. I would have felt braver facing a tiger than this unkempt and forbidding-looking human creature. He was dressed in a tattered gown and his hair hung about his face in long uncombed strands.

The strain was relieved for me slightly when a bird flew out of the bushes and perched on the man's shoulder. He raised a hand and another bird flew on to it as though in compliance with a silent summons. And all about us other birds kept up a constant movement and twittering.

Then the man spoke—and in English. His voice was loud and had a harsh edge to it.

"Where are you going?"

"I was on my way to the end of the valley," I replied.

"Where are you staying?"

"At a farmhouse."

"What's the name of the farmer?"

"Mr. Soong."

He nodded, then pointed to my sketch-book. "Are you an artist?"

"Yes. At least, I was once."

He smiled, showing a row of strong white teeth. "I was a pirate —once."

Now that he had admitted as much, I saw that the word piratical would be a good one by which to describe him. Everything about him, his truculent expression, his strong body and unkempt appearance added up to a realistic picture of a Chinese pirate. All that was lacking to make it complete was a cutlass stuck through his belt. For no apparent cause, he gave a roar of laughter. I felt more uneasy than ever.

I pointed to the far end of the valley and asked, "Is there a way out of the end of the ravine?"

"Yes, I'll show it to you."

I immediately regretted having asked the question, for now, it seemed, I had no option but to follow him along an unknown route.

He set off, walking with long quick strides and I following behind him.

As we were passing another pool, I stopped and held my breath. A baby rhesus monkey, still wobbly in the legs, walked to the pool while its mother watched it from behind a clump of sedge. The infant monkey bent down over the water, resting his weight on his front paws, and started to drink. Suddenly a stone whizzed through the air, hitting the little creature on its flank. It let out a high-pitched yell, horribly childlike. There was a guffaw of laughter and the ex-pirate walked back to where I was standing. The mother monkey, meanwhile, dashed forward and seized her offspring, letting out a stream of rhesus invective at the human offender.

"Yes, yes, I know what you're telling me—go to hell!"

He laughed again, throwing another stone at the pair as the mother leapt into the undergrowth with the baby clinging to her back. I was furious! A charming scene had been needlessly shattered, a little animal terrified and hurt.

"Why did you do it?" I shouted.

"I don't like them—monkeys. Come on. I want to get out on to the hills."

There was nothing else I could do but follow him up a steep bush-covered hillside. The final part of our climb from the ravine almost came into the category of mountaineering. We had to haul ourselves over boulders and bend double under rocky ledges. At last we climbed out on to a plateau.

"Thank goodness that's over," I said. "I would never have come this way if I'd known there was going to be such a stiff climb."

"You won't regret the climb," he assured me. "Hurry up. I want to show you something."

He strode on. Ahead of us were hills and beyond them, mountains. I looked about me, trying to get my bearings, but I could spot no familiar landmarks. I thought my best plan under the circumstances was to keep walking with this strange individual until I caught sight of a landmark I knew, and then bid him a hasty good-bye.

Although he did not speak, I had the impression that he felt friendlier towards me now. He covered the ground at an exhausting pace and I had difficulty in keeping up with him. We began climbing a hill, on the summit of which grew several pines. One stood apart from the rest, a lonely sentinal, its branches twisted by the winds. We walked towards it. Rocks were scattered about as though strewn on the grass by some giant hand.

"Here we are," he said. "Sit down. I'll make you some tea."

"Tea!"

My obvious surprise seemed to give him a childish pleasure.

"Yes, a cup of tea. You are probably thirsty after that climb."

Mystified, I sat down on the grass. He put one of his long arms into a hollow under a rock and pulled out a primus stove, then a pan, a tea-pot and wooden tea-box, and a bucket filled with water. A box of matches made its appearance from a pocket of his gown. He set about pumping the primus, then put the pan of water over the pale flame.

"Did I surprise you with my offer of tea?" he asked.

"You certainly did."

"I've been living up here these past few days," he explained, "and I put my belongings under this rock when I go wandering.

Tomorrow I may move on to somewhere else. I never stay long in one place once the hot weather starts."

"And in the winter?"

"Then I live in a hut or cave. There are several empty ones in the valleys and on the mountains."

I changed the subject and inquired, "So once you were a pirate?"

"Yes, for a short time. And I've been many other things besides that."

"What are you now?"

"I suppose I'm a hermit."

The water bubbled in the pan. He poured it into the enamel tea-pot.

I ventured a more personal question. "May I ask your name?"

"I have no name. Call me Kwong, if you wish. I left my name behind me when I said good-bye to my old life. Now I'm both nameless and homeless."

He put an arm under the rock again and this time pulled out two cups. Unless I was mistaken, they were of green jade. He saw me looking at them and confirmed my opinion.

"Yes, they are jade. Two ancient cups of the Ming dynasty."

He held one up to the sunlight and the thin shell of jade turned a luminous yellowy-green, the colour of a young fern-frond.

I thought it wiser not to ask how he had come by these lovely cups, much as I would have liked to. Perhaps they were part of some loot acquired during his dubious past. In sharp contrast to the cups, the tea-pot and pan were of cheap enamelware, painted with a design of red bats.

The tea tasted particularly good sipped from such a cup. Every so often the ex-pirate would hold his up to the light and gaze at it with pleasure, like some connoisseur of antiques.

I asked, "Were these cups what you wanted to show me?"

"No. I want to show you my birds."

He walked out from under the pine tree, clapped his hands and shouted something in a Chinese tongue, raising his arms above his head. Some birds flew from the pine branches and hopped about at his feet. He took a bag from his pocket and tossed them some crumbs.

"Birds are very sensitive creatures," he told me. "They are fully aware of a person's intentions towards them, good or bad."

Birds started to arrive in answer to his summons. Magnetism seemed to flow from his outstretched arms. The birds chattered and squabbled as they ran for crumbs, and they seemed to fall out of the sky on to his broad shoulders. The flock continued to swell, and contained sea birds and land birds, common varieties and rarer ones. Kwong looked about him and up at the sky as though still awaiting the arrival of yet another winged visitor. Then he gave an exclamation as a beautiful long-tailed bird flew down and gracefully settled on his arm. He stroked its neck, speaking to it gently all the while and offering it a palmful of crumbs.

"I love them all," he told me, "but this one is my favourite; a rare blue magpie."

The bird had a white underbelly, a blue head and throat, and its tail-feathers were about twice the length of its body. It showed not the least trace of fear as it sat on Kwong's arm and ate the crumbs proffered it. When it had eaten its fill, it did not linger, but flew off again, like some rare visitor from another realm who may only remain briefly among mortals.

"Good-bye!" Kwong called after it.

Then he turned to me, saying, "This sparrow is the greediest of the lot. Over there are three of my pets—see?—in the grass. They do not really care for these heights."

And he pointed to three tiny flower peckers, barely visible in the grass, the Colony's smallest birds.

"Have you noticed her?" he asked. "She is another rare one, a ruby throat, a species of robin. Come and stand by me and let's see if she'll sit on your hand."

I walked over to him, birds scattering before me, and placed my hand beside his. He dropped some crumbs into my palm and the bird hopped without hesitation from his hand on to mine.

He emptied the remaining crumbs from the bag and said, "Now I must be going. I have promised to visit a recluse who lives in a cave a few miles from here. Don't try and find your way back through the ravine. Go down this hill until you reach the coast, then look over to your left and you'll see the farm where you are staying."

I thanked him for the tea and for showing me his tame wild birds; then we parted, he walking further inland and I going downhill towards the coast. When I reached it, I could see the farm in the distance.

That evening I asked Mr. Soong if I might rent the room for as long as I stayed in the Colony, and to this request of mine he willingly agreed.

CHAPTER SIX

BIRDS OF PASSAGE

THE PALE MAUVE blossoms of the bauhinia tree were out in Hong Kong. Spring was well advanced and tourists were pouring into the Colony by boat and plane.

When I got back to the flat from Lantao there was a letter waiting for me from a Brahmin woman friend in India. I had got to know her when she was a student in London. On her return to Kerala, she had married into her own caste and was now the mother of three children. She invited me to stay when later I left for India, and suggested that I rent a small house from them for a few months. This would give me the chance of getting to know life in that part of the sub-continent. I thought this an excellent idea and wrote back accepting her invitation to stay and her offer of the house.

There was another letter waiting for me, this one from an English friend, Siriol Hughes, who had just arrived in the Colony with her husband and two children. They were staying at the Peninsula Hotel in Kowloon which overlooks the harbour. From Hong Kong, she informed me, they were going on to Japan for a quick look-see, and then flying to Australia where they were emigrating. She asked me to go over and have tea with them.

I caught the ferry. It was packed with local residents and tourists. Many of the latter were wearing the conical yellow coolie hats which seem to be a 'must' for every visitor to Hong Kong, and some of the women were dressed in tight-fitting cheong-sams, a costume not always flattering to the European female figure.

A Chinese youth dressed in linen trousers and a gaudy shirt sat next to me, the transistor radio on his lap turned on fortissimo. A singer screeched her way up to dizzy heights in the scale. It might seem to the uninitiated that all Chinese singers are in danger of wrecking their vocal chords. Such is not the case, however. Chinese singers very rarely damage their vocal chords, which are as tough as the Chinese nervous system.

The youth asked me, "Are you a tourist?"

"No, I'm not a tourist," I answered. "I'm living in Hong Kong."

"For how long?"

"About a year."

"Then you go on to some other place?"

"Yes."

"Like all English people. They stay one year, three years maybe, then they leave. Perhaps I leave, too, one day. You like Hong Kong?"

"Very much."

"You like Miss Jasmine Cheung?"

"Miss who?"

"This is her singing now. She is my favourite singer."

There our conversation ended. Water churned violently as the ferry slowed to a stop.

The hotel is only a few minutes' walk from the wharf. I crossed the road. Coming towards me was a group of children, blond-haired, barefooted. The boys were dressed in rough linen trousers and high-necked shirts which were caught in at the waist with a belt. The girls were in dirndl type skirts, blouses, and some had their heads covered with a kerchief. They ran past me, talking in an unknown tongue. They were followed by a group of adults dressed in identical styles. All had round, simple faces and sturdily built bodies and were obviously peasants. One of the men, in spite of the warm weather, was wearing a fur hat. I realised on seeing him that they were White Russian peasant refugees from China. They looked just like pictures of peasants I had seen in books about the Russia of the pre-Communist period. Many White Russians of different classes escaped from their homeland during and after the Revolution by the 'back door' into China. Some stayed there until Communism swept over the country, when the majority decided that it was time to be moving on again if they could.

Hong Kong receives all these Russian emigrés when they leave China. They stay in refugee centres until entry permits are granted them into other countries, such as Australia and Brazil.

The emigrés went by, seemingly cheerful, although they must have gone through considerable mental anguish prior to their arrival in the Colony. Then along came Tolstoy, a white-bearded patriarch leaning on a stick. He sat down on a bench and I sat down too. I was not going to miss my chance of a meeting with this interesting-looking character. Some of the other Russians had stopped and were waiting for him to catch up. He ignored them.

"Ingleez?" he asked, giving me a dignified stare.

"Yes, I'm English," I replied. "And you are Russian?"

"Yes, me Russian—from China."

He went on to tell me in halting English that he and the others had arrived in Hong Kong about a month ago, that it had taken them over a year to get the necessary exit permits from the Chinese authorities, and that in a few days' time they would be flying to Australia. He was going to live with a daughter in Melbourne who had preceded him there.

An ancient woman came along supported by a younger one. They sat down next to the patriarch.

"Is she your wife?" I asked him, indicating the old woman.

He drew himself up. "No, not my wife. She is old, old woman. My wife dead many years."

"Oh, I'm sorry."

"This old woman, how many years is she, do you think?"

I guessed—"Eighty-six?"

"My Ingleez not good. Fingers—hold up!"

I held up eight fingers, then six.

"No," And he held up eight fingers, then one.

"Eighty-one," I said. Well, I had not been so far out.

"Now me—you guess," he said.

This time I was going to be tactful. I held up six fingers, then two.

He laughed delightedly. Seven fingers were held up and then four.

"Seventy-four!" I exclaimed—"no, I don't believe it."

"Yes, seven, four. Me old man, but not so old as her," and he gave a hearty laugh. "Too old for my wife, yes?"

"Of course."

"She no speak Ingleez so I can tell you that when we get to Australia she is going straight into home for old people. Sad, yes?"

What a grim life, I thought; straight from a refugee centre in Kowloon and then into an old people's home when she reached Australia, though she may well have been feeling thankful at the thought of ending her days there.

My talk with the patriarch had made me late. When I reached the Peninsula I saw an elderly couple—two more White Russian refugees—standing at the bottom of the steps. But there was something different about these two. They were unmistakably, in spite of their none too smart clothing, what used to be called gentry. The woman was wearing a faded skirt and a white blouse with a silver brooch pinned to the collar. As I approached, the woman asked me if they might go into the hotel with me.

"We are shy," she confided. "This is the first time we have been to such a smart hotel for many years. My husband is treating me to tea here to celebrate our arrival last month in Kowloon. But now we are afraid to go in."

"Please come in with me, then."

"Thank you so much."

They introduced themselves as a Mr. and Mrs. Zambrowski.

There is a huge high-ceilinged central lounge on the ground floor of the Peninsula where people meet and tea is served from trolleys by white-jacketed Chinese waiters. On either side of this lounge are passages lined with boutiques where the more select wares of the Colony are displayed. As we walked past them, Mrs. Zambrowski gazed in astonishment at the wealth of silks, jade ornaments, jewellery, and ivory Buddhas and Kwan Yins on view in the windows.

"All this is just like fairyland for me!" she said. "The China where we have come from, everything is so drab."

A wide archway led into the lounge, and here the two paused nervously as though summoning up courage to walk into this enormous room where smartly dressed men and women were chatting together at the tables and the waiters moved silent footed among them, serving tea.

"Oh, no, Sergei, I can't..." Mrs. Zambrowski began.

Seeing how nervous she was, her husband walked boldly in.

"Of course you can," he said.

We followed after him.

"You can sit where you like," I told Mrs. Zambrowski. "A waiter will bring you tea."

"This is lovely," she said, her nervousness vanishing. "I am going to enjoy myself so much."

My friends were sitting on the far side of the lounge, the children impatiently awaiting my arrival so that they could start tea.

"Sorry I'm late," I said. "It's lovely to see you all again."

"Isn't it strange, us meeting here in Kowloon?" said Siriol.

Her husband Ian, an engineer, ordered tea and then we began talking about the life we had left behind us in England. Presently I asked the inevitable question, "Why are you emigrating and why Australia?" And I added, "You must both be quite tired of answering that question by now."

Tea arrived: neatly cut sandwiches and delicious cakes.

"Not really," said Siriol. "Answering it has helped us to get clearer in our own minds just why we are going. But we both decided before leaving England that even if we don't manage to fit into Australian life we won't go back; we'll try somewhere else. We aren't going to Australia as assisted immigrants so we'll be free to move on any time if we want to."

"But why are you going there?" I asked again.

"There are several reasons, I suppose. The idea of emigrating has been growing on us for the past five or six years now. We've both done a fair amount of travelling and neither of us is a greenhorn so far as living in another country is concerned. Even so, it's a tremendous decision when you finally decide to leave your own country for good, particularly when you've got two children. I don't suppose that we would have managed to make the break if Ian hadn't spent a working holiday out there."

"And liked it?" I asked him.

"I liked it a lot. Not everything, of course. But I loved the sunshine and the casual way of living, and the different flowers, birds and so forth. So much *is* different out there. Everything looked so fresh. When I got back to Britain I realised very forcibly how used up our country is becoming."

"Used up and a little stale," said Siriol. "I hate to say it because I love Britain and I'm definitely not one of those English English-haters who abound in the country these days. But even the air smells less fresh than it used to. And the crowds and the congested traffic! Well, you know yourself what it's like—and it's getting worse each year. We want to live in a country where there's less of a crush. Even if we never visit the outback at least we know it's there, miles and miles of open, unspoilt countryside where there's no treading on other people's toes nor they on yours. Well, those are the main reasons why we're going."

"I hope Australia measures up to your expectations," I said.

They left the hotel directly we had finished tea, as they were going on a drive through the New Territories.

I went and joined the Zambrowskis who appeared reluctant to leave these pleasant surroundings. I told them that I had met a group of Russians on the way to the hotel.

"That would be the group we journeyed with to Kowloon," said Mr. Zambrowski. "They used to be farmers in the Canton district."

"One of them told me that they would be flying to Australia soon. I expect you'll be going there too?"

"No, not to Australia," said Mrs. Zambrowski, "though we were given the chance of settling there. But I did not think we would ever feel at home in that new country and we are both too old now to make the necessary adjustments. Of course, some of us have no choice and must go to whatever country offers to take us in. But my husband and I have been lucky; soon we shall be flying to Sweden."

"Really?"

"Yes. I cannot tell you how happy we are to be going there." Tears filled her eyes and for some moments she was unable to speak. Her husband carried on the conversation, saying, "For years now my wife has had a wish to see birch and fir trees again, trees which grow in profusion in Russia."

Mrs. Zambrowski dabbed her eyes and said, "Those trees have become something of a symbol for me. As a girl I used to walk through the woods in winter and the branches of the firs would be weighed down with snow. I would walk out of the woods and over the steppes where the birch trees grow. Their slender trunks would look silvery in the winter's light and their branches would be coated with ice. Those beautiful, frail-looking trees always survived the weather, however harsh it might be.

"When things became more and more difficult for us in China after the Communists took over, my husband used to say to me that somehow we must leave and start yet another new life in some other country. I would say, 'Yes, we must get to some friendly northern European country where the birch trees grow.' "

"I told her to put such nonsense from her head," said Mr. Zambrowski. "First, we must get out of China. Then, we must not be too particular but go to whatever country offered us refuge, probably Australia. We knew that many White Russian refugees from China had gone on there from Hong Kong. But my wife always refused to think of settling in Australia. She insisted that we must try to get to a northern European country where birch and pine trees grow and the winters are snowy."

"Yes, I refused to give up hope," said his wife. "Our requests to leave China were turned down again and again, but at last the papers came through giving us permission to go to Kowloon by rail. When we arrived, the authorities here held out very little hope of our being able to emigrate to a European country, but I insisted that they put in an application for us to go to Sweden. We had heard that this country sometimes takes in a few people like ourselves. Yesterday we were told that our application had been accepted. So this tea is a double celebration; for having managed to get to the Colony and because soon we shall be leaving for Sweden, the country of our choice."

"That's wonderful," I said.

"Yes, it is wonderful," said Mr. Zambrowski, "and if my wife had not insisted that we try for Sweden, then we would be going with the other Russians to the land of the gum tree!"

I left them still sitting happily in the hotel lounge. I was filled with admiration for that determined Russian woman who had succeeded in gaining permission to live in Sweden.

Friends and strangers whom I had encountered briefly were just a few of the many thousands these days who had left the countries of their birth and were moving on to other lands, because they were compelled to, because they wanted to: young and old, all hoping for better conditions and seeking to start new lives.

CHAPTER SEVEN

WALK TO A MOUNTAIN

A WEEK LATER I was back in Lantao. Mr. Chan had managed to get over too and he offered to take me to several places of interest on the island, including a visit to a Buddhist monastery which lies on a plateau between the twin peaks of the island's highest mountains, Sunset and Lantao Peaks.

One day we took the ferry to Silvermine Bay which lies on the opposite side of the island, and we spent some time exploring the old mine workings. It is at Silvermine Bay that there is a stretch of surfaced road—the only stretch on the island when I was there. It leads from the Bay to Cheung Sha further along the coast.

The next day we were due to visit the monastery but we went first to visit an old fort at Tung Chung and followed a path which went through bright green paddy fields. Small stone houses with tiled roofs and the fort lay at the bottom of a picturesque wooded spur. Inside the stone-walled fort were cottages and trees. We climbed some steps, half hidden by creepers, which led to the top of a wall. Pointing seawards were several ancient cannons. Mr. Chan translated the Chinese hieroglyphics on one, which read: This gun was made in the first moon of the tenth year of the Emperor Chia Ching and weighs 1,200 catties.

"Which makes the year of casting 1806," he said. "Before the British took the island over, this fort used to be a pirate stronghold."

There is a pathway near here which leads up to the monastery, but Mr. Chan wanted to show me the fishing village of Tai O and so we were going to walk to the monastery from there.

We caught the ferry to Tai O, the largest village on the island. Fishermen were awaiting the ferry's arrival in their sampans which were loaded to the gunwhales with tubs of live fish destined for

Hong Kong. We stepped into a sampan and were rowed to the village by a strong-armed girl.

Most of the houses in Tai O are built on stilts and the 'streets' are waterways. The main waterway is intersected by narrow thoroughfares up which boats were coming laden with cargoes of fish, vegetables, and fowls and ducks in wicker baskets. Fish were laid out on the wooden verandas of the houses to dry. The smell, as the girl rowed us down the main street, was somewhat overpowering. We got out of the sampan by a little tea-shop and had some rice cakes and cups of jasmine tea. But the delicate aroma of the tea was not strong enough to counteract the much stronger smell of fish, dead, drying, and alive.

We continued on our way in the sampan, going down a narrow waterway which brought us close to dry land. Nets were spread out and men were busy building boats. The girl rowed us to the head of a creek where we disembarked.

Tai O is surrounded by hills. The final approach to the monastery, which stands at a height of 2,000 feet, is very steep. We followed a path which led to the only opening in these hills. It went through a ravine in which a stream flowed seawards. The twin summits of Sunset and Lantao Peaks reared up in the distance. Flowering rhododendrons made bright splashes of colour during the early stages of our climb.

The distance from Tai O to the monastery is four miles. The views on the way up were wonderful. Behind us, wild hilly country stretched away to the distant ocean. Much of the hillside up which the track wound is covered by a thick scrub but the plateau itself is free of this scrub. Here the monks had planted orchards and gardens.

We were shown into the guest-house by a friendly Buddhist monk. It consisted of one large room. In the centre portion were a table and some chairs and here the vegetarian meals were served. On either side of the dining-space were wings divided into sleeping cubicles. To the rear of the guest-house were the simple sanitary arrangements.

The monk brought quilts for our beds and served us a meal. We were the only visitors there on our arrival, but later a party of tourists appeared. They had come up via the flagged pathway on the other side of the range, the route which most visitors follow. Two older members of the party had been carried up in sedan chairs. It is only in Lantao that this mode of conveyance is ever used in the Colony now.

I went and had a look at the monastery grounds. The monks produce a large part of their own fare, which consists mainly of fruit and vegetables. Rice is bought from local farmers.

As I was standing at the far end of an orchard admiring the distant views, the monk in charge of the guest-house came up to me and we started to talk. He told me that a few weeks ago an elderly German actor who had been filming in Hong Kong visited the monastery. He had been carried up in a chair while his wife, a girl in her early twenties, had walked all the way, bare-footed, by the side of her husband's chair.

"It was very pleasant to see this young wife paying such respect to her husband," he said. "It is not often one sees such behaviour these days, particularly, if I may say so, from a western woman."

I did not disillusion him by telling him that, undoubtedly, the only reason the young woman had walked up was because she had preferred to do so and not because she had any thought of paying respects to her elderly husband.

After a night spent in the monastery guest-house and an early breakfast, Mr. Chan and I walked back to Tai O, caught the ferry and returned to our respective farms.

Mr. Soong's nephew was there when I got back, a youth called Yung-Lee. He had been helping his uncle in the vegetable garden.

"Tomorrow," said Mr. Soong, pointing to a large pack in the living-room, "he take food to hermit."

"May I go with him?" I asked.

Mr. Soong called his nephew and they had a brief conversation together; then, turning to me, he said, "Yung-Lee say alright you go with him but very long walk and he start early in morning."

"I'm a good walker," I said, "and I don't mind an early start."

Through his uncle—the young man could speak no English—

he told me that he would be starting at half-past five and would call me with a cup of tea at five.

We started off in the early dawn. The atmosphere was pleasantly cool. We kept close to the cliffs. Presently the ground started to decline sharply until the land was little above sea level. A coastal village with its square fort stood by the shore and there were sampans and a junk tied up on the beach.

Some dogs were chasing each other across a field not far from where we were walking. They were tearing along as if pursued by demons. To my surprise, Yung-Lee clambered up on to a rock, indicating by urgent gestures that I was to do the same. I climbed up beside him and the dogs dashed past. They were being pursued by another dog which was no larger than they were. But there was something seriously wrong with this rusty-coloured pi, as I realised when he passed under the rock on which we were standing. The dog's mouth was foaming and his reddish coat was streaked with dark lines of sweat, while his eyes were staring and demented looking. The animal must be mad, I thought. Then I realised with a shock that it was suffering from rabies.

The dogs ran in a wide circle, then approached us again. The youth raised his staff, ready to ward off any dog should it attempt to clamber on to the rock. But the group out in front were far too intent on escaping from the slavering jaws of the rabid dog to bother about us. The afflicted animal followed them in swift pursuit. It had only gone past us a short distance when it rolled over, howling and snapping its jaws. Then it was still, released from its agonies by death. I was glad; there is no cure for a dog which contracts rabies.

We got down off the rock and continued on our way, each thinking our own thoughts as we were not able to converse with one another.

Anyone unfortunate enough to be bitten by a rabid dog on Lantao would be in for a pretty horrible death, I mused. It was unlikely that the victim would be able to reach Hong Kong in time to receive an anti-rabies injection. These injections, a series of agonising pricks right round the back and stomach, have to be given shortly after a person has been in contact with such a dog in order to be effective. Otherwise, death is inevitable. But it is not the certainty of death which is the worst part of contracting rabies but the agonising hours preceding it: hours of intense thirst, but if a drink is offered the patient, he refuses it. Sanity goes and is replaced by madness. The human being froths at the mouth and howls just like a rabid dog and is liable to attack anyone who comes near him.

Every dog owner in Hong Kong is compelled by law to have his animal injected against rabies. Strays are periodically rounded up and destroyed. But this is not the case in Lantao.

We started to walk inland. Low hills gave place to lofty ones; before us towered mountain peaks. We were now in country of bare and wind-swept ridges and precipitous rocky cliffs, with seldom a tree to be seen. But there was one delightful stretch through a wooded valley which resounded with the songs of birds. We emerged from under the trees and followed a steeply climbing track. It swept round a high bluff. Several large boulders were perched to one side of it, on the other side was a sheer drop. Yung-Lee stopped and pointed to a wisp of smoke blowing from behind a boulder. We walked around the boulder to investigate.

Crouched over a tiny fire of sticks and dried grasses was a human being so old that it was impossible to tell at first glance whether this gnarled and bent creature was a man or woman. He or she was stirring a pot of herbs with a stick held in a clawlike hand. The rheumy eyes which gazed at us through the smoke-haze were by no means friendly. I felt that this ancient resented our sudden appearance. Yung-Lee spoke a few words but received no reply; the creature went on stirring the green brew. I had brought some rice cakes with me to eat on the way and I proffered one of these. A claw was raised in a gesture of refusal. As I leaned forward, the cake in my hand, I caught a glimpse of two leathery breasts down the dirty brown robe. So this creature was a woman and, as the robe indicated, a hermit of sorts. But the hard battle against the elements her life had entailed, combined with loneliness and an insubstantial diet, had taken a heavy toll. All traces of personality had vanished from her face. Nor could I detect any aura of spirituality about her. Had the struggle been worth it? I wondered.

We left her still stirring the pot of herbs like an old witch, and started to climb further up the trail. I wished I had got myself a staff like the one Yung-Lee was carrying. It would have been an aid to climbing and acted as a brake going down the inclines.

As we were going up a bush-covered slope there was a sudden stamping of hooves and a herd of wild pigs dashed away. Barbets called to each other. Among the rocks was a profusion of wild lilies and bamboo orchids and here and there the deep blue of gentians.

We crossed from one mountain to another by way of a shale-filled valley. These mountains, like the majority on the island, have no names.

We reached the mountain on which the hermit lived. No discernible track led upwards. Huge outcrops of rock appeared like battlements. Among wiry patches of grass and on rocky ledges grew clumps of sea-pinks and mauve snapdragons. Gulls flew past and wheeled above us in the sky. The higher we climbed, the more magnificent the view and the fresher the air, which was scented with ozone. I thought, this hermit, whoever he might be, was not so crazy after all. It must be wonderful to live up here if one's tastes were simple enough, at least in the summer; winter might be a different proposition.

Perched near the summit of the mountain was a small hut built against a fissure in a huge slab of rock. It was facing the sea. Standing on the edge of a sheer cliff-face and looking towards the ocean was an old man dressed in a long grey robe.

Yung-Lee called out a greeting. The old man turned towards us and raised an arm. A strange feeling swept over me as I approached the hermit. I felt certain that somewhere we had met before, although this seemed highly improbable.

Yung-Lee finished the climb at a run, pulling off his heavy pack and dumping it by the open door of the hut. The old hermit, his hands tucked into his long sleeves, smiled as he watched the youth's final, gasping spurt. Then he walked towards me and said, "So you are back again after all these years."

Then I knew. We had indeed met before. This was the same old man I had seen in the Botanical Gardens and whom I had known as a child when he was a younger man and kept a herbal store on the Peak. I wanted to greet him by name but I did not know it.

"Come," he said briefly, and led me to his hut.

There was a wooden bench outside it on which we sat. For some moments neither of us said anything, then he asked, "So you remember me now?"

"Indeed I do. But I have forgotten your name."

"Never mind my name. I threw my old name away a long time ago. But one must have a name sometimes in this world so call me Fo."

I had brought a small box of tea to give to the hermit. I took it out of my rucksack and handed it to him.

"I hope you still drink tea," I said.

"Thank you. A most welcome gift."

He passed the box to Yung-Lee. "We'll have a cup straightaway," he said. "I'm sure you are ready for one."

Yung-Lee stopped unpacking the supplies. He went into the hut and came out again with a primus stove and an earthenware jar of water. While he set about making tea, Fo and I continued our talk.

"When I came over here for good," he said, "I chose to be as anonymous as this mountain. What do you think of the view?"

"It's a marvellous view."

"This is feng-shui country—wind and water country. Even in the hottest summer there is nearly always a cool breeze up here. In winter I sometimes get almost blown away by the gales. But at any time, I have only to open the door of my hut to see the ocean. When the tide is in I can hear it too."

"How long have you been living in Lantao?" I asked.

"I left the red dust of Hong Kong behind me ten years ago."

Red dust means the world.

"But you still go across there occasionally?"

"The last visit I paid to Hong Kong was eight years ago. I have not been back there since."

"That's strange," I said. "Not long ago I saw you in the Botanical Gardens at the time of that severe storm. I was sitting on a bench and you were by the lily-pond. I closed my eyes for a moment and when I opened them again, you were gone.

"As you walked towards me some minutes ago I recognised you at once as the same man I had seen in the gardens and whom I knew as a child when you kept a herbal store. Yet you say you have not been to Hong Kong for eight years now?"

He smiled but said nothing, and I felt that he did not wish to discuss the matter.

Yung-Lee handed us each a cup of tea. He appeared surprised that the hermit and I apparently knew each other, as well he might be.

Everything on the mountaintop, I noticed, had a pristine quality about it. A breeze bent the grasses and tossed the heads of the pinks.

"The wind up here must blow away a lot of life's trivialities," I remarked.

"Yes, it does. And up here one learns to discard and not accumulate, either material goods or worthless mental baggage. In fact, it's only possible to live up here by possessing next to nothing—living light."

"I should love to stay up here for a while."

He gave me a penetrating look and said, "Then you may do so."

Getting up, he motioned me to follow him. He pointed to a broad stretch of grass which wound under an overhanging projection of rock and close to the edge of a precipitous drop.

"About ten minutes from here, along that grassy way, is a piece of vacant property—an empty hut. You may stay there if you wish and do a little experimenting with living; throwing away unnecessary mental baggage and learning to listen to the deep silence which surrounds this mountain. Well, what do you say to my proposal?"

"I should love to come."

"Good."

"When may I return?"

"Whenever you like. The hut is empty and ready for occupation at any time."

"Then I'll come as soon as I can."

Yung-Lee stood ready to leave, staff in hand.

"Haven't you got a staff?" Fo asked me.

I shook my head. He went into the hut and came out with one which he handed to me.

"Thank you. It was just what I needed," I said.

Then Yung-Lee and I started off down the mountainside.

The walk to the mountain had been a long and arduous one but I did not feel tired, and on our journey back to the farm I was filled with a sense of exhilaration. Destiny had decreed that I should meet the herbalist again all these years later. I could hardly wait to return to the mountain where there was an empty hut ready for me to move into.

We reached the farmhouse as the brief dusk was darkening to night. Lamps were burning in the living-room. Mrs. Soong had cooked an appetising supper which was waiting for us when we got in. I was a little weary in the legs by then but in excellent spirits.

CHAPTER EIGHT

MOUNTAINTOP

I HAD TO return to Hong Kong. I timed my arrival back in Lantao to coincide with Yung-Lee's weekly visit to the farm as I wanted to be certain of going with him on his next trip to the mountain.

When I got back to the farm Mr. Soong and Yung-Lee were fixing a wooden stake under the branch of a mango tree. The youth had a defiant expression on his face and Mr. Soong looked glum. I sensed that something was wrong, and when I asked the farmer whether it would be alright for me to go with Yung-Lee on the morrow to the mountain, Mr. Soong replied that his nephew was not going to make the trip any more; next week he would be off to Hong Kong, where he hoped to find more congenial work and higher wages.

So that was that. I would either have to get to the mountain by myself now or not go at all.

After I had eaten supper I went for a short walk to think the matter over. Now that Yung-Lee was not going to take any further supplies to the hermit, would I not be a burden if I stayed on the mountain, presuming I was able to find my way there? How would Fo manage without his weekly supply of provisions? If I attempted to walk there, I would be able to carry only a very small amount of food, enough to last me and the hermit for two or three days perhaps.

I was still pondering the question—to go or not to go?—as I walked back to the farm. As I was passing some out-buildings I suddenly found myself in the middle of a truculent herd of pigs. Mr. Soong was urging them into their stye for the night but the pigs were reluctant to leave the green outdoors. I tried to push my way through the converging mass of black bodies while Mr.

Soong, unsmiling, landed several hard whacks on the rumps of the squealing animals. At last they were all in the stye.

Mr. Soong and I leaned against it. He was looking unusually serious. The pigs were grunting their displeasure. For a while neither he nor I said anything, then I broached the subject of Yung-Lee's departure next week for Hong Kong and I asked the old farmer whether he would be able to find anyone else to help him on the farm. But Mr. Soong was not eager to speak about the matter and so I let the subject drop.

Presently we began to talk on the non-controversial subject of his slump-backed pigs. Pointing to a pregnant sow, the farmer told me that her last lot of piglets had been sold in Tai O for a very good sum, and that the tusker in a corner of the stye was destined to be killed for the Autumn Moon Festival.

When I went to bed that evening I still had not decided whether or not to set off alone next day to the mountain. I thought of the rabid dog Yung-Lee and I had encountered, of the possibility of meeting with thieves, and of the steep and arduous climbs up mountainsides and along precipitous ridges. Better not risk going, was my last thought before falling asleep.

But when I woke up next morning sunshine was streaming through the uncurtained window and I began to think otherwise. The chance of living on those clear heights in the company of Fo was too good to miss and I resolved to at least make the attempt to get there. Nothing venture, nothing gain, as the saying goes.

I told Mr. Soong that I would be away for several days, perhaps longer. Then I shouldered my rucksack and set off. The weather was delightful: hot, but not unbearably so. Up above, a jet airliner sped across the skies on its way to Kai Tak Airport.

By mid-day I had reached the tree-filled valley which lay in wild mountainous country. On emerging from the valley, I followed the ribbonlike track which led steeply upwards. I came to a large boulder. It was here, I remembered, that we had seen the old crone huddled over her stick fire.

I walked behind the boulder but there was no sign of her. Some white ash and blackened stones showed the spot where she had done her cooking. Further on was a hollowed rock which formed a kind of cave. I looked inside. Propped against the rear wall was the old woman hermit. Her mouth was hanging open and flies were crawling over her withered lips. She must surely be dead, I thought.

I turned and continued up the track, anxious to get away from the place.

By three o'clock by my watch I had reached the hermit's mountain. In the distance was Sunset Peak, the second highest mountain on the island, a prominent landmark which had served me as a useful guide. I had made better progress than I had expected. Even so, it was a relief when I had crossed the shale-filled valley and found myself on 'Fo's Mountain', with the great rock-face, like a battlement, facing me.

I was tired now and kept stopping to rest. An azure sea glittered in the distance. I found it strange to look down on the empty beach up which the waves advanced and retreated. It was so unlike the crowded shorelines of Hong Kong.

When I reached Fo's hut I found the door closed. I did not knock but followed the grassy track which he had told me led to the empty hut. In ten minutes or so I reached it. Like Fo's hut, it had been built against the side of towering slabs of rock. I tried the door. It was not locked and I went inside, thankfully taking off my rucksack.

The hut was little more than a shelter from the wind and weather. Some planks had been laid over two boulders to form a rough bed. There was no window in the hut, which was three-quarters natural rock, so when I wanted light I would have to leave the door open. By one end of the 'bed' was a small cavity in the rock into which someone had inserted a wooden shelf. I arranged my cooking utensils and some enamel crockery on this shelf, then I undid my roll of bedding and made up the bed.

The last occupant of the hut had left a pile of sticks to one side of it. Nearby, a narrow rivulet of water trickled down a rockface and formed a shallow pool of water in a basin of rock below.

I built a fire with dried grass and some of the sticks and laid a ring of stones around it on which I set a pan of water. I was dying for a cup of tea.

I sat on the grass sipping the brew and gazing about me. There were only mountain ranges and hills to be seen: rocks, sky and a strip of ocean.

Then I thought I heard footsteps, so soft that I was not sure whether in fact I had. I glanced round and saw Fo walking towards me.

He sat down, saying, "So I have chosen the right moment to come." And he pointed to the tea-pot.

"Just right," I said. "I'll fetch another mug."

When one lives in a Chinese society, whether in a crowded household or on a lonely mountaintop, one is expected to be able to produce a cup of tea for any guest who happens to turn up. Failure to do so involves one in loss of face and is considered a breach of good manners. So I had come prepared and brought an enamel tea-pot, three mugs and a packet of tea.

As Fo was drinking his tea I broke the news to him that Yung-Lee would not be coming any more as he was going to work over in Hong Kong.

"So you managed to find your way here alright by yourself?"

"Yes, somewhat to my surprise," I said.

Fo sipped his tea slowly, savouring the flavour.

"What kind of tea is this—a black China?"

"Yes. Do you like it?"

"It is good tea," he said, "but you have made it just a little too strong."

I asked, my mind still on Yung-Lee's defection, "Will you be able to find anyone else now to bring the supplies?"

"I don't expect so," he answered. "But we'll manage. I have a good supply of rice and some soya sauce for flavouring. During the summer months there is a plentiful supply of wild fare, so we won't starve. Don't let us turn a lack of supplies into a problem. That would be worse than going a little hungry at times. Problems are knots and too many knots in the mind make one a prisoner."

I refilled his cup.

"A little more water, please. There! that's just right. Did you know that tea is in the middle, like everything else that is best in Chinese life?"

"Please explain what you mean by in the middle," I said.

"Well, the smell of tea is delightful, rather like new-mown hay, and the taste is excellent, neither sweet nor sour—not at either extreme. It is a very refreshing drink but it does not cloud the mind or make one drunk like wine, nor is it insipid like a milk-shake. It is right in the centre."

Presently the old man swept an arm out to indicate the surrounding mountainous country.

"Here we are fortunate," he said, "because there is nothing that needs altering or improving. Things just evolve and grow at their own pace. And so, because there is no need to meddle in the things around one, part of one's time each day can profitably be spent just sitting still, looking and listening. If you feel like going for a walk—go for one. Nobody will try and persuade you not to. You are free."

He got up. A seagull flew past us and swept over a stony ridge below which was a deep chasm. Fo went and stood on the edge of the precipice over which the bird had flown and beckoned me to come and stand beside him.

"There he goes! See him?"

I peered over the cliff and saw the bird flying along an escarpment of rock on outstretched, almost motionless wings.

"Now, here is a puzzle for you," the hermit said. "Suppose that gull was larger and offered a sage a ride. On what part of the bird would the sage seat himself?"

"On its back," I answered.

"Yes, of course. The man would not sit on its tail or on a wing but would seat himself firmly on the bird's back, that is, in the middle. Remember what I told you about tea? The idea is the same in both cases. Seat yourself firmly in the centre of the great bird of life and then you won't fall. People who have bad tumbles are usually those who have been sitting precariously on its tail or clinging to a wing. Naturally, they fall off. The great white bird of life," he went on, "flies swiftly forwards in an evolutionary direction. Its left wing is negative and its right wing positive. Is the spot on which the sage is seated, then, a negative or positive one? Quick!"

My mind whirled. "I don't know," I had to admit.

"Think—where is he sitting?"

"On the bird's back."

"That is, in the middle, where the negative and positive poles meet. So the answer is neither; because the central point is neutral. Sometimes the sage might move out to some other place on the bird, but if he is truly wise he is not going to remain out there long where he is in danger of losing his balance and where he is impeding the bird's progress. He always returns to the neutral central position where he is balanced and poised. It is quite simple."

He walked away, his slim figure upright in spite of his many years, his grey gown merging with that of the rocks.

That night I put a large stone against the door of the hut to keep it wide while I slept. I had no fear about possible intruders entering. Fear and uneasiness seemed unnecessary emotions on these peaceful heights.

Before stretching out on my plank bed, I climbed on to a high boulder and gazed about me. Ahead, there was no light to be seen for miles except for that of a distant fishing-smack, and the only sounds were those of the waves. When I turned and faced south I could see a cluster of lights from Tung Chung and Tai O. Silvermine Bay on the opposite side of the island was hidden by mountains. But between a gap in the range I was able to see the Peak from where I stood. It was ashimmer with lights. The atmosphere was so clear that I was even able to glimpse the electric tram as it sped down to Victoria.

But Hong Kong, though it was only a few miles distant, was a long way from Lantao; it was a different island in a different world.

CHAPTER NINE

HERMITS

I GOT UP early while I was living on the mountain, soon after the sun had risen. About every third day Fo and I would go for a walk in search of provender.

One day we walked to a distant cove where there were various kinds of edible seaweed to be had for the picking. The tide was out and we were able to walk right down the beach, looking into pools as we went. Every so often I plunged an arm into a pool and tugged a piece of weed from its rocky moorings. Our diet was wholly vegetarian, so the shrimps and mussels were left unmolested by us.

Fo picked up a mauve pebble and held it up to the light, then he carefully put it back on the beach again. He handled everything with care even if the 'thing' were only a stone or a bit of driftwood, as though he believed that these seemingly inanimate objects held some inner life of their own.

A long line of surf swept up the beach. The wind soughed. We walked barefooted through the rushing waves. And as we walked, my past seemed to be swept away into oblivion, the future did not exist, and I experienced briefly only timeless moments of wind and foam.

We left the cove and walked inland until we came to a piece of swampy ground. Here we collected our 'potatoes', tubers of various kinds. We pulled up swamp plants, picking off the bulb-like roots.

Near the swamp was a spinney of bamboos. We cut off some of their succulent shoots. These shoots had to be stripped of their outer coverings and soaked in water overnight before being cooked and eaten the following day.

Then we walked on to a group of pines. Here we collected edible fungi.

Fo stopped to pick some cream-coloured toadstools which were growing by the roots of a pine. The air was very still and scented with resin. Patches of sky were visible between the tufts of dark green pine needles. The hermit in his grey gown stood motionless as he inspected the toadstools. The scene was one of harmony and quiet beauty.

As I looked at it, a question occurred to me. Suppose someone from Europe, say, was taken on a mystery flight to Lantao and he got out of the plane near this spot, where would the visitor think he was? As he took in the surrounding scene—which was much like that depicted in many Chinese paintings—and if he caught sight of Fo, then he would certainly guess that he was somewhere in the Far East. The peaceful lonely countryside and the old man in his long gown might cause the visitor to believe that he had somehow slipped back in time to another era, or forwards, perhaps, into a future more harmonious age. But he would be wrong in both cases, for Lantao did not belong to the past nor had it advanced into some future era. It was of the present, but no mundane present. Rather, a timeless now. One felt that some subtle principle had transformed the place and made it altogether different from other islands lying in the South China Sea. Lantao was an enchanted island.

My reflections about Lantao were cut short by Fo asking, "Why are you standing there idle and not searching for toadstools?"

"I was just thinking how different in every way Lantao is compared to other islands in the group," I replied.

"Pardon me for having interrupted your thoughts. But what do you mean by saying that this island is different in every way from the other islands?"

"I have the feeling that once upon a time some invisible being must have waved a magic wand over Lantao."

"Really?" he said, somewhat sharply. "Well, then, different in what way?"

I hesitated. "I'm not sure just where the difference lies. Perhaps it's a difference in quality. It's as though some kind of transformation had taken place here."

"Let's be practical," he said. "Lantao is composed of earth and rocks and is surrounded by the ocean, and so is Hong Kong and the other islands. So does the difference lie in the basic ingredients?"

"No, it can't."

"So it must lie somewhere else?"

"Yes."

He said no more on the subject, but it was as though he had left me with a question to ponder and solve for myself.

We started to walk back to the mountain, stopping on a hillside to dig up some dandelion roots. These we would lay out to dry and then chop them up into small pieces to use to make dandelion tea. Our tea had run out and I missed it more than anything else and never grew to appreciate the rather bitter taste of the dandelion substitute, although it was better than nothing.

Fo led the way back up the mountain. We climbed steadily, the old man walking with slow even strides and always ahead of me. His energy amazed me. He stopped only when he saw that I needed a rest.

When we reached his hut we sorted out the provender, putting each variety of food into separate piles. Fo was a good cook and he went to considerable trouble to make the various dishes we ate tasty and nourishing.

We washed the vegetables and seaweed under a rock spring, scraped the tubers, sliced the toadstools. Everything had to be prepared 'just so'.

Our supper that evening consisted of seaweed soup, baked tubers and steamed vegetables, and sliced toadstools which had been cooked in a soya sauce.

As we sat on the bench eating the meal, I congratulated Fo on his prowess as a cook.

"Cooking has interested me ever since I was a boy and was taught by my mother how to make the moon cakes which are eaten at the Autumn Moon Festival. You've seen them? They look like small pies. Inside the pastry-case is a rich filling and inside the filling is a hard-boiled egg yolk to represent the moon. They keep very well, just like your Christmas cakes."

"Were you living in Hong Kong when you were a boy?"

"Yes. I was born in Hong Kong. My great-grandfather came here from Kweichow Province, and we've been here ever since. When I was ten years old I went on a trip to Kweichow with my father. He was a herbalist and an expert in the art of moxa, which is a form of healing by the use of herbs and other means. We journeyed far inland to a village where we had relatives, and we spent some time in the surrounding mountain ranges gathering rare herbs which are not to be found in Hong Kong."

"Is moxa similar to acupuncture?"

"The treatment is different but the aims are the same: to remove blockages and knots which have been set up in the physical and subtle bodies of the patient. In moxa, small cones of specially prepared herbs are placed on the patient in vital spots. They are lit and burn away slowly as he lies there."

"That sounds painful."

"No. Moxa treatment may sound painful but it's not. The patient has a feeling of heat at the spots where the cones are burning, that is all, and no scars or marks are left. After treatment by an expert the vital energies in the various bodies of the patient should be flowing freely again."

I made the dandelion tea.

"Had you wanted to live in Lantao for some time before actually coming here?" I asked him.

"I think ever since I went on that boyhood trip to China. Wandering about the Kweichow ranges collecting herbs gave me a lasting love for lonely mountainous country. We met Taoist recluses in remote hermitages, men who were exploring interior realms in the silence of the mountains. I longed to spend at least a part of my life as they were spending their lives, but it was many years before I was able to leave Hong Kong for good and come over here. And that was not such a bad thing. I had to learn during those Hong Kong years how to keep an inner calm and silence amongst the bustle and noise of life over there. To have lived in Lantao before I had achieved that would have done me little good and perhaps some harm. Most people can only stand short periods of complete solitude and silence. Too long, and these things begin to act like a poison instead of a vital tonic. But those who are trying to acquire an oasis of calm within themselves while living in everyday surroundings will find that short periods of isolation in a silent countryside will be of great help, because an outer silence and absence of busyness helps one to discover an inner silence and serenity."

"How does one start to discover this inner silence?"

"Well, one way is by listening intently first of all to outer sounds. When you go back to your hut try this.

"Sit outside on the grass and just listen. Don't turn this listening into some kind of duty or discipline. Just listen naturally but intently; first, to some distant sound: the waves advancing and retreating up and down the shore. Then nearer sounds: the wind as it blows through the gullies. Closer again: the hum of an insect a few feet from you—a tiny sound and still outside. Now cross the threshhold of yourself into the inner world and start listening to the sound of your own breathing: in and out, like the sound of the waves sweeping up and down the beach. Then stop listening but keep your consciousness fixed inwards still. Listen! What will you hear? Silence. Merge and become one with it. At first you will not be able to hear this inner silence for more than a second or so. Never mind. Persist, and you'll find that the seconds will gradually increase. When you emerge from this silence, start listening again, first, to your own breathing, then cross the threshold into the outer world and pick up the sounds of an insect, birds, the wind and the distant waves.

"One day you may find that the two separate worlds, the inner and the outer, unite and become one. Silence contains all sounds," he said, "but sound does not contain silence."

I went and sat down outside my hut and started to listen, first to the waves, then to the wind, the sound of a grasshopper, and lastly to the sound of my own breathing. For the space of half a second, perhaps, I became aware of a vast ocean of silence, an invisible and unknown sea.

One evening I saw a fire burning in the valley below and the figure of a man standing by the flames. I wondered who had chosen such a remote spot in which to spend the night.

Next morning I caught sight of a figure coming up the mountain. I guessed it was probably the same person who had lit the fire the previous evening. Whoever it was, he seemed to know his way up. He walked with quick sure strides, seldom pausing. As he drew nearer, there struck me as being something familiar about him. He came into full view round an escarpment of rock and then I recognised him as that strange individual who was able to attract wild birds. I watched him approach the summit with mixed feelings. He disappeared from sight as he climbed the final stretch which led to Fo's hut.

In the afternoon I walked over to find out if the 'birdman' was there. Sure enough, he and Fo were sitting outside the hut drinking dandelion tea and talking earnestly together. Kwong pulled a face when he saw me and emptied the remains of his tea on the ground.

"I'm being poisoned," he said. "If I'd known you were out of the proper stuff I'd have brought some along with me."

I was longing to see this man summon birds to him again and presently I asked him if he would do so. He wiped his mouth with his sleeve and said, "Very well."

"Yes, call a flock of your friends," said Fo. "Our lives up here are not very eventful and we'd appreciate an afternoon's entertainment."

Kwong strode to the cliff. Slowly, he raised his arms and stood there motionless. I looked about me; there was not a bird in sight. But before long a far-off gull wheeled towards him like a homing pigeon, and a few minutes later there was a flock of white seabirds around his feet and perched on his broad shoulders. Some yards from him, Fo walked among dozens of squawking birds. They did not appear to be afraid of him but they did not seem to be particularly attracted to him either. Kwong, meanwhile, was stroking a gull on the neck much as someone else might stroke a pet cat. As I watched him gently petting the bird I remembered the incident of the baby monkey. Creatures, it seemed, either rushed away from him in fear or were drawn to him by some powerful attraction.

Fo and I stood watching the milling flock of birds around Kwong.

"It's amazing!" I said.

"No, it's quite natural," said Fo, smiling.

"If it's natural, then why can't I summon birds to me as he does?"

"Why can't I? Well, you must have noticed that this man has a very magnetic personality—even birds find him irresistible!"

Kwong, hearing the remark, laughed loudly and then clapped his hands, whereupon the birds flew off and wheeled in a huge semi-circle, flying far out to sea where they broke up into smaller and smaller flocks.

I thanked Kwong for the remarkable demonstration he had given and returned to my hut. I set about preparing supper.

As I was dropping some tubers into the pan, Kwong came walking along the grassy way and sat down by the fire.

"How do you attract them?" I asked. "Is it by means of some rare gift you were born with?"

I should dearly have loved to be able to attract birds to myself.

For all the attention he gave my question he might not have heard me speak. He sat there, his chin cupped in his hands, gazing into the flames. Then, coming out of his reverie, he said abruptly, "When will you be leaving?"

"I don't know," I answered.

"I spent some months last winter in your hut and I want to come again this year but earlier, whenever you go."

His question pulled me up with a jerk.

"Perhaps I won't be going for some time yet," I said.

He appeared puzzled and asked, "What do you mean?"

I had put into words something which had been at the edge of my mind for several days. Life on the mountain suited me. Here was a place where one could reflect and discard many of the mundane cares and worries which cling to one like burrs in normal everyday existence. Already I felt that I had dropped a load of unnecessary mental baggage. Why not continue, then, for a month or so to live this simple uncluttered life on the mountain —why leave?

"Do you mean you are thinking of staying here for several more weeks?" Kwong asked.

"Why not?"

"You are thinking nonsense!"

"But why nonsense?"

"A short stay up here will do you good but if you remain for long you'll find you are drinking poison instead of nectar."

"Well, you are living a hermit's life on this island," I pointed out, "so why not me, for a few more weeks, at any rate?"

"I can live such a life because I am a whole hermit and you are only half a one. I came to live here as a recluse after years of turmoil and restlessness. I found my goal at last and I realised that, once started on this life, there could be no turning back for me. My past was over and done with. I was prepared to give myself wholly to this new life I had chosen."

"Tell me something about your past life," I asked him.

"I have told you—it's over and done with."

"I'm interested to know what made you take up the rigorous and lonely life of a hermit over here."

"Oh, very well," he conceded, "if you're really interested I'll tell you a little about it. I was born in a village twenty miles from the capital. That was thirty-six—no, thirty-seven years ago."

A blazing sunset had given place to a dusk which was rapidly melting into night. I threw some driftwood on to the fire and the flames leapt up, illuminating Kwong's swarthy face.

"The capital—you mean, Pekin?"

"Yes. We moved to Pekin when I was eight, my parents, myself, my sister and my young brother. My father got a job there as a minor government official. He was quite ambitious and learnt English in his spare time. He died a few years after our arrival during one of the bitterly cold winters. My mother and we three children made the long journey to Shanghai to go and live with an uncle and aunt, the only relatives we had. My uncle was a wealthy trader.

"He and my aunt treated us well at first but I never liked them. I sensed their bitterness and jealousy towards my mother under a superficial layer of goodwill. They were envious of her because she had three children and they, although possessing wealth, had none. One day my uncle asked mother if she would let them adopt my young brother, but she absolutely refused to have anything to do with this proposal. So later we were told to leave the house. Uncle said that he would keep my brother until we were settled in some other place and earning a little money. So we left him there. We were virtually penniless and one more mouth to feed might have meant starvation for all of us.

"We moved to a very poor quarter and I managed to get a job as an errand boy. I began to grow very uneasy about my brother, and one day I walked almost the length of the city to go and see him. My uncle and aunt were out. Their houseboy led me to the servants' quarters and into a tiny room. On some matting lay a boy who was so emaciated that at first I did not recognise him. When I did, I stood there horror-struck. But I managed to pull myself together and I told the servant that I was taking my brother home. This man was on my side. He summoned a rickshaw and we laid my brother on the footrest. He was too weak to sit up.

"You can imagine the terrible shock it was to my mother when I returned home with this near-skeleton. The last time she had seen him he had been a healthy schoolboy and now, obviously, he was close to death. And not a word had my uncle or aunt sent us that he was in any way ill."

Kwong's eyes filled with tears and he stopped speaking.

Presently I asked, "Whatever had happened to your brother?"

"He had been bled to death," Kwong replied, his voice so low I could hardly catch his words.

"When my uncle and aunt realised that they would never be able to adopt him they became filled with hate for this innocent boy and for us," he said. "After we had left, my uncle had told the boy that he was to go to various hospitals in Shanghai and earn some money as a blood donor. Donors were paid quite good sums for their contributions. All the money my brother earned in this way was handed over to my uncle. If he did not return with any then he was given a severe beating. Almost every day my brother went to a hospital and had blood extracted. These hospitals did not keep too careful a record, it seemed, about their various donors, either as to their ages or as to whether a person had given blood only a short while back. Anyway, a person desperate for money often lied about his age and would give a different name if he returned again soon to the same hospital.

"We learnt how all this happened from my brother's own faint whispers to us and later from the servants who worked in my uncle's house. Both my uncle and aunt fiercely denied that they had any idea of what was going on and that they themselves were responsible for the draining away of his life. My brother died a week after I had brought him home."

"How ghastly," I said.

Kwong nodded. "In later years I was to meet many bad characters, but none so evil as those two relatives of mine. After my brother's death my whole life became geared to eventual revenge. I watched and waited and took any job, legal or illegal, so long as the pay was good. But before I was able to carry out my plan of putting an end to those two evil beings with the help of hired assassins, the police got interested in me and I was forced to leave Shanghai in a hurry to avoid arrest. I came to Hong Kong.

"Some time after my arrival I visited Lantao where I met this man you call Fo. In those days he was living in a hut further south, not far from where they are building the reservoir. How can I explain to you? A little peace entered my soul at last and I knew I had found someone unique and rare in this hermit. I continued to visit him; new thoughts began to enter my mind. I still contemplated revenge but not so often now.

"A few days after I had returned to Hong Kong from one of my Lantao trips I was sitting in the Kee Heung Tea House, the place where customers bring their caged birds to be admired, when I happened to glance out of a window and I saw passing a wealthy-looking Chinese couple whom I recognised only too well. You can guess who they were?"

"Your uncle and aunt?"

"None other. They had fled the Communist regime in China and taken refuge in the Colony. My uncle had managed to get most of his fortune out of China and he and my aunt were living in a pleasant house in the Shatin Valley. All this I found out in a matter of hours.

"Here was my chance: two sitting birds unaware of my presence. I would not have to make the journey back to Shanghai now; they had come to me. But somewhere along the way, perhaps since I had started visiting Lantao, I had changed. I found to my surprise that I no longer wished to kill them. When I thought of what they had done to my brother all those years ago I felt only a deep sadness." He paused, then went on, "For years, as I've said, the aim of my life had been to avenge my brother's death, to destroy his destroyers. But now I found that all desire to murder had died in me and, what was more, I wanted to live a completely different life from the kind I had lived in the past.

"So I threw my past away together with my name and I came over here to live as a hermit."

The flames from the fire had flickered out; Kwong's face was veiled in shadow. I sat staring at the red embers. When I looked at the place where he had been sitting, there was no one there. I was alone by a dying fire.

That night I lay for some time wondering whether to stay on in Lantao for a few more weeks—a month, perhaps—or to leave in a day or two. It had been a wonderful experience living on the mountain where there was not a single jarring note or touch of ugliness. I had no fear that solitude and silence would become eventual poisons for me but I did wonder whether, if I stayed for much longer, I then would find it unbearably hard to leave this remote spot and the company of Fo. Sooner or later I knew I would have to leave, and this thought was like a dagger turning in my mind. A dagger! That could maim and kill like poison. I realised then that if I stayed for much longer I might well be laying myself open to a danger as great as that of solitude is to some people: the danger of a heart-rending ache whenever I thought of the time I had spent here, a deep nostalgia that might well threaten my inner equilibrium. But I would stay on for a day, or two, or three . . . postponing my inevitable departure for as long as possible, for as long as I dared.

A wind got up and roared like a living thing round the mountain. I seemed to hear it calling loudly and then softly, India . . . the country I planned to visit when I left Hong Kong, if I ever did leave ... I closed my eyes and saw the Great Snow Range, the wide rivers; scents from long ago came back to me, the pungent scent of tropical flowers: tuberose and queen of the night, flowers woven into garlands and laid on the stone altars of ancient temples. India! the wind whispered, and I answered, 'Yes, I'm coming, sooner or later. ...'

Only a light breeze was blowing the following morning. I walked round to Fo's hut. He was sitting outside it on the bench, and I had the feeling that he was waiting for me.

I sat down beside him and said, "May I ask your advice? Already I've stayed here for longer than I planned, yet I should love to stay on for a little longer still—a week, two weeks—but only if you are agreeable to this. Kwong told me that he wants to move into my hut when I go."

"Never mind about Kwong," Fo said. "He can move in when you leave, but it is entirely up to you when you go. Why has the matter become a problem for you?"

"I suppose because I'm so reluctant to go."

"If I said, 'Then why not stay on here indefinitely?' what would your feelings be about that?"

He had put into words something that I had half hoped he might, but now that he had spoken them and posed the question I was at a loss as to how to answer it.

"Think clearly," Fo said. "Know exactly why you do this or that. What is it that makes you want to stay here—would it be the mountain air and the scenery?"

"I came because you are here and that is why I want to stay on," I said promptly.

"Very well. I am an old man now and I don't suppose I'll be in this ancient body for much longer. Would you care to live on this mountain as a solitary hermit?"

I laughed. "Goodness no! It would be quite meaningless for me to stay here if you were gone, apart from the fact that I wouldn't be able to manage up here by myself."

"You've answered your own question, haven't you?"

"Yes, I suppose so."

There and then, I firmly made up my mind.

"I'll leave tomorrow," I said, and no sooner were the words out than I had to force myself to keep the tears back.

Fo asked gently, "What are your plans, where will you be going to?"

"I'll be going back to Hong Kong and later on I'll be leaving the Colony and going to India."

He smiled. "While you still have this urge to travel you will keep moving. One day when this urge within you has lessened you will search mainly in another direction."

"Search?" I questioned.

"Isn't all this travelling you've done and will be doing largely a search after something?"

"Perhaps. In part, at least," I admitted.

"You are like a traveller who once or twice has glimpsed a distant land and consciously or unconsciously searches to find it again. This land does exist; it is not an illusion. Persist in your quest and sooner or later you'll find the path which leads to it.

"Don't forget," he continued, "that the hermit's life can be led anywhere. For many years, as you know, I earned my living as a herbalist on the Peak and I have never regretted those years. Only when I had reached late middle age was I able and ready to come over here permanently. And when I eventually came over here for good, people said I had become a recluse. They were wrong. For years before coming here I had been a 'hidden hermit' in Hong Kong, though few persons had been aware of this.

"It's the inner attitude which counts, you see.

"A man could spend years in some lonely Lantao valley and be no more a hermit than that seagull, while another could spend his life in Victoria or London, yet be a true recluse, having gained an inner quiet and a certain detachment from worldly affairs."

He stopped speaking and stared at the wide arch of sky. Then his eyes closed and a quality of remoteness seemed to wrap him around like an invisible cloak. I left quietly.

The mountains and valleys stood out clearly under the blazing summer sun. I caught my breath at the sheer beauty of the scene around me. Then I glanced back at the still figure of the hermit. His serene expression hinted that he was immersed in some realm more lovely and unconfined that the surrounding countryside, a realm where I was unable to follow him.

I went and packed my few belongings into my rucksack in preparation for my departure on the morrow.

In the afternoon Kwong came to the hut and said that Fo wanted to see me.

As we walked over, I said to him, "You'll be able to move into the hut tomorrow. I'll be leaving in the morning."

"Are you? I'll come with you to the farm. It's easy to get lost in this region."

I was grateful for his offer to accompany me and that I would not have to find my way back alone over the wild terrain.

Fo was standing by his hut waiting for us.

"Come inside," he said to me; "I want to show you something."

This was the first time I had been inside. The hut contained a narrow wooden bed, a low stool, a shelf on which were a few books, some jars containing herbs, and a Chinese scroll painting hanging from the shelf.

"I don't want to show you anything in here," he said. "I want you to see my wild garden."

Then, turning to Kwong, he remarked, "She's now going to accuse me of being inconsistent. The first evening she was here I told her that nothing on the mountain needed improving and that time was best spent in looking and listening and leaving things alone to take care of themselves. Well, now I must confess," he said to me, "that I have put in a certain amount of time and toil on my favourite hobby of gardening and doing a little improving here and there on the garden I'm about to show you."

He pushed open a door which lay on the opposite side of the hut and led the way out.

A narrow pathway ran between a high fissure in the rock. It was only possible to walk single file. Slabs of rocks towered up on either side of us and then the fissure opened out and we stepped into a wide clearing which was completely surrounded by walls of sheer rock. Boulders lay about the clearing and growing on and around them were patches of green herbs and drifts of flowers.

"Nearly all the plants in this garden are wild ones," said Fo, "which I've grown from seeds and cuttings collected from the countryside. Not all of the plants I've collected have taken to these heights and the rather arid soil, but these have done surprisingly well," and he pointed to a clump of bamboo orchids. "I dug them up at the bottom of the mountain and transplanted them up here."

We walked through drifts of flowers, white, pink, mauve and yellow, like a Persian carpet. Fo sometimes stopped to point out a particular plant to me and tell me a little of its history like any keen gardener.

We walked to the far end of this wild cultivated garden and here a grassy, flat-topped hill stood against the dark wall of rock. At its base was a clutter of boulders, tumbling like ocean waves, and in the deep shade they cast were pools of vibrant blue, not pools of water, but flowers. I recognised these flowers immediately with a feeling of delight. I had only seen them once before in my life many years ago outside Fo's herbal store. But once seen, never forgotten.

Seeing my pleasure, Fo bent down and picked one of the blossoms and handed it to me, saying, "It is not surprising that these Himalayan or blue poppies do well up here because they are flowers of the heights. In China they are sometimes called Flowers of Heaven. See,"—and he pointed to the bright gold stamens surrounded by the intense blue petals—"there is the sun in the centre of blue skies."

Kwong started to walk up the grassy hill. Fo and I walked behind him, I carefully holding the poppy.

The view was panoramic; miles of ocean strewn with islands, and the Chinese coast clearly visible. On the far horizon the blue sky merged with the ocean's rim.

A few yards of grass bordered the flat top of the hill but the centre was entirely covered by a slab of white stone. I noticed as we walked over it that this stone was not a piece of natural rock. It had been carved by some person or persons into a circle and was about twelve feet across. A small circle had been incised in the centre and round this inner circle were various hieroglyphs.

"Do you know what this stone is for?" Kwong asked me.

"I haven't any idea," I said.

He went and stood in the inner circle. "On this stone I am slowly learning to become a wind-walker," he said. "My teacher,"—and he nodded towards Fo—"is an experienced walker of the skies."

He and Fo both laughed, but in spite of their laughter I did not have the feeling that Kwong had been joking and I was puzzled as to how to accept his remark.

Wind-walkers are often mentioned in Oriental stories and legends about the sages. They are men who, because they have jettisoned a load of mental ballast and know many of the hidden laws underlying nature, are able to fly, to 'walk the wind and the sky.' But surely, I thought, gazing at the great circular stone, these tales are not meant to be taken literally but rather in a metaphorical sense. Yet I had to ask myself, if Kwong had in fact been joking, then what was the stone for? Who had carved it and who had brought it to this remote mountain, or had it been carved on the spot? These and other questions raced through my mind.

"Come and stand behind me," Kwong said. "We'll try an experiment and see if we can get you airborne."

Both he and Fo laughed again loudly and this time I joined in the laughter.

I went and stood behind Kwong on the flat stone and said, "I'm looking forward to flying. Tell me what to do."

"Do nothing. Just stand where you are. Fo will stand behind you. Ready?"

"Yes," I said.

Ready for what? A flicker of uneasiness went through me.

Kwong raised his arms, forwards, first, like a swimmer about to make a dive, then sideways. His broad figure, just in front of me, was not like a swimmer's now but like a man poised for flight, ridiculous as that may sound.

The wind blew against my face. Ahead was the sea and down below us was the garden surrounded by stone walls of natural rock.

Presently I began to be aware of a current. It was intangible, yet as strong as electricity. The force of gravity seemed to be lessening and there was a feeling of a strong upward pull which increased in strength with every passing second. This force—whatever it was—became so strong that I began to sway on my feet like a person standing in a fierce ocean current. But this current's force was directed upwards and I had the extraordinary feeling that at any moment I was in danger of being swept off my feet and impelled up into the air. I struggled to keep my feet on the stone but in spite of my efforts I could feel my grip on the earth's surface was being loosened. The implacable force was about to whirl me up and away. My uneasiness changed to fear. I knew that unless I quickly acted in some way this force would have me totally in its grip and in a matter of seconds now sweep me off the ground.

I cried out—"Stop, please stop! I can't bear any more..."

I was tossed sideways by invisible waves of force, my feet slithering over the stone, but already I could feel the current lessening a little.

I had been holding the blue poppy in my hand all this while, but in my struggles against this strange force I inadvertently opened my hand and, like a bird released from my grip, the poppy flew upwards, whirling higher and higher, until I lost sight of it against the blue skies.

Kwong had lowered his arms. The current was ebbing. My feet were firmly on the stone. Down below in the garden the blossoms tossed in the wind. The wind!... it could have been the wind which had given me those extraordinary sensations, so strong that I had felt that at any moment I was in danger of being swept up into the air—it could have been the wind, but I knew that it wasn't.

I was standing firmly on the earth again and feeling slightly foolish at having cried out in the way I had done. How gentle the breeze felt against my face after that strong impelling force which had seemed about to sever me from the earth's surface.

Fo was walking down the hill. I glanced once more at the white stone with its engraved hieroglyphs, then turned and followed him.

The three of us walked back through the garden in silence, along the narrow pathway bordered by walls of rock and into the hut, then out. I stood with Fo on the verge of grass which edged the cliff-like drop. There was the trace of a smile on his lips.

Blues and pale greens were leaving the evening sky and it was becoming filled with the fiery colours of sunset. The hermit appeared to be absorbed in the sight. But I paid no attention to the sunset that evening. I gazed at Fo. I knew that I was seeing him for the last time, an old man, yet somehow ageless.

He turned and looked at me, a deep penetrating look which seemed to see into my innermost being and yet was quite impersonal. Then, still keeping me within his vision, his gaze seemed to go past his immediate surroundings into some limitless beyond.

I placed the palms of my hands together and voiced a silent farewell to him.

I walked back to my hut. The moment of parting which I had been secretly dreading had come and gone but I felt no trace of sadness, only a feeling of almost unearthly happiness.

CHAPTER TEN

RETURN TO HONG KONG

IN THE MORNING I left the mountain with Kwong. He took a route that was unfamiliar to me. We went past some marshy land where graceful white egrets were standing in the bright green grass and then we walked over some low hillocks. On the top of one of them were the ruins of a small temple. The day was very hot and much of the countryside was beginning to have a dried-up look.

Around mid-day we rested in a shady bamboo spinney at the bottom of a stony ravine. It was a relief to sit in the shade for a while. Then, as we were about to get up and resume our journey, we heard men's voices in the distance. Persons in this part of Lantao are so rarely encountered that I got quite a shock when I heard the sound of talking. Kwong peered through the foliage and motioned me to move further into the spinney. The voices grew louder. I looked round a clump of jointed bamboo stems. Six men came into view. Two were carrying a large box fixed to poles, another carried a sack. All the men were of rough appearance and the thought entered my mind that they were probably bandits or pirates off to hide some loot in a lonely cavern in the mountains. They walked out of the ravine and disappeared over the crest of a hill. They were talking loudly as they went by, no more thinking, I suppose, that there might be other human beings in the vicinity than we had done. Kwong said he was certain that the men, whoever they were, were up to no good.

In the late afternoon he pointed out to me the farm lying in the distance among the undulating hills.

"You'll be able to find your way now," he said. "Goodbye."

And he turned and started to walk back towards the mountainous country through which we had come.

When I reached the farm I saw to my surprise Yung-Lee, whom I thought was over in Hong Kong, digging in the vegetable garden. He looked up as I approached and then returned to his digging, having hardly given me a glance or sign of recognition. Mrs. Soong was stripping bamboo shoots in the living-room. I asked her by signs where her husband was and she pointed in the direction of Tung Chung. I wanted to tell him that I would be leaving Lantao on the morrow and would not be coming back.

He returned that evening carrying two empty panniers slung at either end of a pole in which he had taken some ducks to the market at Tung Chung.

"You been away long time," he said.

"Yes," and I told him that in the morning I would be leaving the island for good.

The youth came in and sat at the end of the table waiting for supper, morose and surly looking. I asked Mr. Soong why his nephew had returned from Hong Kong. He told me that the only work Yung-Lee had been able to get there was as a porter in a market. It was very heavy work and poorly paid. After a week or so of hard labour carting crates of fruit and vegetables about and with no prospect of a better job in view, he reluctantly left Hong Kong and returned to Lantao, a sadder and now somewhat bitter young man.

I caught the early ferry at Tung Chung next morning. White foam poured from under the stern as we sailed away.

When I got out of the taxi opposite my flat I saw that the new block which workmen had been busy building next to ours was now completed. The bamboo scaffolding had been taken down and people were going in and out of the front entrance. A large crowd was standing outside as though waiting for something to happen and there were two ominously large strings of crackers hanging down from windows on the first story to ground level.

I had only just turned the key in my lock and walked into the flat when there was an explosion which seemed to rock the building. It continued for what must have been close on five minutes.

Laughter and shouts came from the crowd down below. The block next door had been declared open.

This new block was literally only two feet from ours. When I leaned out of my side bedroom window I had easily been able to touch the ledge of the window opposite. Now, as I looked through my window I found myself staring straight into the eyes of a Chinaman, no doubt the newly arrived tenant. For a second his expression revealed surprise at my sudden appearance, then a blankness came over his face and he turned away from the window, seemingly oblivious of me.

One often sees this blank look in Hong Kong, where most of the population live cheek by jowl with other human beings. It is assumed as a kind of defence mechanism and means that there has been an erasing from the mind of the fact that complete strangers are living in all too close proximity with oneself.

I closed the window and fastened the catch. From now on it would be kept fastened. For all I knew, the occupant of the flat opposite was a perfectly law-abiding citizen, but just in case he was not, I thought it as well to keep the window closed and secured. There is a great deal of breaking and entering in the Colony. I put the thought from my mind that anyone intent on entering my flat from the one opposite would have little difficulty in doing so. A penknife would probably suffice to undo the catch.

I opened my mail. There was a letter from my landlady asking whether I wanted to rent the flat for another year. Had I really been in the Colony for close on a year? I could hardly believe it. Time had gone by so swiftly. No, I would not be renting the flat for a further year.

That evening a noisy mahjong party was held in the newly occupied flat. Mahjong players are supposed by law to finish their games before midnight. When I sat up in bed and looked at my watch I saw that the time was past one o'clock. The talk and laughter and sounds of the blocks being thrown on to the table continued unabated. I felt irritated enough to want to put through a call to the police and tell them to send someone round to stop the party, but I hesitated to take such drastic action. After all, I reasoned, the new tenant might be having a late-night party with friends to celebrate his arrival at the flat and would probably not hold another one for months, by which time I would be gone anyway. There came a burst of screams and shouts and the sound of glasses being clinked together. This was too much! I got out of bed with the idea of leaning across the gap and tapping on his window. Then I got back into bed again, having decided not to. The party continued till nearly three.

One soon comes to think hard before crossing swords with one's neighbours when one lives in a closely packed community like Hong Kong. Should one tell the police that a mahjong party is being held after hours in a nearby flat, the occupants of the flat often manage to find out who informed on them and get their own back on the informer in various ways. The Chinese are experts in inflicting all sorts of subtle annoyances on anyone who does them such a disservice. So most people in the Colony, when faced with the all too common problem of noisy neighbours, take no action and put up with the racket as best they can.

The next morning I went down to Victoria to book a passage. I wanted something different this time and the travel agent suggested I go on a cargo vessel. There was one calling in at the Colony in a month's time and then going on to Mauritius, Ceylon, Bombay and Britain. I reserved a berth on it as far as Ceylon where I wanted to spend about a month, and from there I would make arrangements to go on to India.

The rest of my time in the Colony was largely spent in a whirl of packing and having things taken down to the auction to be sold.

The Vogels were leaving, too, at the end of the year. They invited me to a party celebrating the Autumn Moon Festival due to be held two days before I left Hong Kong.

During a brief respite from packing one afternoon I sat down on the sofa and glanced at the daily paper. I saw to my surprise that Lantao, which only got rare and brief mentions in the local press, unlike Hong Kong which was never out of the news, was the subject that day of quite a lengthy article.

Lantao, the journalist stated, must be developed—and quickly —so as to ease the population explosion in Hong Kong and

Kowloon. There should be reservoirs, factories, and workers' flats built there at the fastest possible rate. Already there were projects afoot, he said, for developing the island but none of these had so far been put into effect. Hong Kong and Kowloon were bursting at the seams with people while Lantao—the largest island in the Colony—had only a mere handful. Get cracking! he urged Government and local officials.

I put down the paper, feelings of hate, sadness and guilt churning in my breast. Hate for that particular journalist for having urged that Lantao be turned into another teeming Hong Kong and sadness at the thought that sooner or later—probably sooner—this would inevitably happen. The solitude and strange mystery of that island would vanish as though they had never been. And I felt the guilt of one who, living in one of the overcrowded, exploding areas of the world, Hong Kong, where one seems to feel the pressure of people around one even when one is alone in one's own flat, still harbours the selfish hope, nevertheless, that one nearby underpopulated island that I loved should remain so. Impossible, of course. At least, thank heaven, I had seen Lantao at its pristine best and for that privilege I should ever consider myself fortunate.

I rang Mr. Chan and told him I was leaving soon. It was he who had suggested that I go to Lantao and who had made arrangements for me to stay at the farm. I thanked him, saying how much my visits to the island had meant to me.

Fortunately, I had acted on his suggestion and thereby discovered an island remote from the rush and turmoil of the modern world; and there I had found the man I hoped I would when I had returned to the Colony, living alone now on a mountaintop. During my stay with him on the mountain I had lived for a while in a totally new and unknown world and become absorbed in it. Things which had seemed of vital importance to me previously had become of negligible account up there. On those lonely heights my consciousness had stretched a little beyond its usual limits. Now I must try to keep on extending the inner frontiers of reality.

Chinese foodshops were full of mooncakes, small pies with a savoury filling and a hard-boiled egg yolk in the middle.

The Autumn Moon Festival lasts for three nights. It is partly a harvest festival but its main purpose is simply to admire the beauty of the moon. Patroness of the festival is the goddess of the moon, the lovely and compassionate Kwan Yin. On the first night of the festival people welcome the moon. The second night, which is the night of the full moon, is when the main celebrations are held. On the third and last night, when the moon is beginning to wane, people bid her farewell.

On the second night of the festival I and the Vogels and a crowd of other guests boarded a launch in the harbour and we sailed out into the mile-long stretch of water which separates the parent island from Kowloon. It was even more packed with craft than usual. Many of the boats were gaily decorated and hung with lanterns and multi-coloured fairy lights.

The supper table on our launch was decorated with yellow flowers and down the centre stretched a long yellow and silver dragon. 'Moon colours' predominated in the various dishes. There was yellow egg and lemon soup, a golden carp, yellow rice, white and yellow vegetables and so on. At the end of the twelve course repast all we were capable of doing for some time was leaning back in our chairs and gazing at the bright orb of the full moon overhead.

Our launch sailed on with scores of other craft to Aberdeen, a fishing village on the coast of Hong Kong which is well known for its floating restaurants. These were brilliantly lit and the guests were arriving and departing in sampans. We spent some time in a cafe drinking rice wine and eating a very thin silvery-looking biscuit made especially for the festival from rice flour and ground almonds.

We sailed back to Victoria, disembarked from our launch, and got into waiting taxis clutching balloons, paper lanterns and papier-maché images of Kwan Yin. It was in the early hours of the morning when I arrived back at the flat.

Two days after that party I boarded a cargo vessel which was to take me to Ceylon. The vessel looked very small in comparison with a huge passenger liner docked nearby and our departure from the Kowloon wharf went virtually unnoticed.

I was shown to my cabin by a crew member. It was bright with flowers which kind friends had sent to wish me bon voyage. Amongst them were some sprays of peach blossom tied together with a red ribbon. I read the attached card:

> I wish you a very pleasant voyage and hope that these sprays of autumn peach blossom will remind you of happy days spent in the Colony.
> With kind regards,
> Chan.

I went up on deck taking the bunch with me and leaned against the rail with some of the other passengers. There were only sixteen of us altogether. The vessel moved away from the quay. The day was warm and sunny, very different from that on which I had arrived. Now the Colony was looking its loveliest and everything was vivid and clear-cut. As the minutes passed and the vessel sailed out into the ocean, Hong Kong became only a small triangle of land on a blue sea, then a dot, and then it was gone. I had seen Hong Kong for the last time and saying good-bye to it was rather like bidding farewell to a gay and charming but somewhat dissipated friend. I felt both sorry and glad at the same time to be leaving the island. I regretted that I had not seen more of it during my stay, but my life had become absorbed in the life of another nearby island.

I looked out for Lantao but we did not pass it. The island is off the main shipping route. But it was there, not far from Hong Kong, unassuming and reticent, unlike brash and extrovert Fragrant Harbour.

I looked at the flowers in my hand and I suddenly realised that, like the fisherman in the story, I had lived for a while in a remote 'Peach Blossom Country'. It was unknown to the mass of tourists and virtually unknown to the inhabitants of Kowloon and Hong Kong. Some words Fo had spoken came back to me. He had said that Lantao was composed of earth and rocks and was surrounded by the ocean, just like any of the other islands in the group, so the difference in Lantao could not lie in its basic ingredients.

I returned to my cabin still holding the bunch of peach blossoms and thinking about where the difference could lie. This was the question that Fo had silently handed to me as we stood together under the pine trees, but the answer to it still evaded me.

CHAPTER ELEVEN

MAURITIUS

MOST OF THE sixteen passengers on board were missionaries returning to England and Ireland after having worked for several years in the Colony. Fortunately for me—my feelings about Christian missionaries are very mixed—there was also on board an Anglo-Greek couple, a Mr. and Mrs. Mikhalaidis, and a young Englishman called Raymond. We four spent most of our time together on deck.

A pair of albatross followed our vessel until the evening before we reached Mauritius. They sometimes swooped right down to the waves, then rose with a fish or scrap of food thrown from the galley. The captain told us that these great birds, the largest in the world, can go to sleep on the wing.

The island of Mauritius, to which we were heading through the Strait of Malacca and then right down and across the Indian Ocean, is off the mainland of East Africa. It is 720 square miles in extent and, like Hong Kong, is one of the most densely populated areas on the earth's surface. The island was once a French colony and the French brought over large numbers of Negro slaves from their African possessions to work on the island's sugar plantations. When the island was taken over by the British, the slaves were freed. But the British brought in indentured labour from South India. Indians and Africans form the majority of the populace today and neither race gets on well with the other. There is also a large number of Creoles, people of mixed coloured and white blood, and a small number of English and French residents.

We arrived at Port Louis in the early hours of the morning on a hot and sultry day. Mr. and Mrs. Mikhalaidis, Raymond and I crowded into a taxi. Our ship was being unloaded of cargo for a full day and a half, which would give us passengers quite a lot of time to see the island.

Our driver, an Indian by the name of Mohan, drove us out of Port Louis and along a coastal road lined with feathery casuarina trees.

"That mountain in the distance is called Pieter Both and is the best-known one in the island," said Mohan. "It can always be distinguished from the others by its three crags."

We passed cane fields and campments dotted with rondavelles, straw huts built on the lines of primitive African dwellings, rushing streams and deeply forested areas. On the limpid blue sea fishermen were throwing out their nets from pirogues, long slender boats rather like canoes.

The four of us kept on exclaiming at the beauty and variety of the scenery.

"Ah, but if only you'd seen it before Carol devastated the place," said Mohan. "Before Carol it was the most beautiful island in the world."

"Carol?" we inquired.

"Surely you have heard of hurricane Carol? It put us back on the world map for a few weeks."

"Oh, yes," Raymond said, "I remember now," but he did not look very certain.

We got out at a sandy beach and spent some time fossicking for shells. In a short while we had collected a wide variety.

Further north, we stopped again at a place called Cap Malheuraux, a spot immortalised by the French author Bernadin de St. Pierre in his book *Paul et Virginie*.

On again to Grande Bay, a smart beach resort. Here we sat on the sand and ate mango ice-creams while Raymond, who had had the foresight to bring along bathing trunks and a towel, went for a swim.

Next, we drove inland to the town of Curepipe, which lies fifteen miles from Port Louis. Here we were to have lunch. We sped up a winding road and the atmosphere, which previously had been hot and sticky, now began to get quite chilly. Mohan, who looked rather like an animated parrot, turned round and said, "The town gets its curious name from the days when stage-coaches went up from Port Louis. They stopped there to change the horses and the men lit and cleaned their pipes."

There were some attractive houses in the town; some of them were surrounded by hedges of gardenias, the white and pink blossoms shining like mid-day stars against the dark foliage. I kept shivering as we strolled along the streets because of the changed atmosphere. Curepipe is said to get about one sunny day a week whereas in the coastal areas seven blazing days of sunshine are quite usual. Yet residents here, Mohan said, love the town and would not willingly live anywhere else.

"It is not as fashionable as Floreal but people seem to like it better."

He went off to lunch at a snack-bar filled with taxi-men cronies, and we went into a restaurant.

We sampled some Creole dishes which were spicy but not as hot as Indian food. There were various delicacies on skewers laid on a mound of fluffy rice, a delicious vegetable dish of aubergines, tomatoes and green peppers, followed by a fresh pineapple salad. We had sherberts to drink and excellent coffee.

Our glance was caught by two exquisitely beautiful children who were having lunch at a nearby table with a young woman, obviously their mother. They were blonde and blue-eyed, sensitive looking, with fine well-shaped limbs and peaches-and-cream complexions. When they left, the owner of the restaurant, who had noticed our interest in the children, came over to our table and told us a little about them.

"Not Angles but angels," he said, no doubt to let us know that he was well up on English history.

He told us that the family had been living in Mauritius for several generations and until recently had been the owners of a large sugar plantation. A short time ago, owing to rising costs, they had sold it. Most of the big plantations, he said, were and still are owned by French families. Theirs had been one of the few owned by an English family.

"Where are they living now?" asked Mr. Mikhalaidis.

"In a house in Curepipe. Very pleasant but nothing like their old place. When those two children walk down the street everyone turns and looks at them because of their great beauty. Yet, I assure you, they are both completely unspoilt."

They were very lovely, certainly, but something had struck me about them both. They looked, not like modern up-to-the-minute English children, but like many English children looked about twenty years ago. There was nothing decadent looking about either of them, they simply had looks which were twenty years behind the times. And they were not the only ones who had given me this impression. Ever since I had set foot on the island I had felt that I had slipped back a quarter of a century or so and I think it was mainly the people themselves who gave me this feeling. Mauritius, for all its beauty, is a backwater. I was glad to have visited it but I should not like to live there because, though I love the wild and unspoilt places of the earth, I have never cared for backwaters. There is a wide difference between the two.

Oddly enough, Mr. Mikhalaidis must have been thinking similiar thoughts, for as we drove off in the taxi he said to Mohan, "Mauritius is very beautiful but it gives me a strange feeling of being completely out of date. Many of the people I've seen gave me this feeling of being a long way behind the times."

"Yes, that's so," Mohan said. "Many other visitors have told me that. But in the past this island used to be a busy and up-to-date place with ships calling in at Port Louis from all over the world. Then trade and shipping trailed off and now we are just a sleepy little island right off the map. But I'll tell you what would put us straight back on to the map again, if only we could find one. Oh, if only we could—just one!"

"One what?" we asked.

"One dodo. That is all we need to have people pouring into Mauritius from all the corners of the earth. Surely you know that once this island was famous for its dodos? It was the only place where they lived. Then—I admit it was mainly our own fault—they became extinct."

We were driving down the Route Royale into Floreal, the

smartest town in the island. The houses exuded opulence. The cars looked larger and shinier and the people better dressed than elsewhere. We sped past old colonial-style buildings and along wide tree-shaded streets back to Port Louis.

"You must go and visit the dodo," said Mohan. "You cannot leave Mauritius without seeing him."

"But you've just said—" Raymond began.

"Extinct, yes. But we have one in the Port Louis Museum—stuffed."

We naturally had to go to the museum. In a glass case was the skeleton of a dodo and in another case a stuffed dodo. The huge bird was not a particularly good-looking creature but what he lacked in looks he amply made up for in rarity.

I had been surprised at the number of places of worship we had passed on our drive: Anglican churches and Methodist chapels, and Hindu temples. As we drove through Port Louis we passed a Chinese pagoda and a Muslim mosque. Mohan, ever ready with a bit of local information, told us that in the mosque were the remains of a saintly man by the name of Pir Jamal.

When we got out of the taxi near the quay he said that he had been talking to a driver friend in the snack-bar who had told him that there was going to be some Sega dancing that evening at a beach near Port Louis. This was the national dance of the island and we should not miss the chance of seeing it.

Mr. and Mrs. Mikhalaidis said that they had done enough for the day, but Raymond and I said we would like to go along, so we arranged for Mohan to collect us in the taxi at eight o'clock.

Promptly at eight we were back on the quay and Mohan was waiting for us, dressed now in a very gay shirt, white trousers and a straw hat.

As we drove along the coast in the twilight he explained to us that Sega dancing is only performed in Mauritius and mainly by the Creoles. All the singing and dancing is completely spontaneous, the words and steps of the dances being made up on the spur of the moment. Sometimes performances are given during the day but it is much better watched at night under the moon.

When we reached the beach, quite a large crowd had already gathered there. Overhead in the night sky a sickle moon was just visible. A log fire was burning and not far from it were some big cauldrons and 'ovens', holes dug in the sand, and people were busy preparing supper. Other persons were chatting together in small groups. Mohan pointed out the musicians, who were standing near the blaze: an accordianist, a maracca player, and two drummers. One of the drummers was holding his instrument over the flames in order to tighten the skin and get a good sharp beat.

Presently the talking and laughter grew less and a feeling of expectancy filled the air. We spectators formed a large circle. Many of the Creole women in the crowd were wearing long brilliantly patterned skirts and white blouses with full sleeves and some had scarves tied round their heads. Four kerosene lamps had been lit and placed to form a square inside which people would dance.

The crowd parted and a man walked into the centre of this natural stage and down to the far end, where the waves were lapping the beach. He turned his back to the sea where the surf glowed in a long silvery line. In one hand he held a triangle. He stood motionless and alone for a minute, then he lifted his head and let out a piercing, beseeching cry, as though begging any other human being to step on to the stage and join him. Two dancers, a man and a woman, leapt on to the white sand and the three started to move off in a circle, the leader tapping his triangle and the drummers clapping their hands in time to the beat.

Sometimes one of the dancers would let out a shrill cry and then the pace would increase, gradually building up. More and more dancers stepped on to the 'stage', forming a long snaking line on the white moonlit beach, their bodies casting weird shadows. The pace became faster and faster. Someone was singing a song and the rest of the dancers chanted a wordless chorus. They surged inwards and then out again, they whirled and stamped their feet. And then, as though they had received some invisible signal, the singing stopped, the surge of the dance ebbed. There were three sharp taps on the triangle and the dance ended.

Someone called out, "Supper is ready!"

We moved towards the cauldrons where plates were being heaped with food and for a very moderate sum we received an excellent picnic supper. There was Indian fried bread, roast yams, fish, roast meat, brews of tea and piles of fresh fruit. Some people were swigging rum.

Supper over, the dancing started again. Many more people joined in now. Raymond and I even had a go, as you were allowed to make up your own steps as you went along. Then the arena was cleared and some Creole women in their long skirts, their arms gleaming with gold bangles, did a slow haunting dance called a Kalinga.

We left after that. Mohan told us that the chief dancer, the man who had held the triangle, was one of the foremost Sega dancers in the island and came from the Black River country, an area from which many of the best performers come.

As we were driving back to Port Louis along a lonely stretch of road we heard the distant sound of drumming coming from the direction of some hills.

"Those are voodoo drums," said Mohan. "Not good. Many of the Negroes here call themselves Christians and go to church on Sunday and they hold voodoo ceremonies at night."

Voodoo rites are still performed, apparently, in remoter parts of the island by sections of the negro populace. When the Negroes were brought over by the French as slaves several centuries ago, they brought with them their dark African gods.

I dropped into my bunk and slept till ten next morning. There was only time for a quick visit to the public gardens at Pamplemousse before the ship sailed. Here, it was the same old cry: "If only you had seen them before the hurricane!" Even so, they were well worth a visit and contained many rare trees and plants as well as a statue of 'Paul and Virginie', the hero and heroine of Bernadin de St. Pierre's novel.

Then back to the boat. We sailed away in the afternoon.

Raymond said that he had liked the island so much that one day he would try and return for a longer visit. Mauritius was not quite my idea of a heaven on earth, but I had greatly enjoyed our visit to this little island, a tiny speck of land in the vastness of the Indian Ocean.

CHAPTER TWELVE

CEYLON

Two of us were leaving the cargo vessel when it docked at Ceylon, myself and an elderly woman missionary. We had both planned to stay there about a month; then I was going on to India and she was leaving for England, where she was retiring after many years of missionary service in the Far East. We had both stayed in Ceylon before, I as a child on brief visits on the way out to the Colony and again when my father was posted to India from Penang. Those visits had remained vivid in my mind. Ceylon was then under British rule and my memories of it in those days are of an island inbued with a happy harmony, of sunlit streets and white palm-fringed beaches and of a light-hearted and charming people. The hotels in which we stayed had seemed fabulous and right out of this world. Of course, it is not possible to judge a place as a child as one would as an adult; moreover, I was seeing the island from a privileged position. Even so, I do not think that these pleasant memories were altogether without foundation. Since those days Ceylon has gained its independence.

News and reports which had reached me about the island while I was in Hong Kong had been gloomy. 'The Pearl of the Far East,' as Ceylon is often called, seemed to be in a state approaching disintegration. Corruption was rife, apparently, and ran right down from the top of the social scale to the lowliest manual worker. The Prime Minister had been murdered and a Buddhist priest—of all people—had been deeply implicated in the crime. He was in jail awaiting sentence. The murder rate in the island was the highest in the world. The standards in the once excellent hotels had dropped to zero.

I had booked into a Christian hostel for the first week of my stay where, I had been told, standards were still high and the atmosphere very pleasant. The woman missionary, a Mrs. Braithwaite, had done likewise.

Our vessel docked outside Colombo harbour and we were taken to the customs shed in a launch. There was a dock strike on. Mrs. Braithwaite and I said good-bye to our fellow passengers, who were off on a morning's sight-seeing trip and were allowed out of the building quite quickly. We sat down on a bench to await our turn at the counter.

It was the worst customs I have ever been through. We sat there for ages and watched some frightened-looking passengers from another ship being marched into cubicles to strip and be searched by the customs officials. Our turn came and Mrs. Braithwaite was told curtly that she would have to let her hair down so as to allow the official to see that she had not got any valuables hidden. She wore her white hair piled in a bun on the top of her head, and she looked dumbfounded when told to undo it. But there was no relenting on the part of the petty dictator, and she had to go off into a cubicle with a sari-clad woman official to let her hair down. Meanwhile, the man who was going through my belongings told me to open my handbag. He turned it upside down and emptied everything out on to the counter.

"Two cheque books," he screamed—"that is absolutely illegal!"

I explained that one cheque book was from my London bank and the other from the bank I used in Hong Kong and that if there was anything illegal in possessing the two I was sorry but I had not been aware of this.

"You've left Hong Kong, yet you've still got this cheque book. You should have handed it in," he snapped, producing yet another form—I had already filled in three—and telling me to count up all my money, loose coins, travellers' cheques, the lot and then fill in the form.

I counted, he counted, our total amounts were different, so he told me to count again.

It was two hours before they finished with us and then Mrs. Braithwaite and I had to get our baggage out of the building and on to the kerb. Not one of the officials lifted a finger to help us.

There was no taxi or any other vehicle outside the building. We sank on to our suitcases in a state of exhaustion and, after our grilling at the hands of the customs officials, feeling like a couple of criminals. A cruel sun blazed down on us as we waited and waited for a cab to come in. Mrs. Braithwaite appeared utterly dejected and in a state of near collapse, while I, who had been eagerly looking forward to visiting the island, was now fervently wishing that I had booked my passage through to Bombay on the cargo vessel.

At last a taxi came in.

"I can't take all that baggage," was the driver's first remark.

We begged, we pleaded and finally bribed him and he eventually agreed to take us and our baggage to the hostel.

"You have bad time in customs?" he asked as he drove through the congested central area of Colombo.

"Terrible," I said.

"Careful!" Mrs. Braithwaite whispered to me.

We sped up a hill leading to the suburb in which the hostel was situated.

"Many people have bad time at customs these days," he said. "People searched and all their luggage unpacked."

"Why is that?" I asked.

"There is a lot of smuggling in and out of the country and we lose a lot of gold that way, so they try to stop it."

With a blast on his horn, the driver swerved down the drive and pulled up in front of the hostel.

We found we were back in civilised surroundings once again. The other guests were finishing lunch. After we had been shown our rooms, places were laid for us and we were served a late lunch. Mrs. Braithwaite told me that after her treatment at the customs she would not be staying in Ceylon for a month and she had planned to be leaving at the end of a week.

"And me too," I confided.

In the afternoon I visited the city centre to have a look at the shops. Touts followed me along the streets asking me whether I had any pounds or dollars to exchange for Singhalese currency. They were blatant and one even tried to do a deal under the eyes of a passing policeman, who appeared quite indifferent to this pest who was telling me that he would give me a very good rate of exchange for any English money I cared to hand over to him. This was in one of Colombo's main thoroughfares.

"Nothing doing," I said.

Having extricated myself from the touts, I thought, for old time's sake, I would have tea in the Galle Face Hotel. This hotel, where I had stayed as a child, is situated on the sea-front and used to be one of the finest hotels in the Far East.

When I went in, having walked along the front, workmen were swarming about the entrance-way and lounge. Dustcloths had been draped over half the furniture and there were step-ladders and buckets dumped here and there. Two men were whitewashing the ceiling of the lounge and another was hammering away in a corner while a posse of disgruntled-looking guests were having tea and trying to make themselves heard above the din of hammering.

I ordered tea. The waiter returned with my tray and wound his way between workmen and buckets to set the tray on a table in front of me. The tea consisted of two sandwiches with curled-up edges and a slice of stale cake. But at least the Kandy tea was good to drink.

I knew one person who lived in Colombo, a Mr. Shaheed, whom I had first met in London. After tea, I went and phoned him. He had told me to be sure of looking him up if I ever visited Ceylon.

"Are you free tomorrow morning?" he asked. "I'm going on a trip which I think you'd enoy and you'd see something of the countryside on the way. The place I'm visiting is only twelve miles from Colombo."

I said I would like to go along and he said he would pick me up at the hostel in his car at nine.

When I put the receiver down I realised that I had not asked him what we were going to see, but I suspected that the object of the trip might be to meet some Veddhas. Mr. Shaheed, I remembered, was deeply interested in these primitive people who were the original inhabitants of Ceylon and were now fast dying out.

In the meantime, I had a quest of my own to embark on, a search for a particular reclining Buddha about which I had read some years back. It was a Buddha with azure-coloured eyes.

But neither the clerk at the reception desk nor the taxi driver he had got for me had ever heard of this Buddha.

"Do you mean the new Buddha at Asokaramya Temple?" the driver asked me.

"No, the statue I want to see is a very ancient one."

I asked him to take me to the Mount Lavinia Hotel, which lies on a high promontory some miles out of Colombo, just off the main Colombo-Galle highway, and to ask persons on the way there whether they knew of the whereabouts of this Buddha. I felt sure that the temple in which it was housed must be somewhere along this stretch. But although the driver stopped many times and made enquiries from vendors and shopkeepers, none seemed to know anything about the Buddha.

When I had read about this huge reclining statue I had determined that if I ever visited Ceylon I would seek it out for myself. In his book *A new model of the Universe*, in which Ouspensky writes about this Buddha and the deep impact it made on him, he does not mention its exact whereabouts. By omitting this detail he no doubt hoped to discourage the mere curiosity seeker in going to look at it. He himself, he states, had come across the statue almost by accident but he had realised directly he saw it that he was gazing at one of the world's masterpieces. He had been staying at a hotel near the sea which was situated a few miles south of Colombo and one morning had gone for a walk along the beach and had then crossed the main road and walked up one of the numerous side-roads running off it. At the end of this road he came to a temple set on a low hill. A Buddhist priest had shown him round and then unlocked the door of a long low building in which was the recumbent statue, a hundred feet or so in length. It had been painted yellow and the Buddha's eyes were of a deep azure blue. The statue was not known at all in the western world and was not all that well known even in Ceylon. Ouspensky, who had embarked on a journey through the Far East in search of what he called the miraculous, realised that this statue was the kind of miracle he had been hoping to come across.

My drive out to the hotel had not brought me any further clues as to the statue's whereabouts. I walked down the steps leading to the beach. Guests were lazing on the warm sand and bathing in the crystal-clear waves.

The girl at the reception desk had not heard of the Buddha either. I began to realise that finding this statue was not going to be as easy as I had thought it would.

Another taxi and another driver. He looked blank when I described the Buddha, but he said he would take me to a nearby temple before returning me to the hostel, as the caretaker there would almost certainly know where the statue was.

There was a huge garishly painted statue of the Great Teacher in this temple. The hot air was heavy with the scent of flowers, big wax-like blossoms, laid on the altar. The caretaker followed me round.

"A Buddha with blue eyes? No, I've never heard of it. Could you mean the Golden Buddha at Kelaniya? That is the most famous reclining Buddha in Ceylon," he said.

"No, it's definitely not the Golden Buddha," I said.

A group of small novices with shaven heads were gathered about the door watching us. They were alert and intelligent-looking boys, none of them much more than eight or nine.

I asked the driver to take me to the hostel. I had drawn a complete blank that day in my search for the Buddha with the azure eyes.

That evening I went down to the Anglican cemetery to look for the grave of a great-uncle of mine, although I had little hope of finding it. This was the relative for whom, when he had been in bed with some childish illness, the poet Robert Browning had written the 'Pied Piper of Hamelin' to amuse him. As a young man, Willie had joined the East India Company and had died in Ceylon at the age of thirty-nine.

Many of the graves had obviously been untended for years. Some were only just distinguishable as low grass-covered mounds, others were buried under heaps of broken stonework. But even where the crosses and headstones were still standing, the lettering had often been erased by the elements. I soon gave up the search.

I walked back to the hostel. Crowds swirled along the pavements, food vendors shouted their wares and from the distance came the sound of a temple gong.

I spent the remainder of the evening reading up a little of Ceylon's history. I knew that the first man, Adam, is believed to have descended from heaven on to what is now called Adam's Peak or Sri Pada and that the island had a line of monarchs stretching back for many centuries.

The Singhalese, like the English, often refer to their country as 'this Sceptred Isle,' and with good reason. In 544 B.C. an Aryan prince from India, Vijaya, landed in Ceylon or Lanka, to give the island its Singhalese name, with several hundred followers, thus starting a line of Singhalese kings, one hundred and eighty in all, who held sway over the island in unbroken succession for 2,300 years, which must be one of the longest spans of rulership in history.

In the 3rd century Buddhism came to Ceylon, and with this noble and gentle faith the civilisation of the island burst into full flower. The arts flourished, huge sculptures were carved, vast man-made lakes and cities were built, including the ancient capital of Lanka the Resplendent. The great ruined city of Anuradhapura was in its heyday larger than London and lasted for longer than the ancient cities of Athens and Carthage, thirteen centuries, before its decline began and the jungle swept over it like a vast green wave.

The first Europeans began to arrive in 1505. They were the Portuguese, the most cruel and fanatical of the colonisers of this once peaceful island, and they are hated down to the present day. They murdered, tortured, and destroyed many of the wonderful buildings and sought to convert the populace by force from Buddhism to their savage Catholic faith. The Singhalese bent before the terrible wind of the invaders and it was something of a miracle that, in spite of the pressure brought to bear on the inhabitants to become Catholics, very few did and the people remained true to their faith as they do to this day. But much of Ceylon's great civilisation was swept away by the Portuguese.

They even laid their desecrating hands on the islanders' most sacred relic, the Buddha's tooth, and ground it to powder. But the priests at the temple of Kandy said that they had expected this to happen and so they had substituted a false tooth for the real one. It is this tooth which is paraded through the streets of Kandy at the annual Perahera Festival.

The Portuguese, like the Spanish, colonised their territories with a sword in one hand and a Bible in the other. After them, the Dutch came to Ceylon and they were more enlightened colonisers. They did not seek to force their own Christian faith on an unwilling populace. They built forts and their high-ceilinged houses, which can be seen to this day.

The Dutch ceded the island to the British in 1796. Like the Dutch, they never imposed their religion upon the inhabitants. They built houses and churches, roads and railways and started the big tea plantations.

During the Second World War the island was the base for the South East Asia Command. And on the 4th of February, 1948, Ceylon gained her independence and elected to remain a member of the Commonwealth.

Mr. Shaheed arrived for me next morning and we set off in his car through Colombo.

He had a round friendly face and an enthusiastic manner. Every so often he stopped the car to point out some temple or building of interest. The first of these halts was to show me a large pillared edifice in an open space which had been opened by the Duke of Gloucester. The opening ceremony had been the last in Ceylon in which a member of the British royal family had officiated.

Then we stopped outside the house in which the late Prime Minister, Mr. Bandarainaike, had been murdered. The family had since moved out of the house and his wife had bravely stepped into her late husband's shoes to become the world's first woman prime minister.

"When it was found out that a Buddhist priest had been implicated in the crime, there was a sense of shock which was felt throughout the Buddhist world," said Mr. Shaheed. "Buddhism, as you know, preaches harmlessness towards all living beings, and this precept, by and large, has been strictly adhered to down the ages. We have had no inquisitions or holy wars and we don't use ugly words like heretic and infidel. Buddhism, as I think you must agree, has been the least blood-stained and guilty of cruelty of all the great religions. So when a priest was found to have been involved in the murder of the Prime Minister, Buddhists throughout the world were deeply shocked."

"Was it a purely political murder?" I asked.

"I believe it was, though some people think other issues were also involved. Everyone on the island has his own ideas as to the why's and wherefore's of the crime. But you see, there is this thing—a monk being involved in politics, something that would never have happened even five years back. It is only in the past few years that Buddhism in Ceylon has become contaminated with politics. The priests these days seem to have less and less time for spiritual things. More's the pity."

"From which temple did this monk come?"

"From Kelaniya, the temple which houses the great Golden Buddha. And not only did he come from it, but he was the chief incumbent there."

"How extraordinary!" I said.

"Yes, until not so long ago Buddharakkhita Thero was its abbot. If he is sentenced to death, that will be the first such sentence passed on a Buddhist monk for many centuries. There has only been one other such case. And here is a strange fact: this one other death sentence was imposed on an abbot for having converted to Buddhism the wife of a Singhalese king. The king sentenced him to be thrown into a vat of boiling oil. And this monk was none other than the abbot of Kelaniya Temple."

"That is very strange," I said. "What sort of man is the present abbot or, rather, the ex-abbot?"

"He is a highly intelligent and powerful man with a magnetic personality—women find him very attractive. He entered the order when he was fifteen and during these past few years he's been actively engaged in various political schemes."

"He sounds an odd mixture for a monk."

"He's a mixture of vices and virtues. Monastic rules slipped rather badly while he was abbot of Kelaniya. The monks' quarters are next to the building which houses the Golden Buddha. Buddharakkhita Thero lived there in a pleasant air-conditioned flat and he slept in a double bed—seldom alone. He was known to have indulged in several love affairs with attractive women. Have you seen the Golden Buddha yet, by the way?"

"No, I haven't," I said.

"You should make a point of seeing it. The recumbent Buddha is one of the most magnificent carvings in the Far East."

I had not been particularly keen to see this famous statue, partly because it is so well known. But that is rather like admitting that one does not wish to visit the Taj Mahal because of its world-wide fame. Now that Mr. Shaheed had told me that the late abbot at the temple was one of the men involved in the murder of the Prime Minister, I felt even less inclination to go there.

We were driving along a road lined with palm trees and little thatched huts and stalls piled high with green and brown coconuts. I made some remark about the ruins of a big white dagoba we passed. These great hemispherical structures can be seen everywhere on the island, usually within the precincts of temple grounds, and they often have sealed up within various sacred relics.

Mr. Shaheed's smiling face became suddenly grim. "That dagoba was built by one of our kings and was torn down by the Portuguese—and that temple over there, too," he said, pointing to another ruin. "I can't help it—I detest them. No other race has done us such harm."

Some minutes later his grim expression was replaced by his usual smiling countenance.

"By the way," I said, "I still don't know what it is you're taking me to see. Would it be some Veddhas?"

"Oh, no. Veddhas don't live anywhere near Colombo or any other town. You find them only in remote country areas, usually deep in the jungle. Have you read your Kipling?" he asked.

"I've read some of his books."

" 'The Jungle Stories'?"

"Yes."

"Well, we are going to see a Singhalese Mowgli."

"Do you mean a boy who has been brought up by wolves?"

"Not by wolves, but by monkeys. He was found by an elderly couple in the Nuwara Eliya District. When they first saw him he was stark naked, and bit and fought for all he was worth. They had great difficulty in catching him, but after they got him they found he was too much of a handful and gave him to a man who lives at Bandarawela. This man called the monkey-boy Sumanasekera; Simbo, for short.

"As a toddler Simbo probably lived in a jungle village and one day must have strayed away from his mother when she was gathering sticks or collecting wild fruit. Then some monkeys must have found him and accepted this human child into their midst.

"The boy's parents have never been traced," he said. "When the elderly couple had him, the boy gibbered and climbed trees as well as any simian. He was more like a wild animal than a human being. The man at Bandarawela tried to train him but the boy had no sense of right or wrong. He could not speak a single word but would gibber with annoyance if anyone provoked him. He would climb trees and try and hit people on the head with fruit or coconuts who were walking underneath. And he ate his food just like a monkey. When people weren't looking he would slip into their huts and steal various objects which took his fancy and he would suck the milk from cows' udders. Altogether, he was a thorough nuisance and a bit of a menace. There were so many complaints against him that finally his guardian had to hand him over to the police and he was put into a school run for young criminals, which was unfair because he is mentally handicapped and has no real sense of right or wrong. Anyway, he stayed at the school until he was about sixteen, when the inmates have to leave. The question then arose as to what to do with him, for he'll never be capable of looking after himself.

"He was accepted by the Sucharithodaya Social Service Centre at Maharagama. The head of the centre is a Buddhist monk called Ambegoda Gnanananda. He took pity on Simbo and agreed to have this strange youth at the centre and do what he could for him. The other children found him very odd but he eventually settled in quite well. We are going to the centre now. It's a big place with a children's home and a home for old people and a weaving school."

"Was Simbo retarded before he got lost or did he only become so after he started to live with monkeys?" I asked.

"Almost certainly he was not retarded before the monkeys found him and took him up, so to speak. There is one sad fact about all these children who have been brought up by wild animals," continued Mr. Shaheed, "whether by wolves, bears, monkeys or other species, and that is those who eventually return again to the human fold have become severely retarded and physically deformed in some way. Kipling must have known about this, but of course, to have made Mowgli a mental defective would have spoilt the story."

"Is Simbo severely retarded?"

"I'm afraid so. He has the mental age of a child of five although his actual age, so far as can be judged, is around seventeen. His face, as you'll see, has a marked simian look, while the fingers of his hands have become very like those of a monkey.

"I first became interested in these jungle children," he said, "when I lived for a while in the Indian province of Bihar. A girl was found not far from where I was living who had been brought up by bears. I saw her. She was quite wild and ran around on all fours. Her parents were eventually traced but when they saw the state she was in they were appalled and refused to take her back to their village. The girl had been a perfectly normal child, but when she was about two she had been stolen by a female bear and when she was found again six years later she was anything but normal. Like most of these unfortunate children, she died quite soon after she had returned to humanity. Before her death she had managed to learn to walk upright and could perform a few simple tasks."

"Why is it that these children should become defective and physically deformed?"

"Well, they are normal children living, of course, among humans. Some may even have learnt to speak a little. Then one day they become lost or are snatched away by some animal and are adopted into an animal community. Think of the shock to begin with! Then they have the tremendous task of having to adapt to the animals' way of life if they are to survive. Many learn to run as swiftly as wolves. They hunt for their prey with the rest of the pack and devour food like a wild animal. They bite if attacked, and howl, grunt or gibber like their animal friends. The animals who adopt these children treat them kindly after their fashion and the children are not retarded or deformed so far as their jungle, animal lives are concerned; they have made the tremendous adjustment to it.

"Then a few of them are found and brought back to humanity again and they are by now hopelessly unsuited to live a human life. But once again they have to try and adapt themselves to a completely new way of life with human beings. This task, the new environment, is too much for them. They just can't make the grade, or, at least, only to a very small degree."

"That's tragic," I said.

"Yes, it is. For some extraordinary reason in their karmas these children have slipped back into an animal existence. Nature usually shuts the door on such happenings. It is as near to impossible for a human being—except, perhaps, one living in a very primitive tribe—to slip back into an animal state as it is for the majority of us to shoot ahead and become godlike beings, something which lies ahead of humanity in the distant future. But at least those jungle children who eventually return to humanity do not die in a completely animal state. They become a little more like a human again."

We pulled up in a large rambling estate. A young monk offered to take us to the monkey-boy.

Simbo was sitting on the steps of a bungalow playing with some cups and bowls. The monk told us that most of the other children were still in school but there was no point in giving Simbo even an elementary education, as he was incapable of taking in even the simplest lesson.

The boy was dressed in a shirt and shorts and gave us a wide smile. One was immediately struck by his simian appearance. The monk took hold of one of Simbo's hands and showed us the fingers and thumb, which were extraordinarily monkeylike in appearance.

The monk pointed to a bottle filled with water among the utensils—Simbo still could not understand any words or speak the shortest sentence—and made signs to fill a cup with water.

Carefully, as though he were executing some tremendously difficult task, Simbo poured some water out of the bottle and into a cup and then, both hands round the cup, drank the water.

This simple little human act, the monk said, was quite an achievement on Simbo's part. It had taken many months to train him to drink from a cup and eat his food off a plate.

"What else can he do?" I asked.

"He runs messages for people—he is extremely fleet of foot. And that is about all. If the other children tease him, he is still liable to bite."

Two dogs came by, chasing each other and snarling in mock ferocity. Simbo made a movement as if to join them and then thought better of it. Then three small children came up to us, a girl and two boys.

"Have you seen Simbo climb a tree?" the little girl asked me.

"No, I haven't."

She looked at Simbo and the three of them shouted, "Hi, hi!" and pointed to a large spreading tree a few hundred yards away.

Simbo sprang to his feet and like a well-trained animal began to race towards the tree at an amazing speed, a happy smile on his face. In a trice, he had shinned up the trunk and a minute later was waving to us from a perch in the topmost branches.

"That was clever," I remarked to the children.

"Yes, but what's the good of it?" said one of the small boys.

Poor Simbo, I thought; the things he was really good at, such as climbing trees, were of little use now among the human beings he had rejoined after his jungle life, while human speech and the simplest human tasks were well nigh beyond his capacity.

We left him up in the tree and went to have a look at the weaving school where a very fine range of products was being turned out by members of the community.

We passed the bungalow again on the way back to the car. The two dogs were still brawling on the grass. The three children were seated in the shade of the veranda talking to one another. Simbo had come down from the treetops and was on the steps where we had first seen him. But he was not smiling now. Tears were trickling down his cheeks. It was easy to sense his isolation: the dogs playing together, the children talking among themselves, and he sitting alone, unable to really communicate with either the children or the canines.

The monk did not appear to be worried by Simbo's tears, rather the reverse.

"A good thing," he said. "Tears are human. By crying he becomes a little more like a human being. The children enjoy watching him climb trees but it is not really a very good thing. We monks at the centre are trying to detach him gradually from everything connected with *that* part of his life."

He meant, presumably, Simbo's past life in the jungle living with monkey friends.

We thanked him for showing us over the centre and started back for Colombo.

We made a short detour down an unsurfaced road because Mr. Shaheed wanted to show me a stretch of jungle country.

"It's not real jungle," he said. "You have to go further inland to reach true jungle country, but this stretch will give you some idea of what it's like. Most Europeans when they think of a jungle imagine dark, steamy, liana-tangled tracts of land. But our jungles aren't like that and have none of the sinister atmosphere of the jungles in black Africa. They are open and light, like an English wood, and in them grow many beautiful and valuable trees."

We drove through a forested area of vivid green and Mr. Shaheed pointed out ebony trees, palms and satinwood. There were groves of bamboos and bright open meadowlike areas where there were villages with grazing bullocks and cows.

He took me back to his house in Cinnamon Gardens where we ate a very late lunch out on the veranda, cooked by his wife. It was a Singhalese curry with various side dishes and the meal ended with jaggery pudding. Jaggery is a thick brown palm syrup full of vitamins.

After lunch Mr. Shaheed showed me a notebook in which he had written down details about various children in different lands who had been reared by animals. Simbo was the latest addition to his volume.

"There are several quite recent instances of these feral children," he said, leafing through the pages. "One of the most famous cases is that of the Wolf Children of Mindapore in 1920. These half-human, half-animal children were found by a missionary. They had been living in a large anthill along with two cubs and a wolf mother. They were caught and taken to the mission house. They were as ferocious as wolves, quite naked, and ran around on all fours. One of them died six months after being captured, leaving the other desolate. She was a girl and it took years of hard training before the missionary and his wife managed to get her to walk upright, to wear clothes and eat like a human being. She also managed to learn a few words. A marriage was planned for her to a young man who worked in the mission. But it was not to be. She died before it took place."

He leafed over some more pages.

"Many of the recorded instances of such children have been in India, but there's one case I made notes of concerning a South African baboon boy who was caught by Mounted Police. Like Simbo, he had markedly simian features and hands. He was eventually trained to do simple farm-work."

He turned a page. "A leopard boy from the North Cachar Hills—India again. A wolf boy found in a cave at Allahabad in 1936. Twins found in the Himalayas, a boy and a girl, who had been brought up by bears. Quite untrainable. Later released to return to their wild existence. There's no case at all that I've heard of from Europe."

"I can remember reading about one such case," I said. "As far as I remember, it occurred between the two world wars."

"Please tell it to me and later I'll write it down in this book."

"Very well," I said, and started off. "It took place in Rumania when a little girl—her name was Joanna—strayed from her village called Sugag. She got lost in a nearby forest but, unlike most children in similar circumstances, she was not scared when she found herself alone in the vast forest and she made no attempt to find her way back to the village. She lived on berries and bits of bark which she pulled from the trees.

"In the autumn she came upon a pack of wolves who were just finishing a sheep, fortunately for her, and were no longer hungry. She stayed with them and did not have any fear of these beasts and the wolves allowed her to sleep in their lairs and live as one of themselves. Wolves were her sole companions for the next seven years.

"Then one winter's evening she investigated the light from a campfire and some lumberjacks spotted her. One of them fired at her strange figure as she sprang away to safety in the depths of the forest. He thought he had seen a werewolf. The next morning they set off with loaded guns to find it.

"Joanna had sped back to her lair but the men had dogs who picked up her scent. Hearing the baying of the dogs and realising that she was cornered, she emerged from her lair, naked but half covered by her waist-long black hair. Just in time, before they fired, the men realised that this was not a wolf but a girl. They seized her. She fought like a fiend incarnate but the odds against her were too great and the men carried her back to their village. Later, she was identified as the small girl who had strayed from the village of Sugag seven years before.

"Her parents took her home and did their utmost to turn her into a human being again. Within a couple of years she became a beautiful young woman who ate with a knife and fork and enjoyed being attractively dressed. A young man called Petru fell in love with her and asked her parents if he might marry her.

"The wedding date was set, the guests invited. But a few days before the ceremony was due to take place the young couple set off for a distant valley where Petru, a shepherd, wanted to count the numbers of a flock of his sheep. The job done, they sat on a hillside and he cleaned his rifle. Wild beasts were quite common in the area and he never went far without it.

"Suddenly he felt Joanna tense and she cried out, 'Wolves are coming up the valley. Oh, I hoped they would come for me one day—I *knew* they would come!'

"The wolves approached. To the young man's horror, he saw his fiancée drop on all fours and rush towards the oncoming pack. He called out, 'Come back—they'll kill you! Joanna, come back!'

"But in the space of a few seconds her character changed completely and all he got was a wild mocking laugh. Wolves were yapping all round the girl. They seemed to be greeting each other after a long separation. Then Joanna started to tear off her clothes. The pack turned and raced back to the pine trees and his betrothed ran with them. Petru had a last glimpse of the girl he loved as her white body sped between the pine trunks and then disappeared from his sight in the darkness of the forest. He called to her, but in vain. All was silence now in the valley. That was the last he or anyone else saw of her. Human companionship, even love, had not been enough to hold her and she had returned to the wilds for good."

"What a very extraordinary and moving tale," said Mr. Shaheed. "And thank you for telling it to me."

Another search for the Buddha with the azure eyes had ended in failure and I was beginning to give up hope of finding the statue. I had meantime booked a passage in a cargo vessel to the port of Cochin in three days' time.

Along the stretch of road between Colombo and Mount Lavinia are numerous side-roads leading off the main thoroughfare. One could well spend a month or more walking up and investigating these various side-roads. I was to leave Ceylon within a few days. If I was to see the Buddha, I must quickly find out the temple's whereabouts.

One afternoon I half-heartedly wandered up a dusty lane leading off the main road. It came to an abrupt end among a group of small shops and stalls. There had not been one temple along its length. To refresh myself, I bought a green coconut and drank the cool milk through a straw. The stallkeeper, who had been watching my slow progress along the lane as I stopped and peered down sidings overhung with plaintain leaves and other greenery, asked me what I had been looking for.

"I'm looking for a temple," I answered. "Unfortunately I don't know its name, but it houses a large recumbent Buddha with azure eyes."

"That temple with the blue-eyed Buddha lies just a short distance from here."

"Are you sure?"

"Yes. Everyone round here knows of it."

A dilapidated taxi had pulled up at the stall. The vendor spoke in Singhalese to the driver, who nodded.

"He'll take you there—he knows the way."

I got into the taxi, still doubtful as to whether the driver really knew of the Buddha's whereabouts.

Bits of horsehair stuffing were coming out of the seat and I would not have been surprised to have seen a couple of mice emerge. In front, pieces of string and wire were attached to the gears and the starting handle. The contraption—it hardly merited the name of car—rattled violently and emitted a series of bangs at every pothole we went over. I had reached a degree of fatalism: if we did find the temple—excellent!—though I very much doubted that we would. And if I should eventually get back to the hostel in this travesty of a taxi, that would indeed be a miracle, though perhaps not of the kind for which Ouspensky had been searching during his sojourn in Ceylon.

Slowly, cautiously, the taxi nosed its way under some banana fronds which almost obscured the entrance to a narrow earth track, and then started to speed along it, speed being relative in this case—perhaps twenty miles an hour. We charged through a herd of pigs whose frightened squeals almost drowned some shattering bangs. We left them standing in a pall of dust. With a tremendous spurt, we raced up an incline. Higher up, on a green hill, stood a temple and outbuildings with tall palm trees silhouetted against the skyline. I could hardly believe my eyes. The driver got out of the cab and opened my door with a flourish.

"Here we are," he said, a note of pride in his voice. "I'll get one of the monks to show you the Buddha."

A monk in orange robes was already coming towards us. I asked him whether this was the temple in which there was an ancient recumbent Buddha with blue eyes and he said it was.

But before we went to look at the Buddha, he took me into the temple where the monks worshipped and we walked round a white dagoba.

According to tradition, he said, the Buddha himself is supposed to have visited Ceylon and preached here.

He unlocked the door of a low building and switched on a light. The entranceway brought one to the feet of the statue. We walked slowly along its length. The statue had been painted and the robes were a clear yellow. As we moved up towards the Buddha's head, the monk pointed out to me that from where we were standing the eyes were wide open. The open eyes symbolised the vast aeons of manifested life. As we moved on a little further the eyes appeared to be closed and the Great Teacher sleeping. This symbolised the period when the Absolute draws back all creation into itself and manifested life comes to an end until, after another vast period of time, he breathes out again and a newly created universe comes into being.

I stood gazing at the face of the Buddha. The deep sapphire eyes seemed to gaze at me and through me. The whole expression radiated an extraordinary serenity.

"Why blue eyes?" I asked the monk.

"Because the Buddha was of Aryan descent," he answered.

That was the only question I asked concerning the statue. Great art, I find, has a way of stilling all idle curiosity.

The monk unlocked another door at the far end of the building and we stepped out into the sunshine again. He bade me farewell and walked with slow dignified steps back to the row of cells. I should have liked to have made a small donation to this temple but there was no one to whom I could hand the money. Buddhist priests are not allowed to touch money themselves.

Later on, in India, I could not help contrasting the invariably courteous and non-mercenary attitude of every Buddhist monk I had met with the often appalling behaviour of the Brahmins in their temples, where they swarm upon the luckless visitor demanding money before he has hardly had time to glance at anything, put a dab of paste on his forehead and immediately demand more coins for this doubtful privilege. They would do well to take a lesson from the Buddhist priests.

On the way back to the hostel the driver asked me whether I had seen the Golden Buddha at Kelaniya. I said no and almost before I knew what was happening he had persuaded me to let him take me there next morning.

"But in my brother's taxi—his taxi much better than this one."

Well, it could hardly be worse.

He was round at the hostel the following morning but, as he had promised, in a much better taxi, for which I felt duly thankful.

Kelaniya is ten miles from Colombo. The entrance is up a flight of steps and under a white stone arch. Over to the right was a great white dagoba.

The temple grounds appeared to be deserted but as I was about to enter the temple by myself a young man came up to me and asked if he could show me round.

He said that the temple is in two parts. There is an old section in which the Buddha lies and a newly erected section which has been built alongside the old.

As in the temple of the blue-eyed Buddha, one approached the head of this huge statue from the feet. A few bare electric light bulbs gave off a dim glow above the recumbent figure of the Buddha. The carving, from the feet and sculptored hem of the robe to the head, was entirely covered in several layers of gold-leaf. It was of a lovely hue and seemed to emit a soft light. This statue, like the other, cast an aura of profound calm. The left arm lay along the top of the body, the right hand lay under the Buddha's cheek. The sense of an almost supernatural peace seemed to increase as we walked slowly up towards the great head. The eyes were wide open and all-seeing. I stood for some minutes looking at the majestic face, the serene forehead and the hint of an elusive smile on the beautifully shaped mouth. The expression was one of an all-embracing wisdom. This marvellous statue might have been carved by gods. But it was not gods who had carved it,

I reminded myself, but men, men who had lived many years ago and whose names were unknown. They must have had something within themselves which had enabled them to give this carving a quality of divinity and timelessness, a hint of the great achievement of the North Indian Prince Gotama, who gave up his possessions and took up the wandering life of an ascetic in search of ultimate truth and who in his lifetime achieved enlightenment.

I remembered suddenly as if struck by a blow that in the nearby priests' quarters the ex-abbot had plotted murder, a murder which had been successfully carried out. My calm was momentarily shattered. But the Buddha's face was serene. It was as if he spoke silently of some transcendant realm which is forever unstained by men's crimes and follies.

The young man led the way through a door into the new temple. There was nothing remarkable about this building. There were some paintings on a wall recently executed by a Russian artist in execrable baby-blues and pinks. I turned my head away from these sickly daubs and walked back again into the dimly lit interior of the old temple and walked down the Buddha's length and out into the open.

We crossed a stretch of grass over to the gleaming white dagoba.

"This is not the original dagoba," said the youth. "The first one was destroyed by the Portuguese."

I sat down on a low wall. Below were fields and peacefully grazing cattle.

The youth said that every month a full-moon ceremony takes place at Kelaniya.

"Crowds come from miles around. Then once a year a big Wesak celebration is held here."

Wesak is the big yearly event in the Buddhist calendar. Shortly before he died, the Buddha promised that he would return once a year to earth at the full moon to show his continued concern in the welfare of humanity and to give it his blessing.

Two days after I had visited Kelaniya I left Ceylon by cargo vessel for the port of Cochin, which lies on the steamy southwest coast of India.

CHAPTER THIRTEEN

ROOFTOP

COCHIN IS A busy up-to-date port. The vessel docked at midday and when I reached my hotel I collapsed on to the bed. I love the sun but this was a bit too much; the temperature was 109 degrees and the humidity ninety seven.

Kuchi Bandar, Cochin's other name, has one of the finest natural harbours in India. The town is surrounded by palm-fringed lagoons and thickly forested islands. During the hot weather most of the populace sinks into a stupor at mid-day and starts to come alive again around four o'clock. After tea, I caught a ferry and crossed over to the old capital of Ernakulam, three miles distant. The cafes were packed and crowds of white-clad men and women thronged the streets. White is the predominant colour of dress in this south-westerly part of India. Most of the men wore a length of cloth which hung from their waist down to their ankles and is called a langothi. The women were dressed in white saris.

I was not feeling energetic enough to do much sight-seeing. I had supper in a Hindu cafe, eaten with my fingers off pieces of green banana leaf, then returned to the hotel.

Next morning I went on a launch trip around some of the lagoons and to Bolghatty Island, which was once the seat of the British Resident. It is, perhaps, the most beautiful island in the district.

Cochin's history goes back into the remote past. The Chinese visited it, but little of their culture remains today. The colony of Jews are amongst the earliest Jewish settlers in India. During the reign of King Solomon, Phoenician fleets visited the coast. A later group of Jews arrived as refugees after the destruction by Nebuchadnezzar of the second temple in Jerusalem in 587 B.C. Both Greece and Rome traded with the sea-ports of this coast.

In 1684 the East India Company set up their first settlement at Anjengo, further south, and in 1795 a treaty was signed by the British and the Travancore Raja and the strip of coastline, once known as the Malabar Coast, came under British rule.

I caught a launch the following day down to Quilon. It is possible to travel hundreds of miles in this part of the country entirely by canals and lagoons. We passed men in skiff-like boats fishing with big butterfly nets. Birds fluted. Sometimes the sea was clearly visible a short distance away while at other times it was hidden between belts of forest and low hills.

From Quilon I caught a train down to Trivandrum, the capital of Kerala. The first thing I saw when I left the station was the soaring and elaborately carved seven-story gopuram, or gateway, of the Padmanabhaswami Temple, the city's most venerated shrine which is dedicated to the god Vishnu, the preserver.

As I passed the temple in a taxi on the way to the hotel where I was spending the night, two of the temple elephants went by with their mahouts. They were returning to their quarters after a walk. The taxi driver told me that this great temple has ten elephants and at festivals they are painted with intricate designs and hung with embroidered and bejewelled canopies and look magnificent in the processions.

I still had not arrived at my final destination. I spent one night in the city, then caught a local bus in the morning to the coastal village where my Hindu friends lived. They were called Ashvin and Yamini Menon. Their house was a modern two-story building.

I stayed in their house for a week and during that time I got to know several of their friends who lived in the village, mostly Brahmins, like themselves, the priestly caste of the Hindus. They were persons whom it was unlikely I would ever have met had not Ashvin and Yamini introduced me to them.

On her return to India after several years of study in England, Yamini had married a Namboodiri Brahmin, a man of her own caste.

The caste system in Kerala is unusual and somewhat complicated, in that many of the castes here come under a matriarchal system, the bridegroom going to live with his wife after the marriage ceremony in the communal home called a tarawad.

The Nairs, the largest caste in the state, were once a martial race but these ex-warriors all trace their descent from a common ancestress.

The Brahmins marry as a rule strictly among themselves and follow a patriarchal system, a system that prevails over most of the sub-continent. But down here they go along to a certain extent with the customs of the local inhabitants. Thus, the eldest son of a Brahmin family marries a girl of his own caste and she goes to his home as a bride. But the other sons all marry into different castes. If a younger son, for example, marries a Nair girl, he will go to live in her home.

Yamini belonged to the Namboodiri caste and she married the eldest son of a Namboodiri family, so unlike many girls down here, she went to her husband's home. The home of a Namboodiri Brahmin is called an illam. Both Yamini and her husband Ashvin, whom I was meeting for the first time, were very conscious of the fact that they belonged to the purest of all the Brahminical castes. The Namboodiris trace their descent directly from the ancient Aryans, that mysterious race who long ago came over the massive Himalayas to become the dominant and ruling race throughout the sub-continent. They brought with them an ancient wisdom and they imposed their philosophy and rule on the other inhabitants, the near-black Dravidians, whom they drove further and further south. Other names for the Aryans are the Nobly Born and the Sons of Light, and the ancient name for India is Aryavarta, the Land of the Aryans.

In the orthodox south, particularly among the Brahmins, life follows a daily pattern. Families get up early, about five o'clock, and an hour or so is spent in meditation. If the man is a Brahmin, it is unlikely he has a job such as working in an office. He probably spends some time in the early morning, as did Ashvin, reading the sacred scriptures and then goes out to officiate in the local temple. The Brahmins are entitled to perform temple ceremonies and from them they derive a large part of their incomes.

One of the first things an Indian housewife does in the mornings if she follows the Hindu way of life is to draw a design in coloured chalks outside the front door. This lets anyone coming to the house know that all is well with the family and that they are not suffering from any infectious disease. On feast days the design is more elaborate. This was Yamini's first task in the early morning.

The Menons were quite well off by local standards. They owned their own home and several palm-groves. The family did not own a car. I do not think anyone in the village did. There were three servants in the house and a gardener, quite a usual number for such a household. Servants in India are still a normal part of even quite poor households, unlike households in the west these days, where they are nearly extinct.

At the end of the week I moved into a small house the Menons owned. They found me a servant, a Hindu called Golan, who was to cook, housekeep and do a little marketing for me. A sweeper woman was to come in once a day to empty the toilet. It was taken for granted that I would not eat any flesh foods and I had promised faithfully that I would not crack an egg while under this roof. The Menons, like the great majority of Hindus, were vegetarians and eggs were as much taboo to them as meat and fish.

The house had a little walled garden but it was much too hot to sit out there during the day with the temperature soaring well above the hundred mark. For most of the day I stayed downstairs in the single room with its flight of stone steps leading up to the flat roof. I went up to the roof in the evenings and I slept up there.

In the mornings I got up early, half-past five or so, went out for a short walk, then did a little desultory painting. As mid-day approached, the very air seemed to be on fire and I had no thought of venturing out again until the approach of evening.

I lay prone on the charpoy, the string bed, waiting for Golan to bring me lunch. The sun blazed down from a sky drained of all colour upon a parched red earth. Plants wilted under its scorching rays; animals, birds and insects were stunned into silence. No cicada whirred or striped squirrel chirped during these burning hours.

Golan was cooking my lunch on a paraffin stove out on the

veranda, using one of the flagstones as a chopping board for the vegetables. The floor is used a lot in Indian cookery. An aroma of spices, ghee, and grated coconut wafted into the room. There were three doors in this room; one led out on to the veranda and into the garden with its coral tree and two mango bushes. Another door led into the wash-room and the third opened out on to the street. Woven grass blinds called tatties hung from the unglassed, barred windows and from the open doorway leading on to the veranda. Golan had sprayed them an hour ago, along with the stone floor, and now the whole room steamed like a Turkish bath. The spraying is supposed to cool the atmosphere a little.

I hoped it would be a bit cooler by the evening, as I had invited Ashvin and another Brahmin, called Satish, to coffee, as well as a young Kathakali dancer called Vishnu, who was staying with Satish. To entertain anyone, even informally, I found next to impossible when the temperature was around a hundred and ten degrees. With luck, it would have dropped to the lower nineties by the evening. Yamini was unable to come, as she had to give the children their supper and put them to bed.

Golan came in carrying a thali, a large stainless steel tray, on which was one of his burning South Indian curries. He had told me that he always added *more* chillies to the dishes during the hot season as they helped to cool one down. I had stopped trying to reason that one out.

I rose slowly to a sitting position. The meal was strictly vegetarian, of course. There was a mound of rice in the centre of the thali, two chapatties, a small salad of chopped cucumber, green pepper and tomato sprinkled with poppy seeds, and in little metal bowls were various vegetables, okra (ladies' fingers) and potatoes, all floating in a fiery chillie sauce. Three other bowls contained curds and dhal (cooked lentils) and grated coconut. A slice of melon and a cup of tea followed the main course.

Lunch over, I washed and then lay prone on the charpoy again. The room was now like a furnace. Golan lay stretched out on the veranda. I could just make out his form through the interstices of the blind.

Thoughts rose in my brain and disappeared like bubbles rising and breaking in a pond. I lay there somnolent, neither asleep nor awake but in a nether state in between the two. Squirrels and birds came in freely under the blind. A squirrel ran along the edge of the charpoy and over my bare arm, then it jumped down on to the floor.

I looked at my watch. Nearly half-past four and time to get up. The squirrel was lying stretched out under the table, not curled up in the way they usually lie. I went and washed again and then made some tea. When I had drunk the steaming liquid I thought I felt a little cooler. Tea is supposed to be cooling and coffee heating.

Golan was sound asleep. I slipped on my chappals—Indian thonged sandals—and went out, locking the door behind me. By keeping to a few feet of shade which ran alongside the buildings, I could reach the shore and its long line of palms unscathed by the sun's fierce rays.

An itinerant vendor was just outside the doorway frying an assortment of pungent food in two large pans on top of a small fire he had lit on the pavement. A customer sat by him waiting for the meal to be served. They both had plenty of time.

At a palm tree further along the street someone had tied an emaciated cow to the trunk with about two feet of rope. I had noticed the cow there when I had opened the door in the early morning. The creature must have been standing there all day— no food and no water, and because of the short length of rope it was unable to lie down or move more than a few inches. This unthinking cruelty to animals is common in India. Deliberate cruelty is rare, no doubt because of a long tradition of ahimsa, or harmlessness to all living creatures.

I walked past the little white-washed temple where the evening arati ceremony was in progress to the sounds of cymbal, drum and the deep boom of the conch-shell. Small family groups and single individuals were also walking shorewards, taking advantage of the relative coolness of these hours. Most of the men were dressed only in the white langothi; some wore the sacred thread of the Brahmin across their chests. Most of the women were in white too, but a few wore brightly coloured saris.

I followed the line of the shore, keeping to the shade of the palms. The sky was streaked with vivid pinks and mauves while the sun itself was a brilliant golden orb. Fiery waves rolled up the beach where the fishermen were attending to their nets and their beak-prowed catamarans. They lived in palm-thatched huts along the shore.

Somewhere ahead of me I could hear the sounds of a flute and presently I came upon a small crowd that had gathered about the player. He turned out to be one of India's thousands of roaming ascetics. This man, whose back was towards me, wore only a narrow length of cloth around his loins and a necklace of dried ruckracksha berries around his neck. He stood there facing the sea, playing a haunting little tune on his bamboo flute. Then he tucked the flute through his loincloth and started to sing, raising both arms high in salutation to the setting sun. Long matted hair fell to his thighs. His body, though thin, was strong and supple-looking. The song he sang was as haunting as the melody he had played on the flute. I could not understand the words; perhaps they were Sanskrit, the sacred language of the Vedas. His voice, now soft, now louder, sometimes cried out in a kind of rapture, as of one singing to his beloved. As the sun gradually sank towards the ocean's rim, the yogi's arms slowly fell to his sides. And when the sun had disappeared under the waves the ascetic bent down, picked up his brass loshta (water-pot) and his staff and started to walk off along the beach without having given so much as a passing glance to the crowd which had gathered about him. But that is often the way with these men: sometimes they are prepared to have a lengthy talk with one, at other times an ascetic is quite likely not to utter a word or to give any indication that he has seen you. He may be engaged in meditation, he may have taken a vow of silence, or he may just not feel like talking.

On the way back to the house I met two more holy men. They were sitting under a peepul tree and the older of the two was cleaning his teeth with a twig. The younger, a youth of about fifteen, was feeding handfuls of dry grass to their miniature white cow. It had a wreath of marigolds round its neck.

Little white bulls and cows are bred in the south, but one comes across them all over the sub-continent from Kanya Kumari at the southernmost tip of India to remote spots in the Himalayas, often following obediently in the wake of some ascetic like a well-trained dog.

The youth, whose hair was piled on top of his head in three large coils which had been dyed to a reddish-brown with cows' urine, said, "We'll be returning to Varanasi (Benares) shortly and from there to our caves high up in the Himalayas."

I made some complimentary remark about the cow and he told me that in fact it did not belong to them. They had it on loan from an ashram in Varanasi at the request of the swami in charge, who had wanted the animal to go on a pilgrimage with holy men as he thought it would be good for its karma.

By this time the older man, who was doubtless the younger one's guru, had finished cleaning his teeth and had flung the twig away. Looking at me and pointing towards the cow, he said, "She is my mother!"

This remark, often heard in India, is not to be taken literally! The Hindu believes that the cow, a sacred animal, by giving man milk, ghee, cheese and curds and thus enabling him to live without taking flesh foods—a degrading habit—is thereby his helpmeet on the road to a higher life and a kind of spiritual mother to him.

I said good-bye to the two men and continued homewards, pausing in the main street of the village—an earthen pot-holed track—in front of a magazine stall. India's favourite cover-girl stared at me from the latest edition of a popular Hindu weekly: a gorgeous white cow, garlanded with marigolds, its horns tipped with gold and its huge tender eyes radiating maternal love. It is extraordinary what glamour Indian artists manage to give their portraits of cows, often imbuing their models with a kind of bovine sex appeal. One has to live in the country to fully realise what depth of feeling this animal engenders in the Hindu breast.

After supper, I made coffee and waited for my guests to arrive. The cicadas were whirring in the mango bushes and striped squirrels were uttering high-pitched squeaks as they darted about the garden and up the sides of the house on to the rooftop. Their paws could get a grip on the tiniest projection or declivity. Fairy creatures, these squirrels, which I never tired of watching, and mischievous, too. One took a nose-dive into a box of crayons I had left on the low wall bordering the roof. Only its long jerking tail appeared over the edge of the box. Then the box tipped over and out spilled squirrel and crayons.

It was growing dark. Golan lit the pressure lamp and said goodnight. I dabbed citronella on bare patches of skin to ward off the mosquitoes. There was another charpoy up here which I used as a seat during the evenings and as a bed later. From a patch of sugar-cane a short distance away came the howl of a jackal.

There was a knock on the front door. Standing outside were Ashvin and Satish and the young Kathakali dancer, Vishnu. They followed me upstairs, barefooted, to the roof.

The three of them sat down cross-legged on the matting. I poured out the coffee.

My three guests looked like some fresco that had come to life. All three were dressed in langothis and each wore the sacred thread. The hair-styles of the men in south India are more varied than those of the women. Satish wore his hair done up in a top-knot. Strictly orthodox though he was, he showed no hesitation in drinking from the cup I handed him, something that would have been unthinkable for a strict Brahmin not so many years ago. On his forehead was a tilak mark showing that he was a follower of Shiva.

Ashvin's shining black hair hung loose to his shoulders. There was no tilak mark painted on his forehead. He was less bound by orthodoxy than Satish.

Vishnu, the dancer, also wore his hair loose and it had been tightly waved according to the fashion of Kathakali dancers.

To look at the two older men, Satish and Ashvin, one would have taken them to be about the same age. In fact, Ashvin was thirty-six and Satish twenty-seven. I knew little about Vishnu. It seemed somewhat strange to me that a man of his caste should be a dancer, but custom is becoming less rigid these days and many of the old traditions are breaking down. Even the matriarchal system which has been practised for centuries is not so strong as it was and many of the tarawads are being broken up.

The three talked animatedly. As we were drinking our coffee, one of the new 'stars' appeared overhead, emitting a greenish-blue light. It was a Russian sputnik. Thousands of people in this part of India looked up in wonder at this marvel of the space-age. We too gazed upwards, following its course, until the sputnik became a tiny green dot almost indistinguishable from the multitude of stars and then faded from sight.

"Our poor monkeys," sighed Satish. "It is typical of our Hindu attitude that while we deplore the killing of an animal outright, we are nevertheless hypocritical enough to let many suffer unbearably without our getting so much as a twinge of conscience. The other day I read that we export hundreds of monkeys to the West, where they undergo horrible experiments in laboratories, while others are shot up into space."

"There are no monkeys in that rocket, so I've heard," said Ashvin. "It only carries instruments which are continually flashing signals to earth. It's wonderful, one has to admit."

Satish made a deprecatory gesture. "Oh, yes, it's all very wonderful and exciting, this space travel, but it's nothing but outward voyaging. The further the astronauts travel to explore space and the planets—as they will be doing soon—the more necessary will it become for others to make the long inner journey which is so much more difficult than a trip to Mars or Venus. If some people don't attempt this inner journey, then the world—humanity, that is—will become completely unbalanced: everything outgoing and on the surface of things and the interior life empty and neglected. Already a lack of balance seems to be becoming more pronounced each year in Western countries; massive increases in mental illness and neuroses and half the population swallowing sleeping pills and tranquillisers—I've read about it."

Satish's face, like his thin intense body, gave an impression of fervour, of an inner fire which seemed to burn him, yet sustain him at the same time. He, like the other two, had never been out of India, yet he, like them, felt that he was competent to speak with authority on Western affairs and the international scene.

Ashvin held out his cup for more coffee. "Yes, Satish," he said, "you are right—inner exploration! That is absolutely vital. But here in Bharat (India) there have always been men in each generation who have devoted their lives to this inward journeying: our rishis and our true yogis. In the West," he continued, "the millionaire is held in high esteem. But in the East it is still the ascetic who possesses next to nothing who is deemed most worthy of respect by our people even in this materialistic modern age. The message of the millionaire is 'More!' But the message of our rishis is and always has been 'Less!'"

"That is correct," said Vishnu. "You must have noticed," he said to me, "that most of us Brahmins are content to lead simple and frugal lives. That is because we remember the message of our great yogis and know in our hearts that true freedom and happiness do not depend upon acquiring a big bank balance but lie in a sane limitation of desires. It is this limiting of their desires that gives our yogis the time and the ability to penetrate deeply into the core of their being. Possessing too many things which have to be looked after and having endless desires which have to be fulfilled robs the worldly man of the time and energy which could better be spent in discovering the secrets of his inner self."

Said Satish, "Some of our yogis who have discarded everyday living with its trivial concerns have managed to break through the worldly barrier and have penetrated vast and unknown regions."

The three continued to discuss the fascinating subject—as it is to all Brahmins—of breaking through the shell of everyday human existence into the limitless sphere of the spirit. Presently they lapsed into Malayalum and I was unable to follow their conversation.

Malayalum is the most widely spoken language in Kerala. English and Tamil come next, with Hindi, the official language of India, a bad fourth. English is still the lingua franca in most regions of the sub-continent and looks like remaining so for many years to come. Many Indians have a habit, as did these Brahmins, of going from one tongue to another with hardly seeming to realise they are doing so.

I sat listening to the eerie howling of the jackals in the cane fields. When I turned my attention to the conversation once more, the three men were talking in English again but the subject had changed.

Satish was saying, "Places and countries are like people; there are some places which repel you and there are others you feel indifferent about. Then there are those places to which one is strongly attracted. They seem to beckon you and call to you in the still hours of the night."

"What place beckons you?" Ashvin asked him.

"Ah, that's my secret! I'm not going to tell you," said Satish, laughing.

"Then I'll take a guess and tell you. The Himalayas beckon you and sometimes, I think, you would like to go and live there, a wanderer among the snow peaks, sleeping in lonely caves and so on. Am I right?"

Satish laughed again but this time I detected a note of uneasiness in his laughter.

"Well, I may wish to visit the Himalayas; there are few Hindus who don't."

"You have evaded my question," said Ashvin. "I did not say visit. I said you have this wish to live there, perhaps as a yogi."

"Are you going to leave and take up the wandering life of an ascetic, Satish?" I asked.

"He is not going to leave," said Ashvin firmly, "because with a wife and five children he has thoroughly burnt his boats, to use an English expression, so far as becoming a wandering yogi in the Great Snow Range is concerned." He got up. "Come, we must be going. It's getting late."

Vishnu followed him down the stairs. But Satish lingered a minute and said to me in a low voice, as though taking me into his confidence, "One is free, if one can put one's affairs in order . . . an aunt of mine—she has left me—"

I had no idea of what he was talking about. As though to explain the point of suddenly referring to an aunt of his, he began, "She recently gave me quite a large sum and—"

"What are you whispering about up there, Satish?"

And Ashvin ran up, took hold of Satish by an arm, and pulled him down the stairs.

I heard their voices growing fainter along the street after I had locked the front door.

For some reason, Satish's words, inexplicable as they had been to me, lingered on in my mind. I walked restlessly up and down the rooftop and then I sat down on the wall and gazed at the long line of distant palm-heads along the shore, the fronds unruffled by the faintest breeze. Then I pulled down the mosquito netting and stretched out on the charpoy. The air was absolutely still. I lay there, sleepless, my body turning restlessly in a futile attempt to get a little cooler.

Sleep must have come eventually, for in the deep of the night I woke up. Through the stillness came the clear sound of piping and I thought, 'He's back—the Pied Piper!' whom I had heard in my early childhood years and whom I had never heard again after I had left Hong Kong. As I listened, I realised that the sounds were not of pipes but the insistent melody of a flute. The music went on and on as though it would never stop. Every so often I half recognised a phrase and felt that somewhere I had heard the tune before, but I could not recollect when or where.

Slowly, still drugged with sleep, I went and sat on the wall and looked down at the street below. On the far side was an open space in which was a large banyan tree. It was from there that the music was coming but I could not see the player because of the deep shadows cast by the branches.

Perhaps, I thought, the musician is Lord Krishna himself, the eternal flautist and the divine actor! The sound of his flute, sometimes heard in the dead of night, does not lull the listener to sleep again. It has the opposite effect. Its message is 'Wake up! Arouse yourself from the deep sleep of Maya (illusion). Men, birds and beasts are enraptured by the sound and run to its source. The music of Krishna's flute is said to be the voice of Eternity heard by the dwellers in time.

The player moved out from under the branches of the tree and stood in a patch of moonlight, the flute pressed to his lips. He was a man, near naked, with long hair which fell to his waist. As he stood facing me I was just able to make out his features, though not very clearly. I felt certain that I had seen this ascetic before and I suddenly remembered the yogi of the previous evening whom I had come across playing his flute on the beach and singing to the setting sun. Was it the same man?

The music stopped abruptly and the yogi started to walk away down the street. I watched him take a turning which led down a narrow track, then past some cane fields and into scrub jungle. For one wild moment—perhaps due to the light of the moon, which is said to induce reckless states of mind—I thought of running out of the house and following him. But the impulse passed as quickly as it had arisen.

I went and lay down on the charpoy but sleep did not return. Soon the first pale streaks of dawn appeared in the sky and spread like a translucent wash over land and ocean. Tired from lack of sleep, I went down to the living-room to get breakfast.

CHAPTER FOURTEEN

MY GOTRA

THE TEMPERATURE WAS still well above the hundred mark. There was quite a lot of sickness in the village. People living in tropical countries are more prone to illness during the peak of the hot season, whereas in temperate lands it is during the winter months that people are more likely to become ill.

Dysentery and stomach upsets were what the villagers seemed to be suffering from most, caused by the intense heat. One of Golan's children came round to tell me that his father was ill and so would not be able to work for me for a few days. I felt quite glad to have the house all to myself for a while.

I went out for an early-morning walk as usual and on the way back I called at the Menons' house. Yamini was not feeling well and was resting upstairs. Ashvin was sitting on the veranda studying a long parchment scroll.

"It's my gotra," he said; "my family tree. The name of each member has been written down by the priests at Nasik, a Brahmin town in central India where for centuries the priests have been keeping the records of Brahmin families throughout the country. My gotra is not quite so long as Satish's, but it goes back now for almost nine hundred years."

The writing on the scroll was in Sanskrit. Ashvin told me that the various entries gave the dates of birth, marriage and death of each member of the family and the profession of the menfolk, most of whom had devoted their lives solely to priestly duties. The gotra stretched back to the time when Ashvin's relatives were living up north in the Gangetic Valley, not far from the mighty Himalayas over which the 'twice born' had come. Some branches of the family had gradually moved further and further south, until Ashvin's branch had finally come to rest on the Malabar Coast.

"How far back can you trace your family?" he asked me.

"So far as individual members of it are concerned, only to my great-great-great-grandfather," I replied.

I did some marketing on the way home and made myself a fruit drink when I got back. I felt I could have drunk the ocean. Drinks, fruit and the lightest of breakfasts and suppers is about all one can manage in this blazing heat.

I swept the room; then, my energies already exhausted, lay down and closed my eyes. I had a momentary recollection of Ashvin studying his gotra. That gave me an idea. I stretched out a hand for a pencil and my sketch-book and began writing down the names of my ancestors, drawing lines to connect one person to another. This did not take long, for my own family, unlike the families of my Brahmin friends, could only be traced back through individual members for some seven generations. Nevertheless, I thought, short though my gotra might be in comparison to theirs, at least several of its members had been talented and interesting personalities.

The air rippled with waves of heat. The house was quite silent and in the stillness my thoughts slipped away from India and returned to Britain and my own ancestors. It was the figure of my great-grandfather—W.C.M. as I shall call him—on whom my thoughts mainly centred as well as on some of his children. He died many years before I was born, yet I felt that I knew him well and he meant more to me than ever my own father had.

My family tree started somewhere up in the highlands of Scotland; then, in the seventeenth century, for reasons unknown, one half of the clan—my half—left Albion, the inheritor of the Greek spirit and the golden mean, and crossed over to the Roman island of Ireland. They lived mainly in the Dublin area and earned their livings in various humble occupations. My great-great-great-grandfather was an upholsterer. But his son, W.M., had no intention of pursuing this dull trade. His heart was set on the glamorous life of the theatre; moreover, he longed to leave Ireland and return to Britain, his spiritual home and the land of his ancestors.

He acted in Dublin with the Smock Alley Company, serving a rigorous apprenticeship. He was thirty before he had managed to save sufficient funds to make the channel crossing over to Liverpool. England did not disappoint; he loved the country from the moment he first set foot on its shore. Before long he was acting in Liverpool and Manchester and had married an English girl, an actress. As feckless as a wild fox, his finances were to range from the moderately stable to the chaotic. But up or down, down and out, he usually managed to maintain an optimistic outlook on life. His wife produced a large family, eight children in all, several of whom died in infancy. Her fifth child, born in London, was destined to become one of England's great actors.

The Irishman had not set the Thames on fire with his acting. He decided he was really more fitted for theatre management. He enjoyed being boss and throwing his weight around. He became manager of the Birmingham Theatre and a company of players at Chester. By paying high salaries and helped by a lot of treacly Irish charm, he was able to attract many of the leading players to his theatre.

One evening the hero of Trafalgar and his mistress turned up and were given the best box. The audience went hysterical when they saw Nelson and Emma and kept up a clamour throughout the performance. There was enough of the artist in the old Irishman to deplore the fact that the audience's attention was centred on the Admiral and Lady Hamilton and not on the play. He noted that the noble lord was not at all averse to the adulation and did not make a single gesture to quiet the crowd. When the curtain came down there was a final burst of clapping and cheering—for Nelson.

Finances had never been so good and the Irishman was able to send his eldest son, W.C.M., to a public school. The boy had shown considerable promise as an actor but not the slightest desire to take up acting as a career. He had seen at all too close quarters much of the narrowness and tawdriness of stage life. The actor of those days was classed as a vagrant, little better than a gipsy. W.C.M. hoped to become an Anglican priest.

The boy was enjoying public-school life but his father's

finances meanwhile had taken a sudden dive and the Irishman had become deeply in debt. He was unable to pay his creditors or his son's school fees. At the age of fifteen, W.C.M. had to leave school and start to help his father at the theatre.

The debts kept mounting. Eventually W.M. was forced to go into hiding to escape his creditors. Every so often he would emerge and have a clandestine meeting with his son and then dash back to his hiding-hole again. But eventually his creditors caught up with him. He was handed over to the sheriff and taken off to Lancaster Castle jail. His son, always emotional, broke down and wept when he visited him in custody. The father told him bluntly to go away if he could not control his tears.

By this time W.M. had lost his management of the Birmingham Theatre. But there was still the company of players at Chester. The fifteen-year-old boy hurried off to take control of them on his father's behalf. They had been idle and unpaid for weeks and he met with a mixed reception. Already a perfectionist, he kept the players' noses constantly to the grindstone and some of them began to think nostalgically of those carefree, albeit penurous days when they had been left to their own devices. But the company prospered under its young manager, who was to take his first professional role some months later in the part of Romeo.

He was a well-built young man with dark chestnut hair and deep blue eyes and he was immensely strong-willed.

It was the Regency Period, one of the most vital and radiant eras in English history. W.C.M. was to combine in himself the romanticism of this period with later Victorian idealism and realism and the vitality of both periods. From the moment he set a reluctant foot on the stage, he spared himself no pains to improve himself in his art and to elevate his profession. It was not the art of the actor that he disliked, as his enemies sometimes accused him of denigrating, but the mindlessness and often sordid and meretricious conditions of the theatre of those days, which he never ceased to hate to the end of his career.

When he realised that there was nothing for it but to take up the theatrical life, he determined to do all in his power to improve the actor's lot and to purge Shakespearean drama of Restoration interpolations and mutilations. Since the restoration of the drama in the reign of Charles the Second, many classical plays had suffered distortions and deletions. These vandalisms had been perpetrated by managers and producers who saw fit to doctor them in this manner so that they could be easily comprehended, in their estimation, by the most infant-minded adults in the audience, including, no doubt, the roistering monarch himself, a keen theatregoer. W.C.M.'s opinion of what the public was capable of appreciating and understanding was high, and this threw him into disfavour with many managers and producers.

Well-read in the classics and contemporary works, he had, like most of his fellow countrymen with an Anglican heritage, a profound love and admiration for ancient Greece and everything that country stood for. He took as maxims the Greek 'Knothi Seutha,'(Know Thyself) and the Roman initiate Seneca's 'Find a way or make one.'

The Irishman, after a period of 'resting' in Lancaster Castle, was out again and looking for some project to which he could devote his energies. As he was no longer the manager of a theatre he decided to build his own and install himself as its manager. Funds were at zero but he somehow managed to lay his hands on enough cash to buy a site in the theatreless city of Carlisle and to engage an architect. Six hundred pounds would have to suffice for building the theatre, and the architect was given instructions that the building was to be designed on the principle of the greatest number of people in the smallest possible space. While this job was underway W.M. went up to Berwick and rented an old malthouse which he converted into a theatre.

Father and son, who had very different temperaments, were finding it more and more difficult to get on together. They finally came to a mutual agreement never to live again under the same roof.

The son was making a name for himself as a player. Besides performing in the classics, he was also acting in many contemporary dramas: one about the legendary hero 'King Arthur', and a turgid Germanic drama by Byron called 'Werner'. Byron in his day was considered a major dramatist as well as a leading poet. Actor and poet were to remain friends until the latter's death in Greece, a country for which Byron had a profound love, like W.C.M. The actor always greatly admired the poet's courage, not so much Byron's physical courage, but his moral courage. He never hesitated to do battle with the vulgarians and Philistines on his own and his friends behalf, as W.C.M. had good reason to know and be grateful for.

The actor was fortunate in that many of the leading novelists and poets of his day were keen to write for the stage: Byron, Browning, Sheil, Dickens, Thomas Noon Talfourd, Bulwer-Lytton and others.

Each day the young actor read some poetry for the great pleasure it gave him. England was still producing that wonderful line of poets and seers and poet-seers, amongst whom in that era were Wordsworth, Coleridge, Shelley, Keats and Tennyson. These men were among his favourite poets. No work made much appeal to him if it did not penetrate below the surface of things, and it was to the mystics, whether poet or seer or both, to whom he was drawn and with whom he always felt a particular affinity.

A poem called 'Paracelsus', about the great French occultist and traveller, made a deep impression on him. It had been written by a young almost unknown poet called Robert Browning. The two met at the home of a vicar. W.C.M.'s closest friends were all poets and authors.

One evening when he was acting in a play at Drury Lane Theatre, he was visited in his dressing-room by one of the most unusual and brilliant writers of his day, George Borrow, author of *Lavengro* and *Romany Rye*. This was the only time they met, but I am always glad to think that my great-grandfather did once meet this fascinating Victorian author and authority on gipsy life.

Acting at the same time as W.C.M., a man several years older than himself, was Edmund Kean. No player before or since has excelled Kean in his portrayal of the flash of human passion. Kean's lightning sometimes eclipsed the greatness of the younger actor, but although Kean's brilliance was unsurpassed, his range was narrow and his triumphs were always in roles where the character was of a markedly evil disposition, such as King John. W.C.M.'s range was much wider than Kean's and he was able to portray the good as well as the evil. It is always much easier to portray the deformed and the mean than it is the noble, sublime and the beautiful. When W.C.M. started his career Kean was first player, but gradually the younger man outstripped the older to become first player himself.

W.C.M., like his father, married an actress. The marriage was a happy and harmonious one in so far as the two partners were concerned, but his wife was to be the cause of much of the sorrow he experienced in life, for the young woman was tubercular and not only was she herself to die of consumption but she was to pass the sickness on to most of their children. Again and again he and his wife would be sitting at the bedside of a dying child who one day might appear to be a little better, thus raising their hopes, only for it to have a relapse a few days' later and die from the dread disease.

W.C.M. was passionately devoted to all his children and he was a wise and loving father. Each child received an excellent education, the girls as well as the boys. They were given every encouragement in their various pursuits and were left free to take up any career they wished, with one exception: on no account whatever was any of them to think of going on the stage. In this respect W.C.M. was the stern, unbending paterfamilias. He said—and meant it—that he would rather see one of his children dead than on the stage. He could not bear to think that any of them might undergo the squalors and despairs of theatre life as he had. Fortunately, with the exception of one of the boys, none of the children wanted to act.

It was when Willie, the eldest son, was ill in bed and feeling bored that Browning called and spent a little time talking to the invalid. Willie was an attractive and warm-hearted boy and he and the poet were firm friends. Browning said he would write a poem especially for him and, true to his word, he returned three days' later, the poem completed.

Browning had read a snippet in a paper about a strange gipsy-like individual who had rid the town of Hamelin of hordes of rats by the tune he played on his pipe, and this snippet was sufficient to set his imagination working and he completed the lengthy poem in three days.

The boy was delighted with the poem and learnt it off by heart. Browning had no thought of getting it published. He had written it simply to amuse a sick child. But W.C.M. heard Willie reciting the poem, read it through himself and immediately saw its great merit. It was he who insisted that Browning get it published and, somewhat reluctantly, Browning agreed to do so. The first illustrated edition was an immediate success.

Browning never showed much interest in this poem in spite o its popularity with the public. He was far more concerned at the time of getting W.C.M. to produce a play he had written called *A Blot on the Scutcheon*.

W.C.M. did not care for the play and had no wish to stage it, but week after week and month after month Browning—a most persistent young man—urged and pleaded with him to do so. Much against his better judgement, W.C.M. at last agreed to the poet's urgent requests and the play was produced. It was a resounding flop, as W.C.M. had feared it would be, and ran for only three nights before being taken off.

This play has long since sunk into oblivion, but 'The Pied Piper of Hamelin', scribbled off in a few days, is still being read with delight by children and adults alike.

W.C.M.'s favourite child was his daughter Catherine. When still quite young, Katie began to make a name for herself as a poet. Two books of her verse were printed and were well received by the public and critics.

A younger son, Edward, went through agonies trying to decide whether or not to defy his father and become an actor. He was the only one who wanted to go on the stage and he knew just what he could expect if he voiced his wish to W.C.M. But acting was the only thing he wanted to do.

Kean's life and career were rapidly disintegrating and the younger actor, his chief rival, had succeeded him as first player.

W.C.M., who was both loved and hated, with many close and

talented friends and several enemies, was beginning to see, thanks to his own efforts, the status of the actor improve and a general renaissance taking place in the theatre. Each play that he performed in was staged under the best possible conditions and he made sure that the production as a whole came first. No actor or actress was allowed to hog the limelight to the detriment of the rest. His first principle as both actor and producer was unity and the realisation on stage of the dramatist's image of the play.

When he was forty he met an author, ten years younger than himself, whose friendship was to have far-reaching effects on both his professional and private life. The man was Bulwer-Lytton.

When they first met, Bulwer was already a leading author and politician and was living in bachelor quarters in London, for his marriage was fast breaking up. Like the majority of authors in England then, he was keen to write for the stage.

Bulwer's wife was having an affair with a Neapolitan prince. One day W.C.M. called to see Bulwer at his lodgings. Tea was laid for the two of them. Then Bulwer's wife put in an unexpected appearance and, seeing the tea-table, promptly accused her husband of keeping a mistress. He obtained a separation from her shortly after this. The whole business of his separation was to cause a public scandal, which eventually forced Bulwer into virtual retirement on his estate.

The two men had long talks together and W.C.M. learnt of the younger man's interest in 'the hidden side of things'. Bulwer believed in the evolutionary progress of mankind. He sensed intuitively that not many decades hence the two great traditions of the East and West would meet and merge as never before, and the West would become acquainted to a much greater extent than previously with Eastern wisdom. Man's evolutionary progress would receive a strong push forwards. But the foundations for this push, he believed, and the coming generations, willingness to accept new thoughts and new ideas for a new age—the Aquarian Age—must be laid in his own era. One of the methods he chose to put across his beliefs and occult knowledge was by 'truth through fiction'.

W.C.M. was much interested in Bulwer's beliefs and he too

had his aims which, so far as his public ambitions were concerned, were the renaissance and transformation of the English stage, a stage worthy of a mature and discriminating public. Actor and author both worked on the theatre's behalf and confided their aims and aspirations to one another.

Both the public and the majority of their friends were unaware of the underlying aims of the two. Byron and Browning and Tennyson were exceptions. The statesman Disraeli was also aware of Bulwer's interests and aspirations.

Disraeli himself was deeply interested in those hidden yet potent currents which affect mankind and he was also something of a seer and prophet. During his lifetime he did what he could to keep those currents flowing in an evolutionary direction. He was a man of quite extraordinary perception. I heard while I was living in the East that he may have been an initiate. I do not know whether this was so, only that he was one of several Englishmen in his era who was deeply interested in the hidden teachings and capable of giving his countrymen a push forward, so to speak, in the right direction.

Disraeli and W.C.M. were never friends. The actor had made some rude remarks about the statesman's long ringlets and somewhat foppish appearance, and Disraeli was always careful to cut W.C.M. in the street. A pity, for both men were working for the same aims, had they but known it.

A very successful play by Bulwer with W.C.M. in the lead was about the French cardinal *Richelieu*. There was a powerful scene in which the red-gowned prelate, who had once wielded the sword, comes to realise that there are finer ways of achieving victory. Seating himself at a desk, he speaks the famous lines:

> "The pen is mightier than the sword . . .
> Take away the sword—
> States can be won without it. Bring the pen!"

This play was followed by a Bulwer comedy called *Money*, with W.C.M. again in the lead. While *Money* was being rehearsed, two of the actor's youngest children became desperately ill with tuberculosis. The little girl Harriet died. The small boy miraculously recovered. The play, meanwhile, went on and was a great popular success.

Acting is an unusual profession in that it often leaves the actor of a strong masculine disposition with a sense of unfulfilment. Perhaps this is because acting is basically a feminine art. Nearly every great actor has at some time in his career turned to producing and management in an attempt to remedy this lack of total fulfilment.

W.C.M. became actor-manager, first of Covent Garden Theatre and later of Drury Lane. As well as performing in London, he went on lengthy tours of the Continent, the United States and Canada.

On one of these New World tours he took a respite from the claustrophobic life of the stage. He and a friend hired redskin guides and went on a trip into the Adirondack Mountains in the Hudson River area. The pine-clad mountains and rushing streams gave him a wonderful feeling of liberation, and the vast and unspoilt wilderness was to leave a lasting impression on him. They slept in shelters made by the guides from hewn spruce branches and cooked their meals over log fires. The trip over, they headed back to Albany and W.C.M. continued his tour.

The eldest son Willie went to work with the East India Company in Ceylon. Edward made one attempt to go on the stage during one of his father's foreign tours but the odds against him were too great. The luckless youth was packed off in disgrace to a military academy and gained a commission in the Indian Army. He eventually took a liking to army life, and the ancient land of India made a great appeal to him. During his leaves he travelled widely, particularly in the north among the snow-clad Himalayas. He got to know various yogis and Brahmins and began to study the Vedas. Unfortunately, he also started to gamble and he became more and more in debt. Perhaps this avid gambling was due partly to frustration at having had to relinquish his hopes of becoming an actor.

After he had left for India, the family rarely heard from him. Then, having been in the army for several years, he suddenly resigned his commission—just why has never come to light. Perhaps he was asked to do so because of his reckless gambling or perhaps he had received the first warning symptoms of the disease which had killed several of his brothers and sisters and was to kill several more, or there may have been other reasons. News of his gambling debts, meanwhile, had leaked back to his father and he was sternly ordered home.

Obedient to his father's wishes, he boarded a ship in Bombay due to sail to Britain. But what had he to go back to? That question must have been haunting him as the time for departure drew near. He would never be allowed by W.C.M. to make the stage a career. His future in England must have looked bleak indeed.

When the ship left Bombay he was not on it, and nothing more was ever heard of him. There was another liner in the harbour at the time due to sail for Australia, and some members of the family came to believe that he swam over to this ship and made a new life for himself in Australia. Years later, there were rumours that he had been seen acting in the town of Ballarat in New South Wales, but they were never confirmed.

My own guess is that he swam back to shore and lived out the rest of his life in India, a country he had come to love and whose ancient wisdom he had been studying. Perhaps he spent the remainder of his days as an ascetic with other men of a like kind, among the towering peaks of the Great Snow Range which he had visited when he was an army officer. But this is only a guess. From the time he boarded the ship in Bombay on which he never sailed, nothing more was ever heard of him. This strange young man had left the world without a trace.

Amongst W.C.M.'s friends, Byron had died in Greece, Browning was living in Italy with Elizabeth Barrett, his bride, and Bulwer-Lytton was spending most of his time on his family estate. There, in the quiet of the countryside, he was beginning to write those esoteric novels *Zanoni*, *A Strange Story*, *The Dweller on the Threshold*, a verse romance *King Arthur*, and *The Coming Race*, novels which enthralled readers of his generation.

In the guise of fiction he gave out much occult data and several prophetic utterances. He foresaw, along with Disraeli, Madam Helena Petrovna Blavatsky and several other seers, that the greatest country in Europe in his age—his own—would be the first to disintegrate and fade. At that time Great Britain—as it was then—ruled over a quarter of the world's inhabitants and had an Empire on which 'the sun never set.' It was a radiant land. In this, our own age, Bulwer's prophecy has come to pass; Great Britain is now Britain and the glow has almost faded. No other great nation has ever declined with such terrible swiftness.

Bulwer further foresaw that as Britain, and then Europe, declined, the sphere of influence would gradually move over to those countries in the South Pacific: Australia, New Zealand and South Africa, countries which today are well into their stride and whose peoples are those of his 'Coming Race'.

Bulwer also wrote about men called adepts and initiates. Prior to his novels, the British public had rarely ever heard of such beings. Their existence had been known only to a few highly developed men in occult brotherhoods in the West and to true yogis in the East. The adepts were men who had advanced far beyond the human average and some of them, possessed remarkable powers called siddhis.

For the most part, the general public regarded these mysterious men merely as fictitious creations on Bulwer's part. But, undoubtedly, a few readers asked themselves whether these beings known as initiates really existed and wondered, too, whether it might be possible to extend their own range of consciousness. It was just this kind of questioning that Bulwer hoped to instigate in the minds of some of his readers.

In later years Bulwer met the Russian occultist and seer, Madam Blavatsky, who was an admirer of his work. That was in Ramsgate in 1851. H.P.B. paid tribute to Bulwer in her magnum opus 'The Secret Doctrine', in which she states that although the public might see him simply as an accomplished dramatist and novelist, she and a few others knew him as a member of the occult or white brotherhood.

An American actor by the name of Edwin Forrest came over to Britain for a tour. W.C.M. did what he could to help make the tour a success but certain persons had whispered in Forrest's ear that W.C.M. was jealous of him and was doing what he could to make the tour a failure. This was quite untrue; nevertheless, Forrest believed these whisperers and conceived a hatred for the English actor. When W.C.M. was acting up in Edinburgh, Forrest paid a special visit to the theatre in order to hiss him, an unnerving experience for any actor. The audience shouted—"Turn him out!" But the culprit remained seated in his box till the end of the act and then walked disdainfully from the theatre, followed by the boos and shouts of the angry audience.

Forrest's tour was not a success but that had nothing to do with W.C.M. But the American actor left Britain vowing he would do what he could to put a hefty spoke in W.C.M.'s forthcoming tour of the U.S.

This was to be W.C.M.'s farewell visit to the States. When he boarded the ship for America he had forgotten all about Forrest's hissing of him in Edinburgh, but Forrest had not forgotten about him.

The tour went well until the company played at Philadelphia, when the Forrest faction began to get busy, throwing rotten eggs on to the stage. At Washington there were rumbles of a forthcoming storm but the rumbles died away as W.C.M. and the company sailed up the Mississippi and toured the southern states. Cincinnati was not so good; someone threw half of a raw sheep's carcass on to the stage.

On to New York and a rehearsal at the Astor Place Opera House for the evening performance of 'Macbeth'. W.C.M. had been warned to expect trouble. The Forrest faction had booked large numbers of seats inside the theatre and others were starting to gather outside. But W.C.M. had his supporters too and as evening approached they started to mill outside the theatre.

When W.C.M. made his first entrance as Macbeth, there was mingled cheering and booing. Volleys of rotten eggs, vegetables and stones rained on to the stage. A banner was raised high. On one side was written, "No apologies—it's too late!" And on the other, "You have been proved a liar!"

Outside the theatre the two factions had started to clash. Some of the mob began to smash the theatre windows with paving stones—the street was under repair at the time. The play went on to the sounds of splintering glass, the whizz of missiles, screams and shouts and the noise of fighting going on inside and outside the building. Stones had broken some of the piping and water began to cascade into the players' dressing-rooms. They squelched on to the stage looking as though they had been through a deluge, which, indeed, they had.

The Forrest faction, besides coming to the theatre armed with various missiles, had also brought bottles filled with horrible-smelling asafoetida and these were now thrown on to the stage. Macbeth and the rest of the Scottish thanes were hard put to it not to pull out handkerchiefs to cover their noses.

Some of the uncommitted portions of the audience had thought it wiser to leave the theatre, others tried to protect themselves from flying missiles and the fighting by hiding behind the seats. As friend and foe fought in the pit, the stalls and up in the gallery, Macbeth duelled gamely on stage. The curtain came down at the fourth act and the cast returned to their flooded dressing-rooms to remove their make-up and lick their wounds.

The mob outside was now trying to get into the theatre and set fire to it. The militia was called, cavalry and infantry, and there was the crackle of rifle fire. In the darkness of the night the soldiery tried to encircle the besieged building and cut the mob off, to no avail. Reluctantly, the general in charge of operations ordered his men to fire above the heads of the crowd, but because of the noise, the troops misunderstood his order and fired straight into the crowd. The derisive mob thought the shots were blanks and flung paving-stones at the troops. The cavalry was forced to retire. The infantry was penned about by more than twenty thousand seething people. There was another volley of firing. Two cannons were brought; one pointed down the Bowery, the other down Broadway. The furious crowd began to break up into small groups.

Inside the theatre, friends urged W.C.M. to disguise himself and leave at once. They knew that if the crowd caught sight of him he would be torn to pieces. W.C.M. put on one of the player's jackets and a different cap to the one he had worn during the performance. The doorkeeper at the actor's exit refused to let them pass, knowing the fury of the crowd outside. So they walked across the stage and over the orchestra pit and joined the last members of the audience who were trickling out of the central exit.

All the street lamps had been put out by the mob and they had to walk in darkness through the rioting crowd and along to a friend's house, where he was urged to get out of New York at the first opportunity. A carriage was ordered. Some straggling members of the mob caught sight of it as it was arriving in the early hours of the morning. A friend had gone out to wait for it and he asked a man who was trying to knock in one of the windows what the fuss was about. Turning, the man said, "W.C.M. is in the carriage. They've killed twenty of us, and, by God, we're going to kill him!"

But seeing no one inside, they wandered away and W.C.M. left New York in an early-morning mist and breakfasted at New Rochelle, twenty miles away.

Forrest had won, if such a disastrous night could be called a victory. Twenty-two people had been killed in the rioting and many more wounded and W.C.M. had only narrowly escaped death himself. Relations between Britain and America were severely strained for some time after that.

The actor had once remarked wryly to Robert Browning that if Browning had suffered from father-in-law trouble for a period of his life then he, W.C.M., had suffered from father trouble for the greater part of his. Browning could count himself lucky.

The Irishman, feckless to the end, kicked over the traces even more in his old age than he had done in his more youthful days. When his wife died—the actor's adored mother—he found a celibate life little to his liking. So he took a mistress. Then a second one, and later on a third. These women had to be maintained on his small income. Each in turn produced several not-so-legitimate children, thus further burdening his already severely strained financial circumstances. He made frequent requests for assistance to his famous son, and W.C.M., after wrestling with his conscience, would usually help his father out. An alley cat's morals would have appeared good in comparison with those of the Irishman's at this period of his life. As his mistresses' children grew older, they would come and blatantly knock on the actor's door demanding funds, and W.C.M., after more soul-searching battles with his conscience, would give them something.

Since he was a young man W.C.M. had been forced to take on heavy financial burdens because his father refused to shoulder his own responsibilities. The actor had supported a sister to the end of her life and had seen a younger brother through a military training college. With all these various commitments, both his own and his father's, W.C.M. was nevertheless far from oblivious to the troubles of those outside his family circle. In mid-life he and an unmarried woman who had done much social work among London's poor adopted ten orphan children. Their father, a widowed actor and friend of W.C.M.'s, had died suddenly, leaving the children alone in the world and almost penniless. These children were taken into the spinster's home and W.C.M. paid for their upbringing and schooling. They were welcome to call at his house whenever they wished.

After his final tour of America he started to think seriously about retiring. He had no intention of dying in harness. He had reached the peak of his acting career and the aims he had set himself as a young man had all been accomplished: the great plays were given worthy productions with their original texts, the player was no longer looked upon as a vagabond and was free to move in whatever social circles he wished, and the theatre itself had undergone a transformation. As to W.C.M.'s attainment as an actor, a perceptive critic once wrote of him, 'The spiritual tendency which was first manifest in the poetry of Wordsworth, Coleridge and Shelley, has found its dramatic exposition in W.C.M.'s acting. If Edmund Kean was the Byron of actors,

W.C.M. in many respects affords a parallel to Wordsworth... in particular his insight into the laws of nature under its varied modifications.'

On the 26th of February, 1851, he gave his farewell performance at Drury Lane Theatre. A dinner was given for him the following evening at which many of his friends were present; the painters Maclise and Landseer, Dickens, Thackeray, Bulwer-Lytton and others as well as the actor's eldest son Willie. The Poet Laureate, Alfred Lord Tennyson, had written a sonnet for the occasion in which were the lines:

> '... rank with the best
> Garrick, and statelier Kemble, and the rest
> Who made a nation purer through their art.
>
> Thine is it that our drama did not die,
> Nor flicker down to brainless pantomine,
> And those gilt gauds men-children flock to see...'

He took nothing with him into retirement to remind him of the theatre. His old friend Bulwer-Lytton had generously offered him a house close to his estate to live in permanently or as an occasional resort, whichever he preferred. But he declined the offer. He wrote to Bulwer telling him that he had already bought a home in Dorset and that 'when I turn recluse I must abandon all hope of seeing you, for not even a single railway-line penetrates to the depth of that seclusion which is to be our home.'

He had bought a lovely old house in Sherborne and he hoped down there to 'retreat into silence' and spend his last years in meditation and study. He was free at last, after forty gruelling years on the stage.

But he was not to remain idle. He had always had a strong social conscience and he saw ignorance as the greatest enemy of mankind. He started a night-school for poor children and young working men in which he himself taught and he also conducted a literary and scientific institute. But although he taught at the school and gave readings at the institute, he looked on himself as a student to the end of his days. He read poetry and re-read the plays of Shakespeare and the Greek dramatists, and he still discovered new insights in the parts he had once played.

He had tried throughout his life to accept the blows of fate with courage and without bitterness. The heaviest blows were still to come. His wife, who had been a semi-invalid for years, died shortly after his retirement and her death was followed not long after by the deaths of two more of his children.

Most of his hopes of these later years had centred on his daughter Katie, and it was with great delight that he learnt from her that she and Bulwer-Lytton's eldest son had become secretly engaged. He was a young man, W.C.M. knew, who would encourage her in her poetic art and give her every support.

But for some time Katie had not been well. She had 'a cold', a 'bad cold', a 'horrid cold.' W.C.M. would not, could not, face the fact that yet another of his children, the girl who had always been closest to his heart, had contracted the same fatal illness which had decimated his family.

In order for her to throw off this cold, it was thought best that she should spend the winter in Madeira and return home in the spring, cured. Then the young couple would announce their engagement. She went out alone to the island of Madeira, already mortally stricken, but refusing to admit that she was suffering from anything worse than a heavy cold, no doubt, more for her father's sake than her own. She had always been a gay and courageous young woman, and throughout that winter she saw what she could of the island in spite of her illness and joined in many of the social events. She had written home shortly before her return voyage that she was feeling much better. On the ship, she was the gayest and liveliest passenger on board. Then, a week after the ship had set out, she had a severe haemorrhage in her cabin at night and was found dead the following morning. The ship was stopped in mid-ocean. Passengers had come aboard with bunches of spring flowers—daffodils, camellias, jacaranda and lilies—and all the blossoms which had not faded were placed on top of the coffin. The captain read the burial service and then the coffin was lowered over the side of the ship and into the ocean.

W.C.M. had gone down to Plymouth to meet his daughter.

There was no wireless in those days and news of her death had not reached him. The passengers were lined up against the ship's rail. The captain walked down the gangway alone and went straight up to W.C.M. He told him that Katie had died and been buried at sea. She was thirty-four.

This was a blow from which he never really recovered. Two years later Willie died in Ceylon at the age of thirty-nine. Out of his ten children, only two were alive: a daughter and the youngest son.

This boy was later to become a famous London surgeon and, except for the surviving daughter, he was the longest-lived of all the actor's children, dying at the age of fifty-seven. He was my grandfather of whom I know very little and whom I never met, for he died years before I was born.

Illness overtook the actor's once strong body. His hands became so paralysed that he was unable to even hold a book and he could speak only in a faint whisper. Yet his mind was still active and as he lay on bed or couch, almost physically helpless, he would silently go over the parts he had once played.

Bulwer-Lytton died. And three months later at the age of eighty W.C.M. slipped from life. He had been conscious to the end. Born in London, he was buried in the family vault in a West London cemetery.

With his passing went a man who had been a servant of the theatre and a true artist.

CHAPTER FIFTEEN

THE DOOR IS OPEN

ONE OF MY more frequent visitors was Satish. We would sit on the living-room floor and discuss such topics as ahimsa, cow slaughter, different kinds of love, sex, passages in the Gita, and he would tell me about his friends and ancestors. Like most Brahmins, he enjoyed talking, particularly on some religious or philosophical theme, and he talked well. Golan would appear at frequent intervals with pots of tea.

Sometimes Satish would arrive at my front door with his father, Sri Kalyanji. They might have just finished officiating in a ceremony at the temple down the road. Father and son looked extraordinarily alike. Both had thin wiry bodies and their hair was done up in top-knots. They talked volubly and made the same quick gestures. Both wore the langothi, but whereas the son's would be somewhat untidily wrapped around his waist and hung right down to his ankles, Sri Kalyanji's would be neatly folded and hang only a little way below his knees, which gave him a somewhat skittish appearance. Although father and son looked much alike, there was a wide difference in their characters. Satish was a highly-strung individual, often in conflict with himself and not always inwardly secure, whereas Sri Kalyanji exuded an aura of confidence and was invariably cheerful. It was difficult to think of anything getting him down. Not so with Satish, who was far more vulnerable.

But both of them seemed impervious to the stupendous heat and humidity and would often arrive at my door in the blazing noon-day hours and stand there talking animatedly under the burning white disc of the sun.

Sri Kalyanji was strictly orthodox. He never invited me to his home and always declined my invitation to come in and have a cup of tea, explaining to me frankly that that would mean his undergoing a lengthy purification ceremony after leaving. He would stand just outside my door in the shimmering heat-haze and tell me about some temple rites or give me his interpretation of a passage from the Vedas.

One noon he arrived with Satish. He stood as usual outside the front door, and told me that shortly he would be relinquishing the cares of a householder to spend the last years of his life living in a small hut at the bottom of a son-in-law's garden, where his time would be occupied in studying the sacred scriptures and in meditation.

"Why not in Satish's garden?" I asked. "He is your only son."

Sri Kalyanji smiled and gave Satish a hard dig in the ribs with his elbow, saying, "Unfortunately the vibrations in his home are not always harmonious and so I won't be retiring there."

Poor Satish! He gave a quirk of a smile and then looked down at his bare feet.

In view of Sri Kalyanji's strict orthodoxy, I was surprised when he went on to tell me that as a young man he had studied at Oxford and taken his degree.

"But how did you manage to live in England as an orthodox Brahmin?"

"Those of us Brahmins who studied in Britain were excused our daily rites and so forth while we were studying there. Of course, I never ate flesh, though I did eat a few eggs. When I returned to India"—Sri Kalyanji clapped a hand to his forehead—"oh, the purification ceremonies I had to go through! Internal and external and very expensive. They lasted for weeks. At the end of them I felt I hadn't got any inside left."

I rashly asked for an explanation and Sri Kalyanji told me that, amongst the various internal cleansing rites the priests made him go through, was one which involved swallowing pints of water and then vomiting up the contents of his stomach, and another 'at the other end' which was a form of enema, only a good deal more stringent than the Western variety. Sri Kalyanji gave me all the lurid details without a trace of embarrassment. No wonder he had been in a state of complete collapse at the end of all these cleansing rituals.

He excused himself as usual from entering my unpurified domain and set off briskly homewards.

Satish and I sat down on the floor. He had previously explained to me that it was alright for him to come into my house. "I am not so orthodox as my father." But he regretted that he could not ask me to his illam, as that would mean a purifying ceremony after I had left, whereas I, a non-Brahmin, had no need to purify my house after he had left it. I had smiled when he told me this and I think he must have felt a bit guilty at not returning the little hospitality which I gave him, for he often arrived with a small present, such as a box containing sweets made by his wife and decorated with gold and silver foil and green pistachio nuts. Very pretty.

Golan brought tea, but when I poured out Satish's, I saw that he had taken a dive into the depths of his being and was oblivious of the cup I put in front of him. I had got used to these dives by now. I drank my tea and waited for him to surface. His eyes were half closed, a hand covered the lower portions of his face, and he was unaware of my presence or his surroundings.

Withdrawing his hand a little, he murmured, "I hate him!"

I thought I could not have heard aright. He looked directly at me, his eyes wide open, and said again, a defiant expression on his face, "Yes, it's true—I have very little love for my father and quite a lot of hate."

"Why?"

"Father stopped me from becoming the only thing I wanted to become and he forced me into an early marriage. Yet he still likes to think that everything he did was for the best."

"What did you want to become?"

"I'll tell you. From a very early age—I couldn't have been more than seven or eight—I had this longing to leave home and become a yogi. Father's illam had never really been home to me. I felt I would discover my true abode and my true self as an ascetic in the homeless state. But Father sensed my secret desire and decided to put a stop to it. He arranged a marriage for me when I was only thirteen. Shortly before the wedding was due to take place, I ran away one night and started off on foot towards the Himalayas, hundreds of miles away. The police caught me five days later and I was brought back.

"Father gave me a severe beating, then locked me up in a room. I was kept there until the day of my wedding. By then I was too weak and cowed to make any further protests about being compelled to go through with the ceremony. I was dressed in bridal finery, my eyelids still swollen from weeping. What a sight I looked! I must have been the most miserable bridegroom in India and I felt sorry for my bride, too, for having so reluctant a groom. We had never met until the day of the ceremony, according to Hindu custom. So I was married and Father prided himself in having achieved his aim and stopped me from becoming a yogi." He paused, then said softly, "But if a person has some deep, heartfelt desire, it cannot be killed so easily."

"Do you still want—" I began.

But he cut me short, saying, "For years I was like a bird in a cage beating my wings against the bars. Then, not so long ago, I resolved to free myself. I did not know how I was going to do this; I simply vowed to myself that I would. Hardly had I determined on this than things started to happen and work on my behalf. It was as if I had set some powerful force in action. A few months ago an aunt of mine—a wealthy widow without any children—gave me a large sum of money, sufficient to keep my wife comfortably to the end of her days and my children till they are of marriageable age."

A minute must have gone by and neither of us spoke; then he said, "When one has truly made up one's mind to free oneself, one finds that the door of the cage is open."

"So you are out of the cage now?"

He leaned forward and whispered, "Almost!" Then he put a finger against his lips, as though to indicate that he wanted me to keep silent about what he had said.

That talk with Satish had a disturbing effect on me. It was as though, by telling me something about himself and his aspiration, he had told me something about myself too.

Three nights later, sleeping up on the roof as usual, I woke with a start. A pebble rattled on the stone floor, then another. I thought some street urchin was probably playing this annoying prank. But when I leaned over the wall, about to tell him to clear off, I saw that standing below and looking up at the rooftop was an ascetic.

When he saw me he beckoned me to come down. I had the strangest feeling as I stared at this late-night visitor. I seemed to half recognise him. Why was he summoning me down? For some seconds I hesitated about opening the front door. Many of the so-called wandering holy men are not holy at all, but criminals. I might be letting myself in for an unpleasant experience if I unbolted the door. Yet I slid the bolt back, then drew the door open.

The man standing before me was slimly built and wearing only a narrow length of cloth. His black hair hung loose about his shoulders. He pressed his hands together, palm to palm, and said, "I'm going. I felt I must come and tell you. Perhaps it will give you the courage to step out into the unknown one day."

"Satish!" I gasped.

"I'm not Satish any longer. I have no name now, no caste and no home."

I noticed that the sacred thread was no longer across his chest.

He raised an arm and pointed northwards. "I know I shall find my guru in the Sacred Range," he said.

Then he turned and walked off along the darkened street.

I went up to the roof and sat down on the bed. I could not think of sleeping. My thoughts were of Satish—or the man who had once been called Satish—who was walking towards the mighty Himalayas where he was certain he would find his guru, stepping out into the unknown, homeless and casteless now, the man who had once been so orthodox.

When I went downstairs, the living-room seemed to be hemming me in with its four walls. I suddenly wanted to leave this little house where I had been so happy and to step out, as Satish had done, into the unknown. I felt an overpowering need for the wild unconfined spaces where I could live, for a while at least, in near-solitude and spend my time exploring, not the outer world, but the inner.

But, I asked myself, just step out—to where? Satish had this intuitive urge to go to the Himalayas, whereas I had no feeling to head in a particular direction. Or had I? How should I set about walking off into the unknown in search of silence and solitude and enlightenment? Where to? But, above all, dare I?

CHAPTER SIXTEEN

TWO EAGLES

THE WHOLE VILLAGE was talking about the disappearance of Satish. I did not mention to anyone that he had called at my house that night before walking off to the Himalayas.

When he had not returned home for two days, his wife and Sri Kalyanji had still been reluctant to inform the police of his absence. Satish had had a habit, apparently, of sometimes going off without notice to some distant shrine and returning again a few days later. But this time he did not return, and on the fifth day of his absence his wife, a quiet young woman who led an almost purdah-like existence, received a letter from him informing her that he had left to become a yogi and would never be coming back. The letter had been posted from a central Indian town. His wife told her in-laws about the letter and asked them to look after the children for the night. During the night she swallowed poison and a servant found her next morning, half dead. A doctor was hastily summoned from Trivandrum and he managed to pull her round.

I had tea with Yamini a few days after this had happened and I asked her, "Do you think she'll try to poison herself again?"

"She may. But I think swallowing poison was really more of a cry for help than an attempt at suicide."

She gave a wry smile. "In India the Hindu wife does not fear 'the other woman.' It's the voice of the guru calling her husband away that she's afraid of. There is always the chance that a man may decide to chuck everything—wife, children, home—and embark on the wandering life of a yogi. Very few who go off in this way ever return again to their homes or are found. Well, that is a risk we Hindu women have to take when we get married."

She stirred her tea slowly for some moments and then, changing the subject, asked me whether I wanted to rent the house for another month.

"No. I think I'll start off on a trip next week and see something of other parts of India, now that the weather is getting cooler. I've enjoyed my stay in your little house very much and I'll be sorry to be leaving."

"I'm glad you have. Come back again whenever you feel like it. Where will you be going?"

"I think I'll start by visiting the southernmost tip of India at Kanya Kumari."

"I've been there. It's lovely. Three oceans meet at the point of land and each one is a different colour. Truly!" she assured me, seeing that I was looking somewhat sceptical.

That evening I began to plan my trip. Although I wanted to see Kanya Kumari, I was even more keen to go to a hilltop shrine on the East Coast which was visited each day by two white eagles. I had been promising myself a visit to this hill ever since I had first heard about the birds when I was a child. The two eagles are sacred, and pilgrims and tourists come from all over India in order to receive the birds' darshan and have a look at them.

'All are sacred but some are more sacred than others.'

I have misquoted George Orwell slightly. The 'some' should include, while in India, certain animals, birds, turtles, rivers, trees and mountains as well as humans.

The way sacredness works in the sub-continent goes something like this: cows are *the* most sacred animals, and they are followed by monkeys, who are a little less sacred than cows. The other inhabitants of the animal kingdom could be called sacred, but . . .

"In the sense that everything is sacred, I suppose you could call a leopard or a dog sacred, but they are not half as sacred as cows and monkeys," Ashvin had explained to me.

Take trees. Under certain trees, the peepul and bo tree, for example, certain great teachers and yogis have sat and meditated, sometimes for years on end, thereby conferring sacredness upon that particular tree and its species.

Mountains. The Himalayan Range is held to be sacred but some mountains in it are more sacred than others, and this holds good for other ranges and peaks elsewhere in India.

When a human being is held to be more sacred than other

humans, he has his praises sung, his feet embraced, is garlanded, worshipped, presented with offerings, and devotees sit in respectful silence whenever he cares to say a few words.

Birds. I would soon be visiting the two most sacred birds in the whole of India. I am tempted to say, in the whole world, for I have not heard of a pair of birds elsewhere being considered anything like so sacred as these two.

Before I left on the trip I did a certain amount of reading in order to refresh my memory and gain more information about this remarkable pair of eagles, a god and goddess in disguise, in the best fairytale tradition. And I had plenty of reading matter to hand: tourist tracts and brochures, travel volumes and religious booklets in which the famous pair are mentioned and discussed. Straightaway, I became aware again that facts are of a different order, generally speaking, in India than facts in the West. Like so much in this country, origins, dates, the where's and when's slip away from one and recede further and further back into the past until they disappear. That is one of the reasons why the phrase 'Since the beginning of time' is used so frequently. One hears it nearly every day, and it is a phrase which applies well to the holy eagles, Busha and Vidatha.

I will call them eagles, although in articles about them they are called alternatively eagles, kites and vultures, sometimes all three names being used indiscriminately in the same article or book. This lack of exact specification does not worry the Indian mind in the least but it often infuriates the European.

"Surely," a Westerner will ask in annoyance, "this one simple fact about the birds could easily be settled forthwith. After all, they are seen every day by hundreds of people and they are supposed to have been coming to the hill for, well ... Are they eagles, kites or vultures?"

How long have Busha and Vidatha been coming to the hill? Ask any Indian and he will tell you: Since the beginning of time, for centuries; right through the Kreta Yuga, the Treta Yuga, the Dwapara Yuga and this Kali Yuga—the golden, silver, copper and iron ages of this world. Anyway, the birds have been coming to the hill for a very long time.

After riffling through pamphlets and worm-riddled volumes trying to get hold of a few facts (Western style), I finally managed to find a date. The date, needless to say, was given by a European. He was a Dutchman called Havart who wrote a book about a journey he made through India. He stated that he visited the shrine and saw the eagles on January 3rd, 1681, and he is the first European, so far as is known, to have done so. He adds, without comment, that the pair are said to have been coming daily to Thirukkalukundram for several centuries, or longer prior to his visit. That was in 1681.

A few more facts about the eagles (Indian style). They are said to bathe each morning in the Ganges at Varanasi, a distance of over a thousand miles to the north of the shrine, before flying to the hill to be fed from the hand of a hereditary priest with pure sattvic food—vegetarian and, in this case, sweetened cooked rice, ghee and dhal. Having eaten, the birds fly off and are not seen again until the following day at the shrine, but they are said to go on to Rameswaram, where they pray, and then on again to Chidambaram, some hundred miles to the south of the hill, where they rest. After flying three-quarters the length of India, one feels they deserve this rest and, one must not forget, they make this stupendous flight daily.

There was another piece of information concerning these flying wonders which appeared in nearly every Indian account I read about them and was, apparently, deemed almost as remarkable as their daily flight and their venerable age. The birds arrive punctually at the shrine every day at noon! Punctually, in India? If so—and I confess I had a few doubts on this score—then the fact must certainly be accounted as much a miracle as the birds' divine gift for healing—they are accredited with curing both human beings and animals of many serious diseases—their endurance, and their long lives. Anyway, I would soon be finding out for myself whether they were as punctual as their many admirers, past and present, claimed they were.

I caught a bus to Trivandrum, spent a night there, then caught an early bus next morning right down to Cape Comorin, or

Kanya Kumari, as it is also called. We arrived in the late afternoon. I booked in at a hotel which overlooks this 'Land's End' of India, then went out to join other visitors and pilgrims who were standing in the sea.

I always wore a salwar-kameez, except in the large cities where I wore a cotton dress. This costume consisted of full white cotton trousers caught in at the ankles, a patterned cotton over-dress slit at either side, and a scarf of chiffon, usually white, which went across the neckline, the ends hanging down one's back. A pair of chappals completed my outfit.

Thus attired, I left my sandals on the shore with scores of others, and waded into the trough of water which borders the enclosure of the temple dedicated to the Virgin Goddess of Kanya Kumari. We moved slowly forward, all of us intent on reaching the tip of land round which three oceans meet. They are the Indian Ocean, the Arabian Sea and the Sea of Bengal. Slipping and sliding over submerged rocks and steadying ourselves against a strong current, we reached a sandy spit and from there stepped into the ocean, or oceans.

It was shortly before sunset and already the sky was filled with flame-coloured clouds. I had thought that when Yamini had told me that the sea here was of three different colours she might have been letting her imagination run away with her, but as I stood waist-deep in the swirling waters, I saw that this was in fact so; the sea was a cerulean blue, a deep emerald, and an indigo touched with violet.

A cultured-looking elderly gentleman, dressed only in a dhoti and with a pair of glasses balanced somewhat precariously on the end of his nose, said to me, "Do you know that from here to Australia there is not a single speck of land—nothing but a vast expanse of ocean?"

"No, I didn't know that."

"Yes, that's so." And he went on to say, "I myself believe, along with many other persons, that a link between India and the evolving civilisations in the South Pacific is being formed, just as in the past pre-atomic era there was this mystic link with Britain, a country of a once predominantly Aryan people, the English."

"I'm glad you said 'once'," I remarked, and we both smiled.

"Prophets of both East and West have long predicted that it will be in the young countries of the South Pacific area that the coming great race—in fact, this race has arrived—will gradually evolve."

We gazed at the flaming colours ahead of us before turning and wading back to the shore. We sat down on some rocks in the shade of the temple wall.

Two youths, who looked as if they might be students, came and sat down beside us. They were dressed in white cotton trousers and shirts and had cameras slung from their wrists. As the old gentleman and I continued talking, the attention of the young men appeared to centre half on our conversation and half on a group of pilgrims who were chanting the name of the Virgin goddess.

The old man was saying, "There is a very wonderful atmosphere down here—I'm sure you can feel it? That is because many great rishis have lived and performed tapas here in this southernmost area. In the Himalayas there is also a wonderful atmosphere, again because great souls have lived and meditated on the mountains, right down to our present day. I'll let you into a secret! Before coming to Kanya Kumari I heard, and on excellent authority, that some of our Himalayan rishis have recently moved south to this area. This whole place is more alive than ever with spiritual vibrations! The reason they have moved south is because of the militant Chinese forces massed on the other side of our mountains."

One of the youths asked sarcastically, "Who told you that— someone from Thomas Cook and Son?"

"Ah, the cynical voice of our modern youth," said the old man.

He got up hastily and said to me, "Please excuse me. I must leave before this young cynic destroys the peace in my heart which the goddess has given me."

He walked away, followed by the laughter of the two youths.

"There goes *old* India," one of them said to me, "with all its silly superstitions and religious taboos. Don't spend all your time talking to old India. It is passing and will soon be dead and gone, however much it may seem to intrude into the present. See something of *modern* India: the dams, the workers' flats, the Aarey Milk Colony in Bombay—an up-to-date dairy plant—and so on. If you don't, you'll be doing India and yourself a disservice."

"We are engineers," the other told me, "and are on holiday. We are working on a hydro-electric scheme which has been largely financed by Canada. It is a moving experience for us, this international helpfulness towards our country. Tomorrow we are going to a village in Madras State where the villagers, who live largely in filth and ignorance, are being helped by a group of volunteers of different nationalities who call themselves the Peacemakers. We shall be digging with them for a few days."

"What are they digging?" I asked.

"Drains. If you like, I'll give you their address. I'm sure they would welcome you too for a few days."

It was now my turn to rise hastily. "Thank you, but I'm afraid it won't be possible for me to pay them a visit; I have a rather tight travel schedule. Good-bye."

The following morning I travelled up to the south-eastern town of Madurai. This city was once the capital of the south. Nowadays it is a modern city too, with old and new mingling together without any great clash. Many of the temples are in the heart of the town while others on the outskirts can be seen for miles before the traveller reaches the city. They are great stone structures with soaring gopurams, elaborately carved.

When one first catches sight of some far-off temple, all that one sees is the gopuram. It symbolises the unconditioned Absolute from which all manifested life springs, the unity which contains the diversity. As one draws closer, one notices that the gopuram is elaborately carved with the figures of gods and goddesses, men and women, birds and animals. These myriad carvings symbolise created life in all its wonderful diversity as it plays, makes love, dances, and so on.

The great Temple of Madurai is the most famous of all southern temples and one is advised to see it at night as well as during the day. It has nine gopurams, some soaring to a hundred and fifty feet. It is, in fact, a twin temple, the southern portion being dedicated to Meenakshi, a fish-eyed goddess, and the northern portion to Shiva the Destroyer.

Brahma the Creator, Vishnu the Preserver and Shiva the Destroyer; all manifested forms of life have to undergo the three processes of birth, preservation and eventual destruction and each process has a literal or exoteric meaning as well as an esoteric one. Shiva destroys all forms, whether human beings, insects, or worlds—everything in due time. In the deeper or esoteric sense, he destroys in his devotees Maya, illusion.

I arranged to spend the night in the Ladies' Retiring Room at the station, which one is allowed to do provided one's ticket shows one still has further to travel by rail. One can break one's journey en route and stay in the rest room a couple of days if one likes, getting what meals one wants from the station restaurant—provided there is one. But one can usually rely on getting a cup of early morning tea at the smaller stations. I booked in my baggage, then took a tonga to the Great Temple which lies in the heart of the town.

It can only be entered by a single gateway in the Meenakshi portion. I walked with a guide through courtyards and along corridors, some roofed over, others open to the sky. They lead to a central shrine which only Hindus are allowed to enter. In some of the courtyards vendors were selling souvenirs and noxious looking drinks. We came to a courtyard where the temple elephants are kept. During festivals they lead the processions. The huge beasts were standing there placidly, their ears occasionally flapping, one foot tethered by an iron ring and chain.

I soon lost count of the number of corridors we walked down and the pillared courtyards we had gone through. We came to the Tank of the Golden Lilies. On the water were big gold lilies, and the walls which enclosed the tank were covered with paintings of the more famous Indian temples.

From the Meenakshi section we went through into the Shiva portion. Along with other visitors, I paid an extra fee to have a look at some of the temple jewels. They were fabulous. Most of the well-known temples have a vast hoard of treasure which has been donated through the ages by rich and poor, rajahs and ranees, visiting potentates and others. It is staggering to think what the combined wealth of these temples would amount to.

Next we went to see the most renowned part of the temple, the Hall of the Thousand Pillars. Each pillar in this hall is magnificently carved and one could spend days just looking at these columns alone. The hall was built in 1560 by a statesman. The guide told me that there are actually only nine hundred and ninety-seven columns, each one of which is uniquely carved.

Outside the hall is an unfinished choultry, or gallery, called Tirumala's Choultry. Even though uncompleted, it is still one of the finest galleries in the temple, with its four rows of pillars stretching down its three-hundred-and-thirty-foot length. There are statues of monarchs and one statue of Tirumala and the ceiling is carved with the signs of the zodiac.

I went and had a meal in a Hindu restaurant and in the evening I returned to the temple.

The atmosphere now was quite eerie. The guide, the same one who had shown me round previously, was waiting for me, lamp in hand. We walked down dark corridors and through silent courtyards. One corridor was lit its length by lamps hanging from the walls, but most were in darkness. In one courtyard, open to the night sky, a group of priests were chanting extracts from the Vedas, and in a nearby small shrine a priest was breaking coconuts in front of a carved god lit by a flaring lamp. The priest turned and dabbed some sandalwood paste on my forehead. We walked on, barefooted, and came to the Tank of the Golden Lilies. The water was black, and reflected in it was the scimitar of a new moon.

It was three o'clock in the morning when I finally left the temple. I got a couple of hours' sleep in the retiring room before being waked by an attendant to catch an early train to Trichinopoly, or Tiruchirapalli, the City of the Three-headed Demon, famous for its Rock.

This rock is of no great height—two hundred and thirty-six feet—but because of the flatness of the surrounding countryside it looks taller and one gets a very fine view when one has climbed to the top.

I did not attempt the climb on the same afternoon that I arrived at Trichy but set off at five the following morning.

One starts on the climb by going through a passage on which are carvings of elephants. Steps lead upwards at a steep incline. *Only* two hundred and thirty-six feet... I soon began to feel that climbing Mount Everest would be less demanding. About halfway up was a small temple and from here the steps began to gradually emerge out into the open. It was a relief to breathe fresh air again after leaving the humid passageway. The guide told me that on these steps in 1849 over five hundred people were killed. Some of them slipped and fell as they were going up and were trampled underfoot by those following behind. This started a general panic which ended in the worst calamity the town has ever known.

On top of the Rock is another temple. I did not go in. I stood on the rock summit watching the rising sun light up the town below and the surrounding palmgroves and nearby villages. The atmosphere was so clear in the early dawn that distant figures of men and animals could be seen distinctly.

Next day I continued my journey by rail to Chingleput, which is the nearest town to Thirukkalukundram. There is little of interest to see in it. It is a sprawling, rather ugly town with two large Christian Mission Schools.

Thirukkalukundram lies nine miles from Chingleput and a few miles from the coast.

When I caught a bus outside the station the following morning, the sky was overcast and heavy drops of rain were falling. It was still early when I arrived at the village, so I went and looked round the Shiva Temple which lies at the foot of the hill. I was followed by a hoard of rapacious priests all demanding money.

The village, which is completely Hindu, is comprised of small white-washed houses, one story high, most of which are situated orund a large tank. This tank is a short distance from the temple. Once every twelve years, so I was informed by a priest, a conch shell rises to the surface of the waters, watched by thousands of pilgrims. These shells are kept in the nearby temple of Bhakthavatsalaswami.

The Hill of the Sacred Eagles is five hundred feet high. There is a flight of steps at the entranceway leading to the top, and another flight leading down to the exit. At the entrance I was charged an admission fee, plus a further sum because I was taking a camera in.

A group of peasants from Bihar, the women dressed in brilliant red saris, walked up the steps ahead of me. Two men were supporting a woman who looked as if she were dying from some debilitating disease. Only a film of waxlike skin covered her bones. One of the men helping her up the steps told me that she had been seriously ill for over eight years, but they hoped that after she had seen the eagles and received their darshan she would be cured. I hoped so too, although I thought that recovery in her case seemed highly unlikely even with the birds' assistance.

At the top of the hill I was shown through some rock shrines by two priests who were as money-minded as those below. The shrines were carved out of solid rock.

When we came out, a priest pointed to the huge rounded rock on which the birds alight. Near it was a stone choultry and here people were sheltering from the rain, which was falling quite heavily. Others, in spite of the downpour, had taken up positions of vantage as close to the base of the rock as an attendant allowed them to go. No one except the Brahmin priests are allowed on top of the rock.

I looked at my watch. The time was close to mid-day. The downpour had stopped suddenly and a fine drizzle of rain was falling. I took my place among those gathered near the base of the rock. A Hindu standing next to me with his three young children told me that he had travelled here all the way from Lucknow.

"This is my second visit," he said. "I first came here with my father when I was a small boy. Now I have brought my own children."

Two priests walked across the top of the rock above us. One was holding a black umbrella over his head, the other was carrying several small metal vessels which presumably contained the birds' food. They talked together for a while, then one left and the other sat down, his back towards us, and arranged the jars by his side. I glanced at my watch; the time was exactly noon.

A ripple of excitement ran through the crowd. The priest picked up one of the metal pots and banged it down hard several times as though summoning the eagles. As he did so, he glanced over to his left where there was a wide mist-filled valley and, beyond it, a ridge of high hills dotted with rocks and bushes. The drizzle had stopped and a few streaks of watery sunlight lit up the countryside of bare red earth, thorn trees, palms and red hillocks. I looked in the same direction as the priest but there was no sign of a white wing emerging from the mist. The priest got up and walked to the edge of the rock and gazed across the valley; then he came back and thumped the pot again. But no birds answered his summons. He left, walking away in the direction of the shrines. The crowd settled down to wait.

Twelve-thirty... The birds were proving to be not so punctual as some people would have them. Nevertheless, I was prepared to forgive Busha and Vidatha for being a little tardy.

We waited and waited. The priest reappeared, sat down and once more thumped on the rock, still with no result. It was now one o'clock.

"These holy kites are said to emit a very wonderful darshan," said the Hindu.

"So I have heard."

Darshan is a potent force which emanates from spiritual beings, and people in their vicinity benefit from it. Sometimes the sick are cured and people's spiritual potential is given a boost, so to speak.

The priest started to collect the vessels together. He picked them up and, leaning over the rock, said something to the attendant down below. The attendant spoke to the crowd in Hindi and a sigh of deep disappointment rose from those nearest to him and swept, wavelike, through the concourse of people. The Hindu translated the attendant's words for my benefit: "The eagles aren't coming today..."

"Not coming!" I cried. "But I don't understand—they are supposed to have been coming here daily for thousands of years and—"

"Yes, yes, I know. I too feel very upset, more on your behalf than on my own. I realise how disappointed you must be."

"But why aren't they coming?"

"Well, it's rather wet, perhaps..."

"Wet!" I could have exploded. "These birds are supposed to fly all the way from Varanasi. Do you mean to say that a pair of eagles who can make such a flight have been put off coming here today merely because of a few raindrops?"

"Please! I'm sorry, but I really don't know the actual reason; I was just guessing. Yet it's very strange that they aren't coming," he added. "They are said not to have missed a single visit to this hill since the beginning of time."

"Except for today," I muttered.

I was beginning to take the birds' non-arrival almost as a personal insult. After all, they had not missed a single visit to the hill since the beginning of time, yet the very day I came to pay them my respects it seemed they were not going to turn up.

A few people started to walk down the steps leading to the exit, but most of the crowd continued to wait hopefully in spite of what the priest had said.

"Perhaps I'd better go," I said. "There doesn't seem to be much point in staying here any longer."

The Hindu picked up one of his children. "Yes, I think we'll go too."

Just at that moment someone in the crowd gave a shout. Hands pointed to the hills across the valley. The shout was taken up by several others. Flying high above the ridge of hills, sometimes disappearing into a cloud and then re-emerging, were two white eagles. Then they were gone again, swallowed up in the cloud. The priest hurried out and set the vessels on the ground.

A great white bird skimmed effortlessly across the valley on extended wings and disappeared round the side of the hill. Suddenly there was the beating of powerful wings and an eagle alighted on the rock, its talons scraping along the surface. It folded its wings and walked confidently towards the priest, who was holding out some food in his hand. The bird's pure white plumage was touched by bands of black on wings and tail. It ate fearlessly from the Brahmin's hand and then put its head into one of the vessels and rapidly devoured the contents.

A second bird swooped down. It was slightly smaller than the first. This was Vidatha, the female of the pair. Before walking over to the priest she carefully tidied a few breast feathers, glanced at the crowd, as though to make certain that we were watching her, and then stepped over towards her mate for a share of the offerings.

Both eagles, I am happy to report, looked remarkably fit and lively and good for another thousand years or so.

They took less than a minute to gulp down the food, then their great wings spread out and they were off, flying swiftly upwards and circling high above the hill against a blue sky. The priest threw the remains of the food down to the crowd and people rushed forward to gather it up. Those lucky enough to get a small portion would carefully preserve it as a keepsake and as something which possessed magical properties, like Ganges water.

When I looked up at the sky again, the eagles had gone. The priest walked away and the crowd began to file down the steps.

There was a bus waiting but I decided to catch a later one. I had brought some lunch with me and I sat near the tank eating it. Several pilgrims were taking a dip in the stagnant looking water. As I sat there, munching a chapatti, I thought about the two white birds which had flown across the valley to take food from the hand of a human being and had then flown off again.

A woman came by. She wore an unbleached off-white sari and her black hair hung loose, denoting that she had freed herself from worldly ties and that she was a yogini (a female yogi). I smiled at her and she came over to where I was sitting and asked me whether I had seen the eagles that morning. I told her that I had.

"I live with my guru over on that high hill which lies opposite the shrine," she told me.

"The eagles flew to the rock from that direction," I said.

"They usually fly over the hilltop on their way there. Would you like to ask me anything about them? Since I took up the wandering life as a girl I've lived mostly in this area. Once a year I go on a pilgrimage to Kanya Kumari."

"I visited Kanya Kumari just a few days ago," I told her. Then I thought for some moments. "Yes, there is a question I'd like to ask you. The eagles are supposed to have been visiting the hill since time immemorial and they are supposed to be able to cure people of various diseases and so on. Whether or not these wonderful stories about them are true or just a beautiful legend, what I would like to ask you is, is there some deeper meaning lying behind all these miraculous tales?"

She smiled and said, "I can certainly understand any doubts you may have concerning all these marvellous stories about the birds. But let me try and answer your question. First of all, forget for a while all these wonderful stories and I'll tell you something else about the eagles that I don't suppose you've heard of. You are perfectly free to reject what I tell you later, but for the time being listen with an open mind to what I say and then you may discover something.

"I was born in Bengal but for many years now I have lived in this southern area, and living here as I do for most of the year I have come to learn several things about the birds which are not generally known and would not interest the majority of pilgrims who visit the hill even if they were; they prefer the more astonishing tales. Both the eagles are vegetarians."

"Yes, I heard the priests feed them only sattvic food."

"But after they fly off and are on their own, they don't hunt for flesh foods, although they would be perfectly free to do so if they wished. Now I'm going to ask you a question. Is it natural for eagles to be vegetarians?"

"No," I answered. "Eagles are birds of prey."

"Exactly. And birds of prey take the lives of other creatures and devour their flesh. To them it is the natural thing to do."

"Yes, it is," I agreed.

"White eagles are rare in India; nevertheless, there are a few about and they are no different in their characteristics to other eagles. All eagles are freedom-loving birds, high-flying and solitary in their habits—they don't go around in flocks—and they are all birds of prey."

"Yes," I said again.

"Busha and Vidatha are two white eagles and they have their species' love of freedom and so on. Yet in one respect they *are* different from other eagles; they have lost the deeply embedded instinct to hunt and kill other creatures and eat their flesh. It's not in their natures to do so. Don't laugh at me if I put it to you like this: They don't say to one another, 'I must not kill. I must not pounce upon that mouse. I must try and subdue this lust for killing which lies so deep in my nature.' There is nothing like that with them. They don't have to make an effort to subdue this trait because it's gone, left them completely, and they are free of it, unlike others of their kind.

"At some time during the past a deep transformation must have taken place in them which makes them different to other birds of prey. Yet, don't forget, they are still eagles."

I nodded.

"Now, the difference between a rishi and other humans is somewhat similar to the difference between the eagles you saw this morning and others of their kind. The rishis are still men, but men of a quality totally different from the average human because they too have undergone a transformation. I hope I've answered your question clearly."

And with that she turned and left me.

I watched her walk along the side of the tank, her hair flowing down her back, a woman as free and fearless, I felt, as those two remarkable eagles, Busha and Vidatha.

CHAPTER SEVENTEEN

PILGRIM SPECIAL

I DID SOME hard thinking in the teeming city of Calcutta. I had gone up there to arrange a trip through India to some of the places I had long wanted to see. So far as the Himalayas were concerned, a 'must', I would have to wait till later to travel there, as the passes had closed. They close in the autumn and open again about May.

The trip over, I hoped to set off on another venture of more concern to me, a trip to some remote region where I could stay for a while and embark on the long inner journey. I longed for another period, somewhat similar to the time I had spent on the mountain in Lantao, where the days were empty of events and the world's gossip, where the countryside was wild and underpopulated and where I had for occasional company a person or persons who, my perception assured me, had attained a degree of inner enlightenment.

In the Colony I had been searching for a certain man whom I had eventually found living in Lantao. But here in India I knew of no one to whom I could turn for guidance as I had turned to Fo, who, often without saying anything, threw light on my own path. I knew that all inner strivings would have to come from me but I also knew what a tremendous help the presence of such a person can be to one. And somewhere along the way since I had sailed to Hong Kong and spent a year in the Colony I had become ever more aware that the only real and worthwhile journeys are the inner ones.

There were people in India whom I could have asked to give me the names of certain yogis known to them and who would have been willing to suggest places I might go to for a period of solitude, but I did not really want to ask them for such information. I felt it would be much better if I did my own discovering.

When I was living in Britain I spent several years with the gipsies and came to learn something of their ways and customs. When the gipsies travel they look for signs along the lanes and roadways which others of their kind have placed there. These signs, which are made of such things as bent grasses, stones placed one on top of another, twigs set at various angles and so on, tell the gipsies all manner of things of the greatest use and interest to them. These roadway signs are called patrin.

Now that I was in the ancient land of Bharat, where the gipsies are believed to have originally come from and where thousands still travel in their bullock carts, I felt that I must be on the lookout during my forthcoming trip for signs, both visible and invisible, along the way which might give me clues as to where I should go in search of solitude and of someone who was well advanced on the path. I could only hope that I would find such clues, for I had no idea as to where I should best search for such a place and such a person. I did feel strongly drawn towards the magnetic north, the mighty Himalayas, but that may have been for several reasons, none of which was sufficiently valid for me to take it as the finger of providence directing me implacably northwards to the great mountain range.

I bought a Pilgrim Special ticket which allowed me three months of travel on the railways at a very modest cost. According to the terms laid down for the granting of this ticket, I had to be in Benares, my final stop, on the date stipulated; otherwise I was free to stay an extra day or so at any of the places marked down on my itinerary or to skip others if I felt like it.

Because of the cheapness of these pilgrim tickets, it means that thousands of poor peasants and others are able to set off each year to visit different shrines and sacred cities all over India. The duration of these trips are usually between two and four months and the pilgrim travels north, south, east and west and through central India, so that by the time he returns to his village he could be said to be a well-travelled man, at least as far as his own country is concerned.

Calcutta, the capital of Bengal and the one-time capital of British India, is situated at the mouth of the Hooghly.

I knew no one in the city. I enjoyed walking alone among the surging crowds.

The city was hard hit by the bloody riots which took place at Partition. Streams of refugees poured into the state capital. Prior to Independence, some three-and-a-half million people had lived here; five years after Independence the number had risen to five million. Many of these refugees were still living and sleeping in the city's streets.

There is a saying in India that everything starts in Calcutta, and a lot does. This city experienced the worst riots in the whole of India during Partition time, and it is still here that riots are most likely to break out during times of duress in the country. Calcutta is still one of the world's plague centres and each year the first seasonal outbreaks of the dreaded cholera start here.

In spite of being one of the country's great ports and situated by the sea and on the banks of a river, the water shortage is so acute and what water there is, so unpleasant, that there is serious talk in official circles that in the not-so-distant future the city may have to be abandoned.

That is the dark reverse side of the coin, but there is a bright side too. From Calcutta in particular and Bengal in general have sprung many new art movements and there is a general feeling of intellectual liveliness about the place. Many of the country's famous poets, authors and artists have been born in the state capital or in Bengal, Tagore being the most famous poet of modern times. Going back further, the English author William Makepeace Thackeray, who wrote *Vanity Fair*, was born in the city on the 18th July, 1811, at 39 Free School Street. He and my great-grandfather had been friends.

I had thought that I might visit the house in which Thackeray had been born, but an Indian artist whom I had met in a cafe advised me not to go there. He said that the street in which the house was situated had become a slum and there were large dumps of refuse on the pavements in which rats and stray dogs foraged. So I did not go.

The city streets were always full of interest for me. One evening I came upon a family who were obviously peasants come to town. They had taken over a few feet of pavement. The woman was cooking a meal on a fire made from a pat of cow dung and a few twigs. A baby was asleep on top of a laden basket. The husband was polishing a copper bowl. Several hens they had with them were pecking for morsels of food. The man put a hand into a sack and threw them a handful of grain which they ate greedily. These hens were not tethered in any way, yet they did not move more than a yard or two from their human family.

Further down the same street I came upon a coin merchant who had his wares spread out on the paving.

Sensing at once that here was a likely customer, he said, "I have coins from all over the world but most of them are from Tibet and India. Some are modern coins and some are very old ones."

He picked up one which was about the size of a farthing and told me that it came from a site in northern India. The design, still clearly visible, showed Alexander the Great on a horse. Another coin he picked up was made of baked clay and dated back to the time of the Emperor Ashoka. It had a design of a fish.

"Where do you get them from?" I asked.

"From Tibetan merchants and refugees and from sites all over India. Villagers dig in the ruins of some ancient town, find the coins which they sell to one of my agents." He gave a wicked grin. "Some villagers are employed as diggers on excavation sites like the semi-ruined city of Mandhu and they manage to smuggle a few coins out."

His prices seemed reasonable and I bought several coins, including the one of Alexander and the clay one. I also bought three Tibetan coins, one silver and two copper ones. They had attractive designs of a lion standing against a background of cloud-topped mountains. Finally I selected two big silver rupees with the heads of George the Fifth and Sixth respectively and the words King Emperor inscribed round the edges. India has a new set of coins now and one rarely sees the old silver rupee any more. Having made my choice, the merchant tossed in a further coin as a free gift, explaining to me that it was of baked clay, very ancient, and had been found in some ruins in the Gangetic Valley not far from Benares.

Some evenings later I had a far from pleasant encounter. I had turned down a side street off the main Lower Circular Road when I saw coming towards me a group of men who from a distance I took to be ascetics. They were dressed in loose cotton garments. One had a piece of cloth over his face and was being led by a companion. As they drew nearer I saw that their faces and limbs were horribly distorted. Then I realised that they were a band of lepers.

I turned and started to walk back along the dimly lit street but the lepers had spotted me and realised that I was a foreigner, perhaps rich. I was wearing a cotton dress and was carrying over a shoulder a woven Indian bag which contained my passport, travellers cheques and loose money. I had hardly taken more than a few steps back in the direction of the main road before the lepers had caught up and surrounded me. One of them seized the loop of the bag with stunted fingers and as he did so his hand brushed the cloth which covered the head of another and before it fell back I had a glimpse of what had once been a face. I shuddered. Another leper whose nose had gone and whose face was a mass of nodules stood in front of me barring my way. There must have been about twenty of them ringing me round. Then one gave me a jab in the ribs with a staff he was carrying and as I fell sideways the one who held my bag wrenched it from me.

As I regained my balance I chanced to glance behind me and I saw the turbanned heads of two policemen coming down the street. I yelled, "Police, help, help!"

The lepers must have seen them too, for they started to run. One of the policemen came up to me, the other went after the lepers.

"What happened?"

I explained to him briefly what had occurred.

"You are very foolish to go walking down a badly lit street like this by yourself," he said.

I suppose I had been.

The other policeman came up and to my great relief he was carrying my bag and, miraculously, my passport and money were still inside.

"They threw it away when they saw me coming after them," he said.

I thanked them both. When I reached the main road I took a taxi back to my hotel.

I was ready to start off on my tour. My first stop was close to Calcutta: Sagar Island at the mouth of the Hooghly. It is a large flat island and among its permanent residents are a wide variety of ascetics and quite a few tigers. A tributary of the Ganges, India's most sacred river, sweeps around Sagar's coast, after having flowed all the way from the Himalayas and across the plains to unite here finally with the ocean. The island is visited every year by countless pilgrims and sannyasis. I stayed on the island two days, then returned to Calcutta and caught a train south to the port of Cuttack, and from there started to travel inland across the sub-continent, stopping off at various places of interest along the way.

I eventually arrived at the town of Dwarka in the far west. It is bounded to the north by the Gulf of Cutch and faces the Arabian Sea. This town is one of the Great Sacred Places of Pilgrimage. The others are Ujjain, Conjeeveram, Ajudhia, Muttra, Hardwar and Benares.

The town was founded by Lord Krishna and the Temple Dwarkanath is dedicated to him. It is one of the holiest in India and the only one, incidentally, that I was not allowed to enter. It is strictly for Hindus only.

This peninsula of land is fascinating and it is connected with Lord Krishna, one of the great Indian Teachers.

There is a legend about Krishna which concerns his slaying of the poisonous black serpent Kaliya. He leaps into the whirlpool in which the monster lives and after a struggle kills it and dances upon its hood. This is the dance of victory after the slaying of man's baser nature within himself, a victory which is achieved by all saints and saviours.

When the early Greek sages travelled to India in search of deeper wisdom, they returned to their country with this legend of Krishna slaying the serpent, which, in the metaphorical sense, is man's baser self, and this slaying of the serpent gradually evolved into St. George slaying the dragon of the early Greek or Eastern Orthodox Church, the oldest and most Christian of all the Christian Churches. This glyph was later passed on by Greece to the sacred island, the Isle of Albion, or Great Britain. And the inner meaning of this patron saint of England killing the dragon is precisely the same as that of Lord Krishna slaying the serpent.

From Dwarka I travelled down to Somnath, still in the same peninsular Here a new temple was being built on the foundations of an old one, and all the carvings were being done, not by hired sculptors, but by the local villagers. In the temple grounds overlooking the ocean, is a newly erected square pillar surmounted by a globe pierced by an arrow. The arrow points in the direction of the South Pole and from here to the Pole there is not a single patch of land.

A mile from the magnificent modern temple is Dehotsarja, at the confluence of three rivers, and it is here that Lord Krishna is said to have passed away. I was told that a statue of him will soon be erected on the banks of the River Hiranya.

Next I went through the Gir Forest Reserve, which comprises some five hundred miles of arid forest land in which roam India's only lions as well as sambur, boars and spotted deer.

I did not see any lions in the reserve but I did see a pair some days later in the zoo at Junagadh. They were the most miserable-looking specimens of the 'Lord of the Jungle' that I had ever set eyes on, listless, emaciated, with every rib plainly visible. I went to the zoo accompanied by a young man called Ranjan, the son of a cloth merchant whom I had met when I was buying a cotton quilt at his father's store. He had taken me under his wing and he went out of his way to show me the sights of the city and surrounding area.

I commented to him on the sorry state of the pair and he told me that most of the keepers at the zoo were Moslems because they did not object to handling meat and giving it to the carnivorous animals. They were meat eaters themselves, and so often kept a portion of the animals' rations for themselves and their relatives.

"The lions' share, I'm afraid," he said, laughing. "Hence the beasts' poor condition."

On our way back to the rest house where I was staying we passed three Negroes.

"There is a community of Negroes in the province," said Ranjan. "They are the only ones in India and were brought in as slaves by a maharaja. When the British ended slavery in the Empire, they were freed. Those ones you saw are descendants of the original slaves. We've never intermarried with them, of course."

The Asian is as reluctant as the European to have Negro blood in his family.

I had come to Junagadh for the purpose of climbing Girnar Mountain, and Ranjan, when he learnt of my intention, kindly said he would come along with me. He had climbed the mountain several times before.

Girnar is visited yearly by thousands of pilgrims. It is dedicated to Bhavanath, one of the names of Shiva, king of the yogis. Girnar is one in a group of mountains and, like the others, it is surrounded by jungle-clad hills in which tigers and leopards roam. It lies four miles from Junagadh.

We set off in a crowded bus very early in the morning. The bus roared through the town and through a huge gateway, the Wagheswari Gate, then sped along a road which followed the bank of a river lined with temples.

The bus pulled up at a spot where there was an Ashoka Pillar and we got out to have a look at it. These pillars are found all over the northern half of India. They were erected in the reign of the Emperor Ashoka as from the year 262 B.C., when he was converted to Buddhism. The Emperor died in 232. Inscribed on these pillars are various edicts which show compassion and a high ethical standard. Most are written in Devangiri, the language of he Boddhisattvas and devas (celestial beings) on which Sanskrit is based.

This pillar was in an enclosure and there was an English translation of the fourteen edicts on a plaque. I copied down several of them. Here is one: While he, the King, is reigning, verily no man among his subjects falls away from religion and there is no one who is distressed or in poverty or in misery or avaricious or who, being worthy of punishment, is put to excessive torture.

We continued our journey. The bus pulled up close to an archway which had wide stone steps leading up to it and continuing on beyond. Several ash-covered ascetics were grouped about the archway, their begging bowls in front of them. A passenger from the bus, a very old man, was being carried up the mountain in a dholi, a chair slung between two poles which were supported by four men. Only the sick, pregnant women, the very old and the very young are excused making the climb on their own legs. For a fit person to be carried would mean losing all the merit that climbing the mountain is supposed to give.

Ranjan and I carried staffs to help us in the arduous climb before us, as did most of the other pilgrims. Some devotees take two days to complete the climb and stay the night at dharmasalas, pilgrim rest-houses, which are situated at intervals along the steps.

These steps, bordered by stone walls, wind the whole way up and over the mountain. Green parakeets flew by. Some pilgrims passed us, striding quickly and purposefully upwards. We passed some slower ones. Soon we were walking alone with groups ahead of us and behind us.

As we were rounding a rocky bluff, there came a peculiar hissing noise and I saw waving about in mid-air what appeared to be two long grey snakes—but snakes covered with fur! A few yards further on and the 'snakes' turned out to be the tails of two grey monkeys who were sitting in a small hole in the rockface above us, holding on to each other around the waist, their tails hanging outside the hole. They had white ruffs of hair round their faces and they hissed and bared their teeth at us as we passed.

The steps wound up more steeply. Over to my right I caught a glimpse of the mountain of Datar, with a white mosque on its summit. Further on, Ranjan pointed out the peak of Mount Kalika, which lies due west of Girnar.

"Kalika belongs to the Aghoras," he said. "They are a depraved sect of yogis." And he went on, "If you go down to the burning ghats by the rivers where Hindus are cremated on log piles you'll nearly always see one or two Aghoras sitting nearby. When the bodies have been burnt and the eldest sons and other male relatives have collected up the ashes of the deceased, then, after they've gone, the Aghoras will go up to the pyre and collect any bits of charred bodies which may have been overlooked by the relatives. These Aghoras are allied with everything connected with death and decay. Their patroness is the black goddess, Mother Kali, Goddess of Destruction, and Mount Kalika comes under her suzerainty."

We stopped and looked at the peak. The sides of the mountain were covered by dense forests and there was not a temple or any other building to be seen.

"Nobody except the Aghoras themselves ever goes on the mountain," said Ranjan. "Not even I, a Hindu, am allowed to go there. Various rumours circulate in the district about what these ghouls get up to on Kalika—perhaps orgies and human sacrifices held in honour of Mother Kali—but no one knows anything for certain. Of course, various inquisitive people have sometimes tried to climb the mountain. There used to be a strongly-held belief that out of every two people who tried to visit Kalika, only one returned."

We walked on slowly and Ranjan continued, "The Aghoras shun all society, and it's just as well for others to shun them because they are not at all pleasant people."

"When you mentioned them gathering up the charred remains at the ghats," I said, "what do they do with the bits—throw them into the river?"

"No. They usually eat them."

I must have looked incredulous, for Ranjan said, "Yes, really! The Aghoras live on these charred remains as well as on all manner of filth, including carrion, both human and animal. They are the scavengers of the human kingdom."

I shuddered. "How on earth did a sect like that ever start?"

"That's difficult to say for certain. One theory is that it may have begun through religious competition. You know what formidable fasts and penances various sects here undergo. Some yogis fast for three weeks at a stretch, and a fast here means going without water as well as food; others get by on a handful of rice a day. Some live only on fruit, while others will live only on the sort of food that most people throw on to the garbage pile—cabbage stalks, fruit and vegetable parings and that sort of thing. To beat all the rest, the Aghoras may have decided that they would live not just on discarded food but on stuff that humans won't eat at all: carrion and suchlike. You can't go any further than that."

We came to a huge rock from which in the past devotees of Bhavanath used to throw themselves, to crash to their deaths on the ground a thousand feet below.

Soon after passing this rock we came to the first group of temples. There were about eighteen of them and most were Jain temples. We entered the largest one, which is called Neminath. In it are two halls. In one of them was a shrine and an image of a Jain Tirthankar or Teacher. It was richly bedecked with gold and jewelled ornaments. Near the temple was a tank in which some pilgrims were bathing.

As we climbed higher still, we passed ascetics who were presiding at small shrines along the way. One was sitting beside a stream which fell between two rocks and he handed me a copper mug filled with icy-cold mountain water which was very refreshing.

The steps still ascended skywards, but Ranjan pointed to a narrow flight which led down into a shallow valley in which were several huts.

"We can get something to eat down there," he said.

As we descended I saw some twenty or more yogis who were cooking food on wood fires and primus stoves. They were all dressed in next to nothing. Some had great coils of hair piled on top of their heads, others had their hair flowing loose.

We were shown into a not-very-elegant hut in which were a

few pilgrims and some more yogis. The hut had a bare earth floor. An ascetic—and this one had hair hanging to his knees—brought me a piece of sacking to sit on. He said he was sorry but he could only serve us a very simple meal. I told him that it was marvellous to be able to get a meal at all up here.

While we were waiting for our meal, an ascetic came and sat beside us. I asked him whether he and the other yogis lived permanently on Girnar and he replied that most of them stayed only for the pilgrim season, which lasted about five months. They helped out with the cooking, attended the shrines, assisted the pilgrims in various ways and, when the flow of pilgrims became a mere trickle, they left the mountain. He had simply come here as part of a pilgrimage and stayed on. When he left he would be returning to his cave in the trans-Himalayan foothills. But a score or so of ascetics lived on the mountain permanently, he said. There were caves scattered about the mountainsides which the pilgrims never saw or knew of. During the height of the pilgrim season, he went on, which was due to start in a month's time, Girnar was visited daily by sometimes as many as a thousand pilgrims. Some of these did their own cooking at the various dharmasalas along the route, but most of them had to be catered for. All the cooking was done here by ascetics on log fires and small paraffin cookers and all the supplies were brought up on the backs of porters. I said it was incredible how they managed to cope with such large numbers of people.

I was even more impressed when our meal arrived. It was far from being a snack and consisted of rice, chapatties, a vegetable curry with chutney, sapotas—a sweetish brown fruit which look rather like small potatoes—and to round off the meal we drank mugs of milkless tea.

At one end of the hut was a shelf of books. I asked if I might look at them. I was interested to see what kind of reading matter they had.

Some of the books were printed in Sanskrit but several were in English. There was a copy of the Bhagavad Gita and Sir Edwin Arnold's *Light of Asia*, and Madam Blavatsky's *Voice of the Silence*. A sannyasi took down a small volume. It was Shankaracharya's

Viveka Chudamani or *The Crest Jewel of Wisdom*. Then, to my surprise, he showed me a book of Shelley's verse.

As I turned the mildewed pages he said, "Shelley was a very advanced being."

"I always suspected as much," I said.

Then he quoted the well-known verse which goes: 'The One remains, the many change and pass; Heaven's light for ever shines, earth's shadows fly; Life, like a dome of many-coloured glass, Stains the white radiance of eternity...'

It was strange, listening to Shelley's lines delivered by a near-naked ascetic in this remote corner of India.

The yogi with the knee-length hair said he would accompany us to the top of the next peak. As we were walking away from the hut, an ascetic ran after us and handed me a small book.

"A present for you," he said. "It's some Karai Siddhar Verses—verses written by the rishis."

"Thank you very much."

I asked the yogi accompanying us whether he had become an ascetic when he was a boy. Judging from the length of his hair, I felt that this must be so.

"Yes," he replied, "I was only ten when I left my home in the Tinnevelly District to seek my guru. I found him four years later in a remote forest glade high up in the Nallamalai Range."

We stopped and looked down at the white temple roofs lying below us.

When we had reached the highest peak of Girnar, the yogi climbed over the wall and followed a narrow path down the mountainside. He had told us that he was going to a cave where he meditated.

We were the only pilgrims on the peak just then. The mountain-top was bathed in brilliant sunlight, but about halfway down there was a heavy mist which blotted out the base and the surrounding hills. The atmosphere of serenity which I had felt almost from the moment I set foot on Girnar seemed to be intensified here on this peak. It is not surprising that there is this atmosphere of abiding peace on the mountain, because for aeons great yogis and rishis have meditated here, clearing the atmosphere of dross, so to speak, and instilling one of serenity. And even the most materialistic pilgrim who climbs the mountain usually endeavours to clear his mind of worldly concerns while he is on it.

We still had another peak to ascend, another three or four more hours of climbing.

By mid-afternoon the patches of mist had cleared and we could see the wooded hills and the roadway lying far below us.

Down, down, past temples and high rockfaces with cascading streams falling over the ledges.

As we neared the rock where we had seen the two grey monkeys we came upon a crowd of brown monkeys. They approached us from all directions, clambering over rocks, swinging from the branches of trees, springing along the wall.

"Hurry!" said Ranjan. "These monkeys sometimes attack pilgrims. They can be very fierce."

The monkeys, as though by a preconceived plan, encircled us and brought us to a halt. One sprang down from a rock on to Ranjan's shoulder and he let out a yell. I suddenly felt my ankles gripped and then a long furry arm shot up and grabbed my shoulder bag. As in Calcutta, I had put various documents as well as money in this bag and once again I was in danger of having it snatched from me—this time by a monkey! No doubt he thought that it might contain food.

I clung on to it but by now monkeys all around me were tugging at the hem of my salwar-kameez and trying to drag my bag from me while others had me firmly gripped by the ankles.

Ranjan had managed to free himself from his aggressor and shouted to me to let go my bag and run; he had no idea that my passport and all my monetary funds were in the bag. I simply could not afford to lose it. But a huge pugnacious beast with a torn ear and scarred face—a simian prize-fighter—wrenched the bag from me and sprang with it on to the wall. I flung myself on top of it just as he was disappearing over the edge and managed to hang on to it for a few seconds. Just as I was losing my grip and felt it sliding away, help came. The brown monster let out a screech of pain as a heavy staff thumped down on his rump and he promptly let go the bag. There were more thumps and screams around me and the monkeys started to rush for safety.

A group of pilgrims, all carrying staffs, had caught up with us and were giving the wretches what for. The monkeys attack on Ranjan had been so swift that he had been unable to use his staff to ward them off.

They screeched and yelled at us as we hurried down the steps and one flung a sizeable stone which missed us by a few inches.

As we rounded a bend and the monkeys' shrieks grew faint behind us, I had to laugh. What a ridiculous situation to have been caught in, gripped round the ankles by monkeys and in danger of losing my bag!

"Ah, yes," said one of the pilgrims who had come to our aid, "but those brown monkeys can be dangerous. They often try and rob pilgrims of any baskets or bags they may be carrying and sometimes they are successful. They bite, and these bites can be very painful and often fester."

The ash-covered sannyasis were still sitting silently by their begging bowls. They made no gesture of thanks or acknowledgement as Ranjan dropped in some coins.

A bus was waiting and when it was full we drove off in the evening dusk and I looked for the last time at the jungle-clad slopes of Girnar and the winding steps leading upwards.

CHAPTER EIGHTEEN

CITY OF TEMPLES

AT PALITANA, MY next stop, I had a friend, a Mr. Sheth Harichand. He had made arrangements for me to stay at a Jain nunnery for a few days.

Palitana is a predominantly Jain city and monks in white loincloths and nuns in long white cotton robes can be met down any street. The place is full of maths, monasteries. White is the colour connected with the Jains; their temples, statues and maths are usually white and they wear white, that is, those who wear anything. There is one sect called the Digambaras or the sky-clad who wear nothing except masks over their mouths. These masks are to prevent any insects entering and thus making the monks guilty of taking life. The other sect wear white loincloths and are called the Swetambaras, which means the white-robed.

The room in the dharmasala in which I stayed was of white marble and contained no furniture. I simply made my bed up on the floor, which was spotlessly clean, and laid my belongings alongside a wall. The room was open-fronted and had a veranda which overlooked a courtyard. Opposite were the nuns' quarters. The math was entered through massive teak gates which were closed and bolted at night.

Mr. Harichand took me across the courtyard to meet the abbess. We seemed to be stepping through a fiery furnace and were followed by swarms of bloodthirsty insects.

"The temperature is a hundred and fourteen today," said my friend, mopping his brow.

The head nun was a relatively young woman and spoke in a quietly beautiful voice. The math was not theirs, she told me. It was owned by Jain laymen who saw to all their financial affairs.

Each nun possessed two cotton robes and a staff. They slept together in one communal room at night.

I had noticed that the nuns, like the monks I had seen, were shaven-headed.

"No, our heads aren't shaved," she said. "Twice a year we pull the hair out with our fingers. The reason for this rule is to make us indifferent to our bodies."

"What is your ultimate aim?" I asked her.

"Moksha," she answered; "liberation from the material world and the round of rebirths and death; that is, union with the Absolute."

She asked if I would like to meet a young nun who was undergoing her first lengthy fast.

We went into an adjoining room where a white-robed girl was sitting on a low plinth. Her hands were lightly clasped on her lap and part of her robe was draped over her head. Before her sat an old woman, not a nun, who had her gnarled hands pressed together in an attitude of prayer.

The abbess told me that the nun was undergoing a six-weeks' fast and had completed four weeks of it. During this time the girl had not eaten or drunk anything. In the evening she moistened her lips with a little water.

I looked at the girl. She might well have been a bag of bones by this time but this was far from being the case. She had a rather plump face and was perfectly calm and assured. The only thing at all unusual I noticed about her face was a slight puffiness of the lips, perhaps due to lack of water.

The prioress said I could ask the girl a few questions if I wished. So I asked her whether she could give up the fast if she felt unable to complete it.

In a low, clear voice, she said that she could give it up any day but that she intended to complete the full six weeks.

"Are you feeling alright?"

"I'm feeling a little tired and thirsty," she replied.

"And hungry?"

"No. All feelings of hunger left me after the first five days."

When we had left the room I asked the abbess what was

achieved by such rigorous fasting and she replied that fasts had two main aims. One was to make the person undergoing the fast indifferent to his or her body, as with the hair extraction. The other was to achieve a state of purification, physical, emotional and mental.

"That girl is taking nothing from the world," she said, "and she is able to concentrate her whole being on spiritual things."

Mr. Harichand and I left the compound. He was taking me to visit some monks of the Swetambara order. The Digambaras do not allow women to visit them.

I felt dizzy with the heat and, although I had drunk a tumbler of water only a short while back, I was already thirsty.

"How *does* she do it?" I asked him.

"The young nun? She accomplishes her fast by self-discipline and the help she has received in spiritual training since she joined the math. It's wonderful how the body acquiesces when told firmly by the mind that it will undergo a strenuous fast. What's more, it won't become sick; just a little tired, perhaps, towards the end."

The monks Mr. Harichand introduced me to were no stony-faced ascetics. They laughed and talked with me freely and answered any questions I asked them with perfect frankness. I was careful to keep a certain distance from them, as one of their rules is never to touch or be touched by a woman.

Many of these men had memorable faces. It seemed that through relinquishing those things which most people hold to be life's greatest blessings they had gained something that was even more precious: an inner vision and a calm that no worldly storms or disasters could ruffle.

On our way back to the nunnery we went into a shop in which were sold prints of gods and goddesses and contemporary yogis and Jain saddhus. Mr. Harichand rolled off a name to the proprietor who was evidently familiar with it, for he went straight to a shelf and brought down a calendar which pictured a seated Jaina.

"My guru," said Mr. Harichand. "He's dead now. For many years he lived at Delawera Temple at Mount Abu and he went for occasional retreats into the surrounding forests. I should like you to have a picture of him."

I thanked my friend for the gift.

Seated on the veranda which overlooked the courtyard, he told me that the link between him and his late guru was as strong as ever.

Picking up the calendar he said, "These wild animals you see gathered about him were not put there by the artist merely to make the picture more attractive. His Holiness had the power of being able to draw wild animals to him and he was left quite unharmed by the more dangerous kinds. He would sit alone in the jungle and no tiger would touch him.

"When I said he had this power," he continued, "I do not mean that he had consciously sought to acquire it. He never sought any occult powers and always advised his devotees against trying to acquire any. This so-called miraculous power came to him as a gift, as it were. His sole aim and his great accomplishment was the attainment of the transcendental realm."

"Do you mean he attained liberation?"

"Yes. He attained moksha and became one with universal being."

He looked at me and said, "There is a question that one really should not ask but sometimes one does ask it nevertheless. Perhaps you are wondering how it is that a man who has merged and become one with the universal principle can still keep in touch with his devotees and give them spiritual help, as I assure you His Holiness still does. To such a question he would have replied, 'Attain liberation yourself and then you will know the answer to it!' "

He got up, saying, "I'll be along at half-past six tomorrow morning for our climb of Shatrunjaya."

When he had gone, I examined the calendar more carefully. It pictured a Jaina who had a singularly serene expression. Seated in front of him was a man. A couple of rabbits gambolled on the grass, while peering out of a thicket were a leopard and a deer. Up in the branches of a tree was a peacock, its magnificent tail hanging down and almost touching the monk's shoulder. He was seated in the lotus posture. Under the picture were the words: His Holiness Yogi Acharyadev Shrimad Vijayshanti Soorishwarji Maharaj in his forest abode.

What names some of these ascetics have!

I propped the calendar up against the wall, then lay down on my bed. As the sultry hours passed, I felt coming over me one of the periodic attacks of chronic fatigue which I have suffered from ever since I was inflicted with the evil nurse Hewlett as a child. Since then I have always had to conserve my energy. If I neglect to do so, then I pay the consequences in a fit of acute tiredness which can lay me out, sometimes for several days.

I supposed that I had been overdoing things lately, but I hoped that this tiredness which I felt at the dharmasala would prove to be only a false alarm which a few hours' rest would cure. But by the time the stars were appearing in the sky, I felt worse and too overcome by fatigue to perform even the simplest task, such as combing my hair. I realised by then that it was useless to think of climbing Shatrunjaya the following day and I would have to call the trip off.

The nuns were singing kirtans —hymns— in the courtyard. Presently the Palitana town band struck up for a practice session in the courtyard next door. The din was frightful.

The old guardian who sat all day by the massive teak gates slipped into my room, placed a lamp on the floor and crouched down by my bed. He held a sheaf of pamphlets in one hand.

"For you," he said.

They were tracts on the Jain religion.

He asked whether he might read out some of the precepts, as he wanted my opinion on his English which, he feared, was getting a little rusty. I told him to go ahead.

"Golden Sentences," he began, as a trumpet blared and the band started off on the first bars of 'Over the Waves', drowning the nuns' voices. "Religion is a prime necessity for all. Master your passions and heaven is not far. Biggest room in the world? The room for self-improvement . . ."

Every so often he would ask me how he was doing.

"Very good," I would reply automatically.

I do not know when he left. I fell asleep listening to the slow drone of his voice and the strident notes of the trumpet.

In the morning I awoke feeling as acutely tired as on the previous evening. I managed to wash and dress. The old man brought me a cup of tea. I decided I had better spend the day in my room regaining lost energy and then, if I felt up to it, catch the evening train to Mount Abu, my next stop.

Mr. Harichand arrived. I explained the situation to him, saying that, disappointed as I was, I was afraid I could not possibly climb the mountain now.

"Look," he said, "Shatrunjaya is one of the wonders of the world. It's unlikely that you'll ever be coming here again and so this will be your only chance to see it. The hill is only a mile from the town. We'll take a tonga there. Men will be waiting with dholis. I'll arrange for you to be carried up."

"Oh, no!" I protested. "I simply can't go up in one of those."

I remembered the old man at Girnar being carried up and I felt that for a person of my age it would be too ignominious a way to see Shatrunjaya, much as I wanted to visit the City of Temples.

Mr. Harichand brushed aside my protest. "We are all invalids at some time or other," he said. "As you aren't feeling well, you've a perfect right to be carried. Why miss the chance of seeing this wonderful city?"

He finally persuaded me to go and we set off in a tonga.

The countryside round Palitana is very flat except where this hill rises straight out of the plain. As we approached it I could see scores of temples on the slopes and a road leading upwards towards the twin peaks of the summit, which were still veiled in an early morning mist.

"There are eight hundred and sixty-three temples altogether," said Mr. Harichand. "Some are of stone, others of white marble dust—not pure marble like the Jain temples at Mount Abu, where my guru lived for many years. A few of the temples date back to the eleventh century. But the Moslems destroyed many of the older ones and the majority date from the sixteenth century onwards. The hill itself is a little under two thousand feet."

I got into a dholi and we started off through the main gate.

At the foot of the hill was a rest-house and here, along with other pilgrims, we were given glasses of water and light refreshments.

The first building we came to after leaving the rest-house was a hall, and here, inscribed on marble stones, were the principles of Jainism. Next we came to two life-size statues of elephants. From then on it was temples, temples all the way. Some stood singly, others were in pairs, others again had been built inside massive fortified enclosures. The temples and roadway had all been kept very clean, a pleasant contrast to some Hindu temples where the floors are often littered with filth.

One temple, Jalmandir, made a particular appeal to me. It was pure white and situated in a lake. It had slim pilasters and lace-like carvings and was encircled by a wide terrace. The temple was surrounded by water and gardens.

Mr. Harichand and the porters walked at a slow steady pace. The road was lined for much of the way with shady trees.

Eventually we reached the southern peak of the hill, which was almost entirely covered by a vast battlemented enclosure with high walls and rounded turrets at the corners. We went through a gateway and inside were temples with soaring domes and carved pillars. These fortified enclosures are called tunks. Here in this City of Temples were wide streets, squares, flights of steps, shrines and trees. Some of the temples looked like palaces, others like mansions and most were covered with exquisite carvings. It was like entering another world.

We left through a different gateway and the men carrying my dholi followed a narrow road which led up above the tunk so that I could look down on it. It appeared a veritable abode of the gods. Far below wound Shatrunjaya River and further off lay Palitana and local villages.

"The Gulf of Cambay," said Mr. Harichand, pointing, "and those mountains to the north are the Sihor Range."

We started our descent.

I was more than glad now that I had made the effort, at Mr. Harichand's urging, and seen this unique hill.

I spent another night at the nunnery guest house and next day caught a train for Abu Road Station.

CHAPTER NINETEEN

A FOREST SAGE

FOR A WEEK I lay prostrated in a hotel at Mount Abu. Then my energy began to seep slowly back. I had left behind me the oppressive heat of the low-lying Saurashtra Peninsula. The weather in the hill town was sunny and bright, with the heat tempered by cool breezes.

My collapse had put me behind in my travel schedule. I could not arrive in Benares now on the date stipulated. So I decided to cancel the rest of my tour and after I left Abu I would visit some of the places marked on my itinerary, taking my own time and finishing up in Benares at a later date.

I could not have picked a more pleasant spot to spend a week recuperating than at Mount Abu, which is set among some of the prettiest scenery in India. Perched on a hill a mile away is Delawera Temple, which is, in fact, two temples. A special pass is needed to visit it.

I set off with a Parsee couple called Ahmedi from the hotel one morning in a taxi to visit Delawera, sometimes called Dilwara.

We passed Nakhi Talao Lake and the old former Residency and English-style bungalows surrounded by orchards and lawns.

Mrs. Ahmedi had already told me that she regretted the departure of the British and she sighed as we drove past the bungalows, each in its own garden, and said, "Oh, those lawns! They remind me so much of the green of the English countryside. This place isn't the same as it was in the old days. When the British left India, all the gaiety went with them. Now there are no more dances or polo matches and very few parties. Everything is drab and dreary these days and the country is corrupt from top to bottom."

She gave another sigh and went on, "Before coming up here

for a holiday from our home in Bombay, I took a prescription to a chemist's. It was for my husband, who has not been at all well—nervous dyspepsia due to worry and overwork. There was the usual notice in the window that one sees everywhere these days in some form or other: 'We are honest and uncorrupt. Our medicines are unadulterated and made up exactly to doctors' prescriptions. Bring your prescription here!' Of course, it was the usual pack of lies.

"My husband took some of their made-up stuff and felt no better. Our doctor had the contents of the bottle analysed. It was nothing more than coloured water with a bit of aniseed or something added for flavouring. Our doctor wrote a sharp letter to the manager and the chap wrote back apologising and saying he would give the assistant who had made up the prescription a telling off. What a joke! He had probably made it up himself. But what can one do about all this corruption which is rife everywhere? Nothing, absolutely nothing."

I agreed with her that the corruption was terrible. No one who has been in India for even a few days can escape it in some form or other. Then I tried to change the conversation to a more pleasant topic. But Mrs. Ahmedi had not finished with the subject.

She continued, "A person coming here from England could hardly believe that corruption is rife even in the banks and the hospitals, but it's true. When my husband was ill recently, our doctor tried hard to get him into a hospital run by one of the Christian missions—their schools and hospitals are the only ones in the country which are not corrupt. No good; every bed was taken. So my husband had to go into an Indian hospital.

"I was worried every minute he was there. If he wanted a nurse to bring him a bedpan, he had to tip her; if he wanted a servant to bring him a meal—and what terrible food!—he had to tip the servant. Even the doctors were not past accepting bribes. No tips, no service."

Mr. Ahmedi sat silent and tortoise-like, the lower portion of his face wrapped around in a long white chaddar.

"My husband is still convalescing," said Mrs. Ahmedi. "You

two invalids must take things easy and not over exert yourselves seeing the temple. You know what the guides are like—they'll take you down every passage and through every courtyard if you give them the chance. I shall be firm and say, 'That's enough'."

Delawera, which is built of pure white marble, gleamed on a hill high above the valley through which we were driving.

"The marble from which the temple was built was quarried in the district," said the driver. "Delawera is the finest example of Jain architecture in India."

Blue and green parrots flew past.

"Is that so," murmured Mr. Ahmedi, unwinding a short length of scarf.

"Don't go getting chilly, dear," said his wife. "You know how easily you catch cold."

Something yellow flashed past the taxi window and Mr. Ahmedi sprang to life.

"Stop, driver, stop! I must get out . . ."

His voice sounded so urgent that I wondered whether he wanted to make a sudden dash behind a tree. Mrs. Ahmedi had mentioned that he was suffering from a nervous stomach or something.

". . . that bird which flew past—a golden oriole. I must try and get a better look at it. So rare and so beautiful—"

"A yellow parrot, dear. You only get golden orioles up in the Himalayan area."

"Nonsense!" he snapped.

In an aside to me, his wife said, "Four years ago we visited Britain and he learnt bird-watching with an old friend of ours, an Englishman who used to be in the Indian Civil Service. Now he thinks he can recognise every bird in England and India."

Another flash of yellow.

"Two," shouted Mr. Ahmedi—"a pair! Driver, *will* you stop."

The taxi screeched to a halt and Mr. Ahmedi tumbled out and started to run back down the road.

"We'll just have to wait," said his wife resignedly.

In ten minutes he returned.

"I didn't actually see them," he said. "They had flown into thick jungle. But listen! Hear them?"

Surprisingly enough, we did: clear bell-like notes coming from the nearby jungle.

We reached the temple, produced our passes and hired a guide.

The buildings are surrounded by groves of mango trees, the dark foliage emphasising the whiteness of the marble.

The guide told us that the oldest of the two temples was built in 1031 A.D. and the later one in 1230.

We entered the newer of the two first. I marvelled at the lace-like delicacy of the carved marble and at the multitude of the statues and pillars.

The other temple was not so elaborate and was dedicated to a monk called Adinath. There was a statue of him in white marble seated in a cross-legged position. This statue was at the end of a room which was lit only by the sunlight entering through the open doorway.

Every so often we would pass groups of Jain monks or come upon one seated motionless before a shrine.

The Ahmedis got tired of sightseeing and wandered back to the taxi with the guide. I walked on by myself out into a courtyard where a group of monks were seated under a tree.

I was carrying the calendar which Mr. Harichand had given me. I wanted to ask at the temple whether any of the incumbents had known his late guru who had lived here for many years.

I went up to the seated group and handed the calendar to one of the monks. He recognised the late Jaina at once and passed the calendar to another monk, who likewise recognised him.

This monk said to me, "He was a great being who attained the ultimate reality in this life."

He asked how I had come by the painting of His Holiness. I told them about my stay in Palitana and said that the calendar had been given to me by a Jain friend whose guru had been Yogi Acharyadev.

Then they told me something about this monk who had lived at the temple and spent periods alone or with a few devotees in the jungle, and they confirmed that he had possessed this power over wild animals.

One of them said that although he knew of no Jaina in the district now who had this power, he did know of a Hindu yogi who lived in the jungle about twenty miles from Delawera and who was visited in his retreat by both humans and animals.

"You mean Yogi Rishabhdeva?" said another.

"Yes." And turning to me, he continued, "Both humans and animals are attracted to this yogi because of his remarkable compassion for all living beings and because of the high state of consciousness he has attained."

I asked whether it might be possible for me to visit this yogi and they told me that it would be if I hired a guide to take me there and was prepared to spend a night or two in the jungle. Although the distance was only about twenty miles, it would take me the best part of a day to get there. A Jaina asked me for a pencil and scribbled down on the back of the calendar the address of a man who lived on the outskirts of Mount Abu. He owned several ponies and would be prepared to take me to the jungle ascetic, the monk assured me.

"Just mention Yogi Rishabhdeva's name and this man will know who it is and the way to reach him."

I thanked the monk for giving me this information and returned to the taxi.

Sometimes in India one's various plans and projects take weeks or even months to arrange and get going. One feels that one may well be sitting around forever without any progress being made. But occasionally the plans one has in mind for some trip or for meeting some particular person move forward at a tremendous speed and one finds to one's surprise that one is setting off to one's destination almost before one had started to get the trip organised.

This happened to me in my meeting with Yogi Rishabhdeva. Two days after visiting Delawera, I set off by pony to visit him. Plans had gone forward so quickly and smoothly that I could not help feeling that this trip was in some way predestined.

The guide's name was Premchad. We set off in the early morning down Abu Road, the ponies' hoofbeats and an occasional chirp from a bird being the only sounds in the tranquil dawn. He rode one pony and led another, which was saddled with bedding, cooking pots and two wicker panniers containing food.

We rode past Delawera and further along came to more temples, which Premchad told me were called Achalgarh. The scenery here was most lovely.

Shortly after passing a large tank, Premchad started to ride down a forested track. From then on we rode along jungle paths which wound over hills and through sunlit glades. The jungle was bright with flowering trees and it was a constant thrill to me to see wild peacocks walking through the undergrowth and crossing our path, their long tails rustling over dry leaves. They appeared almost tame and did not hurry away as we approached.

In the afternoon we rode up a steep hill and came to a village inhabited by tribals. From there, it was only a few miles to a group of kutirs, where we were to spend the night. Kutirs are one-roomed dwellings which are occupied temporarily by pilgrims or permanently by persons who are leading contemplative lives.

One of the kutirs was occupied by a studious-looking gentleman called Mr. Bhandari and another by his servant and a guide.

He looked none too pleased when Premchad and I rode into the clearing in which the row of kutirs was situated. No doubt he had been enjoying the place more or less to himself.

He peered into my room as I was unpacking and pointed to the calendar and some belongings I had placed on the window-ledge.

"If you leave those things there, monkeys will put their arms through the bars and grab them. Who's that?" And he indicated the painting of His Holiness.

Once again I embarked on an account as to how I had come by the calendar. Mr. Bhandari disappeared and returned a minute later with a coloured print which he handed to me, saying, "My guru, Yogi Rishabhdeva, the yogi you've come here to meet. It's a good likeness of him."

I studied the picture. It was of a yogi seated outside a cave, a mature man, neither young nor old.

"An enlightened being," said Mr. Bhandari, who had now become very friendly. "I'll take you along tomorrow to meet him. His cave is about two miles from here."

Premchad and Mr. Bhandari's servant cooked supper, which we ate seated on a cotton rug. The ponies, seven of them, cropped the grass on the far side of the glade. Later they would be put in a covered stockade for the night. It was all very peaceful and pastoral.

I washed in a stream which ran behind the kutirs.

"Be sure to bolt your door before going to bed," Mr. Bhandari told me. "The jungle is full of wild beasts and they often come investigating round here."

I should have liked to have left my door open, but I did as I was told and bolted it. Night birds called softly. I gazed through the barred window at the leafy tops of the trees and the sky brilliant with stars, and I thought of how through untold centuries India's ascetics have lived close to nature in mountain ranges and forests. They have never looked upon nature as evil or as something to be conquered, as has often been the case in the West. The yogi regards nature as an ally which will help him in his spiritual quest and bring peace to his mind. He refers to the natural world as divine nature. Mountains and rivers are often objects of worship, and animals are referred to as 'our younger brothers'.

An atmosphere of serenity seemed to flow down from the starlit sky upon this piece of earth and ascend upwards again to heaven like an invisible Jacob's ladder. I was glad that my thoughts, as I lay down to sleep, were peaceful too, so that they did not mar the almost supernatural tranquillity of the atmosphere.

Next morning Mr. Bhandari and I set off for the yogi's cave.

"It's not worth saddling the ponies to ride there," he said. "Besides, I enjoy a stroll through the jungle in the early hours."

I asked him what our chances were of meeting a tiger.

"I reckon our chance of meeting a tiger and being attacked by it are about equal with being run over by a car in a city, that is, not very likely. Anyway, I have this staff."

He shook it and put on a fierce expression.

"Have you had any personal experience of the yogi's power over wild animals?"

"I've seen a deer come up to him and take grass from his hand. But a friend of mine had an unforgettable experience concerning the yogi and a leopard. He and Yogi Rishabhdeva and another man were walking one day through the jungle, as we are now, when a leopard came out of the bushes and stood in the middle of the trail watching them. My friend and the other man immediately stopped, but Yogi Rishabhdeva walked on calmly right up to the beast, passed it, and continued to walk on, calling out to the other two to follow him, which they did. The leopard turned and began to walk alongside Rishabhdeva like a pet dog.

"My friend had experienced some moments of fear when the beautiful spotted beast had suddenly appeared, but now every vestige of fear left him and he felt no further concern for his own safety. Presently the leopard turned back into the bushes and the three of them continued unharmed on their way."

The track started to follow the banks of a dried-up riverbed and the trees became more widely spaced. We walked into a wide clearing, in the centre of which were some rocks partly hidden by bushes.

The yogi's cave was amongst these rocks. He was sitting outside it, his legs crossed in the lotus posture. Mr. Bhandari pressed his palms together and stood motionless before him for some seconds and then the yogi gestured that we were to be seated.

He continued to sit there in the same posture, still and silent. For a moment I studied him, but I found that it was not easy to look into his eyes. His gaze as he looked at me was penetrating and searching.

But I noted that the yogi's features were well formed. His long hair had traces of grey in it. I put his age at about fifty. His most remarkable feature were his eyes. They were full and luminous, untouched, unlike his hair, by any sign of age.

I gradually felt a subtle link forming between the ascetic and myself. I closed my eyes and I sensed that in some way, not to be described, he was helping me to get off the ground, as it were, and to reach a higher plane.

An hour, perhaps two hours, passed and then, without opening my eyes, I realised that the yogi had ended the meditation and we presently got up and left

When we got back to the kutirs I told Premchad that I wanted to stay on for a day or two longer and he was quite agreeable to doing so.

We visited the yogi and silently meditated with him again on the following day. The man had impressed me deeply. I sensed, as I am sure that nearly everyone did who came into contact with him, that here was an enlightened being who had journeyed far into higher regions.

When we went to his cave on the third day, the yogi asked Mr. Bhandari if he would meditate for a while in a nearby cave, as he thought I might like to talk alone with him. I had indeed been hoping to spend some time alone with the yogi, but now that I had my chance of a few words alone with him, I suddenly felt diffident.

"Would you like to ask me any questions?" he enquired.

For a moment I thought of asking him about this power he had over wild animals, but something told me that this was too trite, remarkable though this power might be. So I asked, as I had asked the Jain abbess at Palitana, what his aim was.

"Samadhi, eternal samadhi," he replied.

He said nothing more and a silence began to flow around us. But after a time he spoke, his words seeming to flow with the silence, not breaking into it.

"That is the only goal. If you make it yours too, you will never stray far from the path and sooner or later you will attain it. Then two will cease to exist; you and me, this and that, mine and theirs, me and the Absolute. There will only be One."

A light breeze swung the branches of the bushes. Squirrels darted over the rocks and into the cave.

"Is there anything else you would like to ask me?"

My diffidence vanished and I began to confide in the yogi my wish to spend some time in the Himalayas, in a remote place where I could live simply and spend much of my time in contemplation.

"I'm hoping to travel there next spring when the passes have opened," I said, "and go right up to Badrinath."

Badrinath is a small temple town close to the borders of Tibet.

"If you have this urge to visit the Sacred Range, then you should go."

"Yes, but after I have travelled up along the pilgrims' route to the Indo-Tibetan border, then where to? Could you tell me of a place in the Himalayas where I might live for a while, and, any person who could help me in achieving my aim of entering the path?"

"The invisible path of Dhyana can be entered anywhere. It is not a question of being here or there. But if you have this desire to spend some time in the Himalayas and feel that you are more likely to get assistance there than elsewhere, then by all means go."

His eyes half closed and I wondered whether he had plunged deep into meditation, but presently he looked at me and said, "I know of someone there who may be able to help you. I cannot give you his address because his 'address', like mine, is a cave, nor is he there all the time. He travels to other caves in the district, staying a few days or weeks at one and then going on to another, where he may spend several months. These caves are in a very isolated and wild region on the south-westerly slopes of the Trisul massif."

"What is his name?" I asked.

"He'll tell you his name if you meet him."

"How am I to get to his cave or know if he'll be there if I do reach it?"

"Listen intently," he said. "I'll give you some directions. Try and remember them exactly. After you've visited Badrinath, go down to Nandaprayag, which you will have passed through on the way up. Find out there about a track which leads in a north-easterly direction towards Mount Trisul."

He then gave me various directions of the kind such as, "You must look out for a pool shaped like a lotus leaf which lies under a towering rock on a mountain range close by Trisul," and, "Look out for a pine tree growing on another tall rock which lies to the right of the trail, and this will lead you to a valley in which grow only a few tufts of grass because it's above the tree line. You will know you are in the right valley if, when you look straight ahead, you see a barren hill with two peaks, the southerly one bent somewhat in the shape of a breaking wave," and so on.

He ended by saying that the cave in which the ascetic sometimes dwelt was situated down a narrow valley that lay close to a high circular plateau of barren land ringed about with snow peaks. If this man was not there when I arrived, I would almost certainly find one or two other hermits in the vicinity who would be able to tell me when he was likely to return.

"But who shall I ask for?"

"They will know who it is that you've come to see."

"When you travelled to this place, Yogi Rishabhdeva, how long did it take you to get there from Nandaprayag?"

"I have never been there."

"Oh... Then this ascetic who you think may be able to help me—did he visit you here?"

"I have never met him but I know him well."

And with this enigmatic remark the yogi brought our talk to an end.

I pressed my palms together and stood before him a moment in silence. Just as I was about to go, he said, "Trust in yourself and in God; then you will find your way there."

Sitting in the glade that evening, I thought over the yogi's instructions for reaching this place high in the mighty Himalayas, a place whose name he had not given me and which probably had no name anyway, where I might find an ascetic whose name I did not know. And many of the directions would be as difficult for me to spot, I felt—a pine tree growing on top of a rock, a pool shaped like a lotus leaf—as had been the gypsies' roadsigns, the patrin, in days past. Nevertheless, they were all I had to go on and I knew that when spring came I would try and get there and find this man, whoever he was.

CHAPTER TWENTY

TOWNS ALONG THE WAY

BUNDI IS A walled Rajput town. Kipling loved and wrote about it in his 'From Sea to Sea.'

By the side of the town is a lake dotted with islands on which are pavilions and temples. The town is dominated by a palace which stands on a hill just above the maze of old houses and winding streets. It belongs to a clan of Rajputs who call themselves 'children of the fire-pit' because they believe that their founders were created by Vishnu in a fiery pit on one of the peaks of Mount Abu. The family, like Rajputs in general, have been noted for their martial and chivalrous qualities. The present Maharaja won the M.C. in the last World War. I was told that he does not live in his vast palace these days but in a modern house which lies a few miles out of the town, but that a suite of rooms is always kept ready for him at the palace and he stays there occasionally.

A pass is needed in order to look over the palace or those parts of it which are open to the public. Having obtained one, I was taken round by an old retainer who had known two of the late Maharajas as well as several Viceroys who had come to stay at the palace. He was a mine of information about life in those days.

We walked through huge rooms and across terraces on which were trees and gardens and shady alcoves. I looked over a wall at the town and lake lying below, a wonderful view which I could have gazed at for hours. But the old retainer wanted to show me a room in which were displayed various family heirlooms. He himself, he said, had suggested to the present Maharaja that these objects should be displayed, as he believed they would be of great interest to persons visiting the palace. I certainly found them fascinating.

We crossed a courtyard leading to this room, and as I entered it I felt that I had stepped back into an era which was now as remote and legendary as that of Czarist Russia. There were photographs of Viceroys and their wives, the men in uniform and the women in long white gowns with diamond tiaras on their heads and ostrich-feather fans in their hands. The photographs were signed with messages of affection and appreciation by the various Viceroys to the Maharajas who had entertained them. Displayed in cases were jewelled swords, bracelets and anklets and other valuables. But what interested me most were several large oil paintings of past Maharajas, all magnificently dressed. One of them had been painted seated cross-legged and holding a jewelled sword. He was wearing full white trousers, over which was a pleated skirt. The top part of his body was encased in an embroidered and bejewelled jacket. Rings gleamed on his fingers, ruby ear-rings hung from his ears, and round his throat was a choker of pearls which must have made a Viceroy's wife green with envy had he worn it while she was staying at the palace.

"What parties and picnics there were in those days," said the old retainer—"boating parties on the lake, picnics in the hills and big processions through the town. No more now."

I said good-bye to him and walked down the huge stone entranceway with its high walls and sharp V-turn into the palace, this, no doubt, to make things difficult for would-be invaders in past centuries.

Peacocks walk through the streets of Bundi and perch in the lower branches of the trees. The town is completely unspoilt. A long line of artists have lived and painted here. I was followed through the streets by men thrusting paintings at me, and was assured that the pictures were very old and valuable, veritable masterpieces. I finally bought one in order to rid myself of my pursuers. It was painted on leather and depicted a Maharaja of Bundi riding a white horse which was magnificently bridled and saddled with a tuft of peacock feathers between its ears. The chief was escorted by retainers who were waving fluffy white fly-whisks. The painting was no masterpiece, of course, but it had a vitality and a certain bravado which I liked and it would be a small memento of my happy stay in this lovely Rajput town.

My next stop was Mathura, or Muttra, again a very ancient town as well as being a centre of pilgrimage. As with Dwarka, it is connected with the life of the blue-eyed god, Krishna. Like all worthwhile cities, it is built along the banks of a river, in this case, the sacred Jumna.

I stayed in the Ladies Retiring Room, which was packed to overflowing with women, children and babies. The men, as is usual in India, did much better and their Retiring Room further along the platform was relatively uncrowded and a veritable oasis of calm in comparison to ours. The men were lolling about in chairs, reading newspapers and combing their hair.

As I was looking with envy into this peaceful abode, one of the men came up to me and said that I could come in here whenever I felt like it! He had a wife and five children in the Ladies Retiring Room and knew just how crowded and noisy things were there. It was a pleasure to get away from his family for a while. He had been travelling with them in a packed carriage and the baby had cried for hours on end. Had I seen the town? I said no, but I was thinking of going out right then and having a look at it.

"I'll come with you," he said.

His name was Shuddhananda Chaudhuri and he came from Orissa. He and his family were on a pilgrimage and had been travelling now for nearly three weeks. Did I know that it was the height of the pilgrim season in Muttra? That was why the retiring rooms and everything else were so crowded.

I had not known this, but I would have done so directly I had walked a short distance down any street. Even as we left the station, a train pulled up and out poured crowds of men, women and children. Amongst this crowd were saffron-robed saddhus and matted-haired ascetics. They are allowed to travel free of charge so long as they are able to satisfy the railway authorities that they are genuine holy men.

Crowds surged through the ancient town. Old houses, four and five stories high, lined the streets and the banks of the river. Most of them were fronted by open courtyards in which talks were being delivered to bands of pilgrims and townsfolk by various pundits and yogis. In one courtyard we watched a play being performed.

The players mimed their parts while an actor standing to one side read out the lines in Hindi. My companion informed me that the play was about one of the Krishna legends.

The parts of the women were taken by small girls, none of whom looked more than about eight. They were dressed in white trousers and velvet jackets and wore pill-box hats on their heads. Their eyes were heavily made up with kohl. In their various roles of wives, courtesans and love-lorn young women, they acted with great skill, flirting with the male actors and tempting them with sensuous gestures. No wonder that girls were once married off so young. One seductive gesture of a tiny hand was able to convey an invitation to her beloved as subtle and compelling as one which might have been made by an experienced English beauty three times the age of the small actress.

There was no scenery, but the players were able to conjure up for the audience moonlit groves, pavilions and secret hide-aways. Although the play was of a quasi-religious nature, it was also somewhat bawdy. In one scene the hero was forcibly ejected from the house of his beloved by an irate father and he crawled around the stage on all fours. A seated sadhu gave him a hard whack on his posterior as he went by and the man let out a bellow, much to the delight of the audience. Then there was a scene where the would-be lover of the heroine inadvertently found himself closeted with the girl's mother ...

Shuddhananda roared with laughter as the actor at the side of the stage recited the lines while the hero was gripped in an unwilling embrace.

"No, I can't possibly translate that bit for you," he said, still gasping with laughter.

In another courtyard we listened to a talk being given in English by an ascetic who had spent thirty years in the Himalayas. Once a year he and his disciple, a bone-thin youth of about twenty, left their mountain abodes and walked all the way to Mathura and, after spending some days in the town, went on to Dwarka. He was apparently quite well known. The talk was delivered by him standing up. Since becoming an ascetic he had trained himself always to stand. He had never once sat, knelt or lain down for the past twenty-five years or so. The young disciple, a member of the audience whispered to me, could now stand throughout the day and half the night. Before long he would be able to stand continuously like his guru. Oh, by the way—the old man had not slept for twenty-five years now.

To believe or not to believe? That was the question—for me, at any rate. One sees and hears so many astounding things in India. I knew that thousands of ascetics do undergo fasts and penances which would be deemed impossible by many people in the West. Now I had been told that the old man delivering the talk had stood for twenty-five years and, moreover, had not slept a wink during that time. Was it true? I simply did not know.

At the end of the talk, which not unnaturally had been about the undertaking of various penances, the old fellow stretched out both arms benevolently to the seated audience with the words of the many-armed Nataraja, "Thou too art I, for all are One."

Near us was an ascetic whose withered arms stretched up to heaven.

"He too visits Muttra yearly," said my informant. "His arms are quite useless now; the bones have set. He can't do anything for himself and has to be fed by his fellow yogis."

Why? What good does it do? Those were the questions I asked myself when I heard this, as I was to ask myself many times again while in India. But I never found a satisfactory answer as to why it is that some men commit these extreme acts of self-mortification. Perhaps there is none.

Shuddhananda wanted to hear another talk which would shortly be given by a very learned saddhu, but I had heard enough for one evening and so we parted and I went down to the river.

A narrow street ran alongside it, bordered on one side by a row of open-fronted shops in which were numerous goods to tempt the women pilgrims. One of these shops was filled with nothing but bracelets. There were several seated women trying on glass bracelets, gold and silver bracelets, and a papier-maché kind which was decorated with small pieces of coloured glass arranged in the shapes of flowers and leaves.

I immediately fell for some of these bracelets and pointed to those which had taken my fancy. The proprietor handed me pairs to try on. Bracelets are bought in pairs and some of the women were buying, two, four or six of the same kind and colour.

"Too small, I'm afraid," I said. "And these too."

My hands are not large, but in comparison to the hands of these women they appeared about twice the size of theirs. I tried to get some larger bracelets over my protesting knuckles but to no avail. I gave up and was about to leave, but the proprietor motioned me to stay where I was and went into the back of the shop. I thought he had gone to look for some larger bracelets but he presently returned carrying a bowl of soapy water. Picking up one of the bracelets which I had put aside as being too small, he dipped it into the water, took hold of my hand and dipped that in too, and then started to ease the bracelet over my knuckles. It was sheer agony; no Chinese torture could have been worse. I groaned and begged him to stop but he took no notice of my pleas, while the women around me exhorted me to endure the agony; the bracelets were lovely ones; I would not regret having undergone a little pain once I was wearing them.

Ouch! one bracelet over—and another. Only when there were six on my wrist did he at last desist. The women congratulated me on having stuck it out.

I continued my walk along the street, refusing to look into any more shops. My hand felt as though it had been crushed under the wheel of a tractor. I wore the bracelets for about three weeks and then got someone to break them on my wrist, as I could not face the agony of easing them off over my knuckles.

Beyond the shops, the ground sloped down to the river where there was a temple and bathing ghats. The evening arati ceremony was being held at the temple and a large crowd had gathered there. A conch-shell was blown, a Brahmin intoned verses from the Vedas. Amongst the crowd, patiently waiting for the service to end, were scores of monkeys and milk-white cows, while lined up along the riverbank were turtles by the hundred; tiny ones, the size of a rupee, and huge fellows measuring some three feet across the shell. When the ceremony had ended, the priests and many people in the crowd distributed food to the turtles, monkeys and cows.

I spent one more day in Mathura and then caught a night train on to Delhi.

The capital is two towns united in one: Old Delhi and New Delhi.

I was staying a week in Delhi and spending the last four days with English friends who had a bungalow in a New Delhi suburb. But they were on holiday when I arrived and so I was putting up at a hotel for the first three days.

Although I had made no booking, I hoped I would be able to get into a hotel in Old Delhi where I had stayed years ago. Most people who had stayed there thought that it was the nicest hotel in Delhi and always went back if they returned again to the city. It was situated in a large garden. The spacious bedrooms had high ceilings to make for coolness, and many overlooked the garden. Nearly every one had its own veranda. Outside the hotel was a wide terrace where guests and their friends had tea and sipped cool drinks. The hotel was not air-conditioned, but I much prefer these old-style colonial buildings, even at the height of the hot season, with their high-ceilinged rooms and individual atmosphere to the skyscraper, air-conditioned modern emporiums where guests sit in their square rabbit-hutches of low-ceilinged rooms. If the air-conditioning is going full blast, I always feel shivery in these dens, particularly on returning from the outside world where the temperature may have been well above the hundred mark. If the conditioning is set at medium, I just feel clammy. All too often there is an electricity failure and then, horrors, the wretched guests sit in their rooms like joints roasting in an oven. Also, these modern edifices seem to me to lack any kind of atmosphere and they always remind me faintly of the inside of a hospital.

When I got out of the train at Delhi and had my baggage seized by a red-jacketed porter, I had pleasant thoughts of the next few days which I was spending, I hoped, in the spacious old-style hotel in its lovely garden situated in the heart of the ancient city. Alas...

The wretch of a Sikh driver drove me all the way there and only when he pulled up outside the steps leading to the entrance, where there were crowds of children and monks going about in their long habits—which struck me as being very odd—did I find out that the hotel had been sold some time back, had been bought by the Roman Church and turned into a Catholic school. So much for that.

We drove back to New Delhi, past the Red Fort and the huge Jama Masjid Mosque, with its great dome set between two minarets, and into New Delhi, with its wide tree-lined streets and fine modern buildings. I got a room in one of the air-conditioned monsters. My taxi fare, of course, was enormous.

No sooner had the hotel porter dumped my baggage down in my small box-like room with its double windows to keep out the heat, than I raced off like a homing pigeon to Connaught Circus, the centre of New Delhi around which the city's life revolves, to have tea in my favourite restaurant, and I spent as little time as possible in my air-conditioned den.

I thought I would do a little sight-seeing before my friends got back and I visited the Red Fort, which was built by the Emperor Aurangzeb in the year 1659. It is vast. One really needs days to see it properly. One of the things there that I remember most vividly was a beautiful screen of a wonderful symmetry, painted in the Moghul manner, which depicted the scales of justice.

Delhi is a city of many periods and many past empires, of modern buildings and ancient ruins. The last Hindu king was defeated in Delhi in 1192 A.D. and there then commenced six centuries of Muslim rule, which was followed by two centuries of British rule.

I went on a tourist bus trip. Our first stop was the Qutb Minar Tower, which is held to be one of the greatest architectural achievements in the city. The tower is 238 feet high and is ornamented with wide floral bands. In the enclosure which surrounds the tower stands the Iron Pillar, which dates back to ancient times. It is twenty-three feet high. When it was dug up out of the earth, it was found to be quite unrusted.

I walked around the pillar looking to see whether there was the slightest trace of rust or corrosion but there is none. The metallurgical skill of those ancient Hindus must have reached an extraordinarily high level.

From there we went to see the ruins and tomb of Tughlaq Shah on the outskirts of the city. This Sultan was a man of fine character. His city of Tughlaqabad was built in the space of four years. Today it lies largely in ruins and jackals howl there at night. Buried in the tomb are the Shah, his Queen, and their son Juna Khan. Unlike his father, the son was anything but a noble character. During his reign he was so cruel that he earned himself the title of Khuni Sultan—the Bloody King—as had likewise Mary Tudor during her terrible reign earned herself the title of Bloody Queen Mary from the British populace.

From this Moghul tomb we went on to see some of the modern buildings of the city built during the period of British rule when the capital was transferred from Calcutta to here.

New Delhi was designed by two English architects, Sir Herbert Baker and Sir Edward Lutyens. It is a wonderfully planned modern city and many of the buildings are magnificent, particularly the President's House, with its Moghul gardens, the Secretariat and Parliament.

After we had seen these buildings, the bus pulled up near a fine statue of one of the last of the King Emperors, George the Fifth. It stood at the confluence of several of the city's main avenues which radiated from it. The King Emperor stood in full regalia, a crown on his head and his cloak falling from his shoulders to extend behind him for thirty feet or so. In the year 1911 a magnificent Coronation Durbar was held in Delhi for this King and Queen Mary.

The statue which I saw has since been removed and one of Gandhi is going to be put in its place.

We were driven back to Connaught Circus for lunch at an Indian restaurant where we passengers ate vegetable sambals, curries, Tandoori chicken and various Moghlai fare which is a specialty of the Delhi region.

The next day I went to an opening of an art exhibition which was being attended by the Dalai Lama. The theme of the exhibition was Buddhism, and all the pictures had been painted by artists who were living in Delhi or the nearby districts. I went to this exhibition not so much to look at the paintings as to see the young Dalai Lama.

Since he had fled from Tibet after the Communists had taken over his country, the Dalai Lama has lived mainly in the small Himalayan township of Dharmsala, but he comes down to the capital occasionally.

There were so many people at the opening that all I saw of him was a brief glimpse of his head and shoulders as he stopped to look at a painting hung close to where I and a few dozen others were standing. Even so, during those few moments I saw him, I was impressed by his serene and smiling countenance. There was no trace of bitterness or resentment in his expression.

Among the people present were several Tibetan lamas who had escaped from Tibet. Some had reached India alone, others in small groups. I was introduced to one of these men, who was an artist monk and prior to his arrival in India over the Himalayas had been living in a very remote monastery in Eastern Tibet.

He told me that since he had come to India he had learnt to paint in oils. Before, he had always used powder paints which he ground and mixed himself, and he had only painted thankas.

Thankas are similar to Chinese scroll paintings but the Tibetan ones are always on some religious theme, such as the wheel of life.

I asked the monk whether he still painted thankas and he said that these were what he worked on most and that recently he had begun to sell a few and had made a little money to keep himself going.

Before leaving Delhi I bought one of his thankas. It was of the Tibetan poet-saint Milarepa. The monk had painted him seated outside a cave and singing, so he told me, one of his own hymns. The painting is edged with red silk and hangs by a red cord.

This artist monk was certain that one day he would be able to return to his homeland, a belief that is held, apparently, by the majority of Tibetan refugees.

I took the opportunity while I was in Delhi to go along to the National Gallery to see the collection of paintings by my favourite Indian artist of modern times, Amrita Sher Gil.

Her work is influenced by traditional Indian art, yet it is also utterly contemporary. There is a marvellous sense of space in all her work, which is free of the fiddly and distracting details which mar the work of many modern Indian painters. The unique vision which is apparent in her paintings and their freshness of style mark her as one of the few artists of genius that India has produced in this twentieth century.

Although her mother was a Central European woman, Amrita felt herself to be Indian in every fibre of her being.

Her life was short and imbued with tragedy. She was the daughter of a Sikh father and Hungarian mother and was born in Budapest in 1913 and came to India when she was eight. She lived on her father's estate in the North Indian hills. Then in 1929 she went to France to study art and returned to India in 1934.

From all accounts of her, she was a bold young woman with an arresting personality, who lived life on her own terms. She was also extremely sensitive and proud, this latter trait being partly due no doubt to her Sikh blood. The Sikhs have a saying about themselves which is: 'Where there is one Sikh, there is one Sikh. Where there are two Sikhs, there is an assembly of saints. Where there are five Sikhs, there is God.'

She travelled the length and breadth of India and met a wide variety of people, but it was the tribals and villagers following the ancient traditional life who made the deepest impression on her and whom she most often painted. Her feeling for her country was very different from that of the national sentimentalist or the casual visitor. While she was living in Paris she had felt a deep yearning for her native land and had written: 'It was the vision of winter in India—desolate yet strangely beautiful, of endless tracks of luminous yellow-grey land, of dark bodies, sad-faced, incredibly thin men and women who moved silently, looking almost like silhouettes and over which an indefinable melancholy reigns. It was different from the India, voluptuous, colourful, sunny and superficial, the India so false to the tempting travel posters that I had expected to see.'

In 1938 she went back to Hungary where she married a cousin and the young couple sailed for India the following year.

Amrita Sher Gil always kept well away from the art coteries in her country and she deplored the superficiality of much of the painting that was being produced in India during her time. The fact that her own work was so often ignored or misunderstood never ceased to rankle with her. In 1939 she was awarded the gold medal of the Bombay Art Society, but this did little to quell her feelings of bitterness.

During the week I spent in Delhi I met several people who had actually known her, but they all gave me oddly differing accounts as to the cause of her death and the circumstances surrounding it. One person told me that she had died quite alone while she was in labour, another that she had died suddenly from a variety of ailments in the middle of the night, attended to by her husband and a cousin.

Her death took place in Lahore at the tragically early age of twenty-nine, when she was in the midst of new artistic developments, with her vision set on fresh horizons.

As in all tropical countries, her funeral took place on the day following her death. A friend of hers who had attended it told me that her Hungarian mother was half-crazed with grief, but that her Sikh father showed a wonderful dignity and calm as his daughter's body was consumed by the flames and hymns were sung from the Granth Sahib, the holy book of the Sikhs.

For the last part of my stay in the capital I thankfully left my impersonal and claustrophobic room in the hotel and moved to my friends' bungalow, which was set in a garden full of autumn flowers and shady trees.

These friends later drove me down to Benares.

I had come to the end of my pilgrim tour and would not be doing any further travelling until the spring of next year, when I would be going up to the Himalayas. I had thought that I might spend the winter months in Varanasi, but after a few days in this city, which many Hindus believe to be the oldest in the world, I decided that it was too noisy and crowded for a prolonged stay and that I would do better to spend the winter months in some smaller place.

I stayed in a hotel run by a red-faced, rawboned Irishman who, in a country where prohibition is in force, somehow managed to acquire plenty of drink for himself, and he would appear in the dining-room in the evenings in that nether state in which heavy drinkers spend much of their time and which lies somewhere between sobriety and drunkenness.

I stayed only a few days in Kashi—yet another name for Benares. I took an early-morning boat trip down the Ganges past the bathing ghats and the spots where Hindus cremate their dead and the ashes are thrown into the river. Hundreds of pilgrims were bathing in the none-too-clean water and rinsing their mouths with it. Others were sitting cross-legged on the wide steps, deep in meditation.

During a tour of some of the temples I was amused when the guide, standing in front of a statue of the black goddess, Mother Kali, told us that she is the patroness of this dark Kali era, the present Iron Age, and that one of her incarnations was England's most evil monarch, Bloody Queen Mary.

The statue was painted black and the goddess had been sculpted in her most usual pose, dancing on a corpse and wearing a necklace of human skulls. I thought that if Bloody Mary had not been an incarnation of Kali, then she ought to have been. She brought the Inquisition to Britain, and 'heretics', amongst whom were some of the most Christian men and women in the land, were burnt in thousands at the stake. And the black tentacles of the Inquisition stretched right out to India and it raged in the Portuguese possessions of Goa and Diu.

An Indian professor who was in our party said to me that the

Inquisition is held to be the greatest of all crimes committed during this Kali era, by sages in the East as well as by those in the West.

The day before I left Varanasi I made the short four-miles journey out to Sarnath, where the Buddha preached his first sermon.

Buddhism almost ceased to exist in the land of its birth around the year 800 A.D. and Sarnath became deserted. But in recent years it has gained a new lease of life and Sarnath today is usually full of pilgrims. A new temple has been built there by the Maha Bodhi Society called Mula Gandhakuti Vihara.

The day I was there a crowd of Tibetan lamas in their deep purple gowns were going round this temple. Several were carrying prayer wheels. A large crowd had gathered at the entrance to the temple grounds. They were standing by to welcome a Tibetan who had measured his length all the way from Benares to Sarnath. His goal was this temple. He was a bedraggled looking individual with a torn robe and dusty hair, but that, I suppose, was only to be expected.

"Four miles," someone said—"that's nothing. I once met a man who was on his way back to Kashi who had measured his length to Lake Manasrowar beyond the Himalayas. The journey had taken him twelve years."

Another man said, "The Buddha never encouraged the practise of such feats. He always preached the Middle Way between extreme austerities and indulgence. It was certain priests who encouraged such things, as well as such superstitious practises as the worship of relics, not the Great Teacher himself."

I returned to Benares, caught a train back to Delhi and travelled on again by train to the town of Hardwar, which lies a hundred miles to the north of the capital. It was here that I had decided to spend the winter months.

CHAPTER TWENTY-ONE

ABODE OF SNOW

HARDWAR IS ONE of the seven sacred cities and is situated on the Ganges at the base of the Siwalik Range, part of the foothills of the Himalayas.

The town has a long main street with sidestreets running down to the river. Once a year a mela, a religious fair, is held here, and once every twelve years a super mela, called the Fair of the Sacred Urn. Pilgrims and saffron-robed sadhus come from all over the sub-continent in order to bathe in the Divine Pool during those auspicious hours of the mela which have been calculated by astrologers. By doing so they hope to gain release from further incarnations on earth. There is a legend that hidden in the pool is an urn which contains the elixir of immortality. During these fairs, processions of sadhus—the word sadhu means one who has renounced—and long-haired ascetics, some of whom, the Nagas, are completely naked, march down to the pool, watched by thousands of pilgrims. Their leaders ride decorated elephants or are carried on gold and silver palanquins. Bands blare, the pilgrims shout, 'Hail to Mother Ganga!' and everyone plunges into the pool. In the evening little leaf boats filled with flowers, each one holding a lighted candle, are floated on the water to drift downstream with the current.

I arrived after the yearly mela had been held and things were fairly quiet in the town. I managed to rent a large room. It was in a tall old house in one of the side streets and from it I could walk down to the river in three minutes. Enormous fish swim in the waters and are fed by pilgrims.

There were plenty of places to visit roundabouts. Sometimes I caught the little train up to Rishikesh, which lies fourteen miles from Hardwar.

As the weeks passed, the weather became cooler and some mornings there was a frosty feeling in the air.

I spent long hours in meditation in my room, and I thought of my coming trip to the Himalayas, whose lower ranges could be seen from the town, and I thought of the ascetic living somewhere among the vastness of those snow-capped mountains whom Yogi Rishabhdeva had told me about. And I wondered whether I would be utterly foolish if I embarked on what, on the face of it, would appear to be a wild, an almost hopeless search for him. Yet I had a feeling that if I did not make the attempt, I might regret not having done so to the end of my life. Commonsense told me no, but my heart told me yes.

I had no illusions as to what getting lost in the Himalayas could mean. After hours of thoughtful deliberation in my room, weighing the pros and cons as much as I was able, I decided finally that I would go in search of this ascetic.

But having decided to embark on this quest, I tried to be as practical as I could about the venture lying ahead of me. I did a few repairs to my sleeping-bag and windjacket and I made out a list of supplies that I would need, both for the journey up to the Himalayan township of Badrinath and later.

In early spring I went down to Delhi to have innoculations against smallpox, cholera and typhoid. No one travelling up along the Himalayan pilgrim route is allowed past the boundaries of Rishikesh if he or she cannot produce a certificate stating that immunisation has been taken against these dread diseases.

Spring came and the trees burst into flower, the Red Silk Cotton, the Flame of the Forest and the Coral tree. The fiery shades of the flowers which cover the leafless branches of the trees in brilliant masses are an unforgettable sight, especially when they are seen against the green of the jungle or a clear blue sky.

Although spring had come to the foothills, the passes remained closed and there were reports of bad weather and snowstorms up in the mountains.

In April the first trickle of pilgrims began to arrive in the town. Some went on to Rishikesh, where buses set off laden with passengers for the Abode of the Gods. But it was not until the first week in May that the authorities declared the passes opened, with warnings that the weather was still far from good in the mountains and that there had been road slips and avalanches in some places, so pilgrims must proceed warily.

Within a week there were reports of deaths from exhaustion and exposure of several pilgrims.

In the third week of May I left Hardwar and went up to Rishikesh and caught one of the buses which would take me three-quarters of the way to Badrinath, which lies on the Indo-Tibetan border. The last section has to be walked, or one can hire ponies and ride. The old and sick can be carried in dandies, which are chairs fixed between poles like the dholis of the south. The distance from Rishikesh to Badrinath is a hundred and seventy miles. Because of the narrowness of the road and the many sharp turns, one-way traffic is enforced.

Soon after leaving Rishikesh, the bus started to climb along the road which ran parallel to the Ganga and the scenery became awe-inspiring, particularly at Devaprayag, which lies at a height of 1,630 feet and where there is a confluence of the Bhagirathi and Alaknanda rivers, the latter being the infant Ganga.

The passengers in the bus had come from all over India, from the far south, Bengal and Rajasthan, and all had set their hearts on reaching Badrinath.

After leaving Devaprayag, the bus went over a steel bridge across the Bhagirathi and from then on it followed the road which wound like a serpent over the mountains.

In the afternoon we reached our first halt, the town of Srinagar and Kirtinagar, which lie on either side of the banks of the Alaknanda. We were told to be ready to start again next morning by five o'clock. Srinagar is the largest town in the state of Garhwal.

No breakfast. We were off at crack of dawn. But after more twisting and turning along the serpentine roadway we stopped for breakfast at Rudraprayag. On again through Gauchar, where a fair is held every winter, and then through Karnaprayag and Nandaprayag. We stopped at Chamoli. Here several passengers left the bus. They were going to follow a footpath which goes to

Kedarnath, by Kedar Mountain. Kedar is another name of Shiva, God of Destruction, who is believed to preside over this area of Himachal. The temple at Kedarnath is dedicated to him. Badrinath is dedicated to Vishnu, the Preserver.

Our next stop was Joshimath, where there was the bus terminus. Before reaching it we passed snow-clad ranges and alpine meadows ablaze with flowers. The lower slopes of the mountains were covered by green belts of pine and deodar forests. These great deodar trees are a species of cedar and the pine-cones have edible kernels.

We had a puncture as the bus neared Joshimath and we got out to stretch our legs while the driver changed the tire. Several of the passengers scrambled down a narrow track to a pool lying below the roadway and they returned carrying bunches of a lily called the Kailas lotus which they had pulled out of the pool. The flowers were a golden colour and had a lovely fragrance.

Joshimath is a religious centre and there is a monastery here which was established by the great Acharya Shankaracharya, and two famous temples. Badrinath now lay only nineteen miles away, but we would have to walk these miles. I spent the night in a crowded dharmasala. The weather next morning was bright and sunny.

There is no chance of getting lost on this last stretch to Badrinath as scores of people were heading there, most of them on foot, some on ponies, while the infirm were being carried in dandies. There were also some army personnel going along with the parties.

I was amazed at the light clothing most of the pilgrims were wearing, the women in flimsy saris and sandals, though many walked barefooted, while the men were in dhotis and shirts and perhaps an old jacket. I was also surprised at the number of very old pilgrims. And of course there were also several ascetics, most of whom were clad only in narrow loin-cloths.

I started off with a party of about ten others. We had not gone far along the narrow twisting path when the blue sky became darkened with heavy clouds and a biting wind started to blow. We walked through a deep gorge which followed the course of the Alaknanda. It was a stony world of precipitous rock walls and loose micaceous shale and patches of ice. Then the gorge opened out into a wide valley. We came to the village of Gobindghat. Beyond it lay the well known 'Valley of Flowers' and Hemkund Lokpal Lake. It really was a flower-filled valley and it was encompassed by heaven-high ridges capped with snow. On their slopes were spruce, pines and maples.

After leaving the valley the path narrowed and became steep and treacherous. We tramped through icy slush. Under some rocks a weary group of pilgrims were resting. They said they had walked the thirty-nine miles from Pipalkoti. Three days ago, they told us, two pilgrims had died in a snowstorm when they were only a few miles from the shrine.

A group passed us shouting, "Jai Badri Vishal Ki!"

The route resounds with this cry, which pilgrims shout to encourage one another on the arduous and often hazardous ascent.

The pathway reached a height of eleven thousand feet and here we caught our first sight of the shrine, with mountains in the background.

On the last few miles we were dragging our weary legs through icy mud and slush but the sun was out again and we could see the triangular red and white flags flying from the golden temple dome.

The small township of Badrinath lies at a height of 10,300 feet. The temple is the predominant building there and the goal of all the pilgrims. It is not a particularly attractive town but there is a vital spirit about the place which is almost tangible, and behind and around it rear the magnificent mountains, the Abode of Snow and of the Gods.

Our morale, which had been flagging slightly, revived as we walked into the town and made straight for the temple, up whose steep flight of steps a file of pilgrims was ascending.

During the Buddhist era in India this temple, like many other Hindu shrines, had fallen into decay. It was restored to its former glory by Shankaracharya, who was a Namboodiri Brahmin and came from Kerala. Since that time the officiating priest during the pilgrim season has always been a Namboodiri Brahmin from the far-off Malabar Coast.

There was a seated statue of Shankaracharya in the main hall. The central figure in the hall was a black stone statue of Lord Vishnu in a meditative pose, which was hung with garlands and various decorations. Round this statue were burning ghee lamps. Officiating in a nearby shrine was a priest. He was dressed in white trousers, a gold and violet turban, and a mauve velvet coat richly embroidered with gold down the front and on the sleeves. With his black shoulder-length hair and striking looks, he made an impressive figure.

Then, as I came up to him, I recognised him.

"Vishnu!" I exclaimed.

It was none other than the young Kathakali dancer whom I had met down south when he was staying with Satish. We could not speak together for more than a minute because he was busy attending to the crowd of pilgrims passing through the temple, but he told me to call at the temple in the morning, when he would be free, and he would take me to a place where I would be able to get a glimpse of Tibet.

I followed a line of pilgrims down a flight of steps which led to the warm waters of a tank. There are several hot springs in the area. Beyond were bathing ghats on the banks of the Alaknanda.

The town has a single paved street. I managed to find a room for the night in a small house whose owner let it throughout the five months or so of the pilgrim season, but I had to share it with two other families.

The town is situated in a barren valley strewn with stones and boulders. On either side of the valley and to the rear tower the mountains, including the shining white peak of Nilkantha, which rises to a height of 21,640 feet.

Next morning I met Vishnu and we walked along the lengthy valley which runs to the rear of the town. The golden ball and spire of the temple gleamed in the sunlight.

"Any news of Satish?" I asked him.

"No, none. I don't suppose there ever will be. He has completely disappeared into the blue."

We started to climb the slopes of a mountain. Vishnu's training as a dancer obviously stood him in good stead, for he ascended the steep incline with the ease and grace of a gazelle. I soon found myself well behind him. He stopped and waited for me. For some moments we stood and looked at Badri, lying below us in the distance.

"The history of the town stretches back into the far-off past," he said. "For centuries pilgrims have been coming here and then, after visiting the temple, going on over the Himalayas to the sacred mountain and lake of Kailas and Manasarowar in Tibet. Of course, they can't do that now. In a cave not far from here at Vyasa Gupha, the Vedas were written down by a great sage, Maharshi Vyasa."

After more strenuous climbing over the rugged terrain, Vishnu stopped and pointed to the pinnacles of a mountain lying perhaps six miles away.

"Beyond that range, all the mountains you see lie in Tibet and behind the mountain I'm pointing at is a Chinese look-out post."

The scene about us was wild and barren but magnificent beyond all superlatives. Towering snowclad mountains, range upon range, reared upwards towards a clear blue sky, and a glacier, a shining river of ice, wound its way down a valley. Just visible between the peaks of the mountains ahead of us was the fabulous land of Tibet, which I had once longed to visit. But not now. I was not at all sure that I should have preferred not to have seen it, now that everything this remote country stood for is being stamped out by the Chinese Communists and their gun-posts are set at strategic points along the length of the Indo-Tibetan border. When I think of Tibet now, it is not of that mystic country's tragic present but of her past, which is the way I think of my own rapidly fading country these days, when the jackals are out in their thousands and snapping at the body of the dying lion.

We started off on our way back to Badri. Vishnu said he would be staying there till about the end of October. Soon after that the snow starts falling and the passes are closed for seven months.

I left Badri next morning, walked back to Joshimath and the bus which was going the one hundred and seventy miles to Rishikesh. I got out of it at Nandaprayag, having next to no idea as to where or how I was going to proceed from there.

I studied my map. There was a road of sorts marked which ran east from the town along the banks of the Pindar River and then turned northwards towards the eastern slopes of Mount Trisul, with Nanda Devi lying north-east. There was also a footpath marked leading from the town and going more directly towards the south-westerly slopes of the mountain, and this, I felt, was the more likely route to take. Even so, to start off along this trail or along the road, with only the haziest of ideas as to where the goal of my journey lay, smacked not so much of mere foolishness, but madness. I would somehow, I realised, have to get some facts in the township as to the rough whereabouts of my goal and how best to get there.

I went for a walk to think things over and I came upon some ascetics who had gathered in an open space near the outskirts. One was sitting a little apart from the rest. He had a well-shaped face and an intelligent expression and he was wearing the saffron robe of a sadhu.

I walked up to him. He did not evince the slightest surprise at my sudden appearance. I asked him if he would give me some advice and he replied that he would do so if he could and told me to go ahead and explain what kind of advice I wanted. I then recounted to him how I had met a certain yogi in the forests near Mount Abu who had spoken to me of an ascetic who lived on the south-westerly slopes of Mount Trisul, and that ever since hearing about him I had wanted to meet this man, but I did not know his name nor the exact place where his cave was situated.

When I reached the end of this rigmarole, the sadhu then asked me courteously the name of the yogi who had spoken to me of the Trisul ascetic and a few further questions. Then he said he was sorry; he could not help me personally. He had been up to Badrinath and was now on his way back to his place of abode, which was in the forest of Brahmapuri near Rishikesh. He had no idea as to who this ascetic might be, but there were several yogis in the town who would be returning to their caves high up in the mighty Himalayas and he would find out from them whether they could throw any light on my problem. He told me to return to the same place the following morning.

Next morning when I was buying a few provisions at a shop I was approached by two ascetics, one of whom was covered with grey ash from head to foot. They asked me whether I was the woman who had asked the sadhu the previous evening about an ascetic who lived in the Mount Trisul area. I said yes. I felt an upsurge of hope when they asked me this. But one of them went on to say that he did not know who the man might be but that they themselves would be returning to their caves which lay on the southern base of the mountain. The journey would take them four days and they would be starting off that afternoon. The following morning they would reach a cave inhabited by three yoginis. I could probably stay with these women for a few days and I might find out something there about the ascetic whom I was seeking. Various holy men lived in the area and they might be able to help or to offer me some worthwhile suggestions. If I wanted to travel with them, I should go to the open space where I had spoken to the sadhu soon after noon that day.

I did not know what sort of people those two men were but they had struck me as being genuine holy men. One of them carried a staff with a three-pronged trident on top, showing that he was a follower of Shiva. If I set off with them I might well be embarking on a wild-goose chase, but that was a chance I felt I would have to risk.

So I made some hasty preparations, bought myself a staff and some more provisions and soon after mid-day returned to the open piece of ground. The sadhu had left, but the two yogis were there. When they saw me, one of them pulled up his staff which he had stuck in the ground and we set off.

We walked towards some pine-clad hills and from there followed a path through the woods, emerging some time later on to a grassy plateau covered with wild flowers. Before us lay a chain of mountains, with the peaks of further chains towering up in the background. Neither of the two yogis spoke as we walked. At the end of the plateau, walled off by lofty mountains, they made unerringly for a narrow gorge. A path of sorts ran through it which was flanked by a crystal-clear stream. From the heights above us cascaded several waterfalls. The landscape became more and more rugged and had a wild beauty which was beyond description.

We came upon a group of five yogis who had erected a small tent by some rocks, made of pieces of cloth and a few sticks. The ash-covered yogi asked them where they were going. One of them replied that they lived in the forests of eastern Nepal and were returning there after having visited the sacred places in this part of the Himalayas. My presence puzzled them and the ash-covered one explained that I was hoping to find a certain ascetic who lived somewhere in the vicinity of Mount Trisul and that I was going with them as far as a cave inhabited by some yoginis. This explanation seemed to satisfy them.

For anyone other than a Nepalese who wants to visit that country which lay to the east of us, a pass has to be obtained. Even Indians are required to have one. But yogis are like birds who can travel freely over frontiers forbidden to others, and they know of secret passes and tracks. They reminded me of the gipsies who likewise in Britain and on the Continent know of secret trails leading across the borderlands and over the frontiers which divide one country from another.

Dusk was falling. We stopped by a group of deodars. No fire was lit. I sat under one of the huge trees a little way from the two yogis and ate a couple of chapatties, some coconut cakes and fruit. Then I unrolled my sleeping-bag and got into it.

There is a wide variety of animal life in the region: various kinds of deer, brown and black bears, snow leopards and wolves. But the odds of being attacked by one of the fiercer kinds of animals are not very great. If a wolf approached when I was asleep and felt inclined for a meal, that would be just too bad as far as I was concerned. Anyway, there would be nothing I could do to protect myself and so I dismissed the matter from my mind. Of more concern to me was how I was eventually going to find my way back to Nandaprayag. I had a large-scale map of the region with me and a compass, but I had not taken any compass bearings while on the way and I was now in the heart of wild mountain territory. But it was pointless to worry.

We set off early next morning. The yogi who was not covered with ash—I never learnt either of their names—said to me as we walked along that human beings should not waste their time in petty anxieties and concern for their safety but should take a lesson from birds and animals who do not grumble at rain and heat or worry as to what the next day may bring, but live at one with nature.

"We trust ourselves to life itself," he said.

Perhaps he had sensed my thoughts of the previous evening, which had not been altogether carefree.

We walked across a grassy meadow, perhaps a mile in extent. Pine forests clothed the surrounding hillsides and the base of the mountains, while their upper reaches were covered with long sweeping slopes of virgin snow. Crowning the summits were clusters of white clouds.

"What do you think of our scenery?" asked the ash-covered yogi.

"It's heavenly," I replied, as indeed it was.

We started to ascend the slopes of a mountain and the scenery became more barren, yet beautiful in its stark magnificence.

The ash-covered yogi pointed to a cavern several hundred feet above us, perched like a swallow's nest on the edge of a perpendicular drop.

"That's where the yoginis live," he said.

We passed some brilliant blue gentians and white velvety edelweiss, some growing in drifts of snow.

The yoginis must have seen us coming, for as we approached their cave two came forward to meet us. They both had long uncombed locks and were wearing unbleached off-white saris. The oldest one looked about thirty and the youngest around twenty-five. Neither seemed at all surprised to see me and the two yogis and I had the curious feeling that they were indeed expecting us. The atmosphere is so clear and uncontaminated in

Himachal, and the great majority of the ascetics here live such simple and purified lives, with their consciousness fixed on the sublime, that it is possible that they are able to see and hear things that most of us are not, and perhaps know in advance when persons are approaching their secluded abodes.

The older of the two said to me, with a charming smile, "Yes, you may stay here."

And these words of hers confirmed my opinion that in some way they had known I was coming.

The two yogis, saying they wanted to be on their way, turned and started to walk down the mountain. Not a word had they said to the yoginis about bringing me here. As the non-ash-covered one passed me, he nodded a good-bye and gave me a piercing, almost amused, look which seemed to say, 'Oh, yes, there may be a few things in this life of which you are unaware!'

I was taken to a small cave which lay a short distance beyond the yogini's. There was nothing in it.

Later, I went down to the women's cave, carrying a packet of rice and some dried apple rings as a gift. Two white saris were blowing out from a line and there was a smell of cooking.

The yoginis were pleased with my gift. I met the third member of the little group. She was older than the other two, in her late fifties perhaps, and grey hair hung far down her back. Her name, she told me, was Yogini Chakreswari. The other two were the Yoginis Savitri and Draupadi.

I was invited into the cave or, rather, caves, for it was a triple one, each cave running into the next. The first, which was open fronted, was used for cooking and laundering. There were several large iron pots in it and one was set over a low fire in which various roots were being boiled. We walked through into the middle cave, which had an opening in the front like a window. On the rear wall was a small carving of Shiva and there were two carved pillars in the centre of the cave. They told me that they usually meditated and read the sacred scriptures in this room. The last cave was in almost total darkness, having no opening to let in the light except that which entered it from the central cave. They said that they slept here.

I asked them what they lived on and they said they ate what they could find in the way of roots, berries, herbs and nuts and they drank only water. Very occasionally they received a gift of food from a passing pilgrim or visitor as they had done from me.

This cave, they said, had been lived in for centuries by various ascetics, as had many of the caves in the Himalayas.

"Some of these caves," said Yogini Chakreswari, "are situated very high up near the peaks of mountains and are inhabited by yogis who have learnt to withstand the bitterest weather. Some caves have been the abodes of great rishis. Most of these are known only to a few yogis and ascetics."

There were some pine trees growing on a wide ledge of rock not far from my cave and I set about gathering some sticks and making a fire. Then I put on some rice to boil. Water was no problem. There were several ice-cold rills nearby.

Yogini Savitri came along to my cave later, carrying a pot of cooked roots for me. She was the one who looked about thirty.

On her face was a look of calm joy. I could not doubt that she was happy in the life she had chosen in spite of its many rigours.

I asked her what had made her take it up and she said that for many years, ever since she was a child, she had hoped to take up a religious life. She had left her parents' house and stayed at various ashrams in different parts of the country but none of them fulfilled her needs. Then, when she was staying at an ashram in Varanasi, she happened to meet an ascetic who was down there on a pilgrimage from the Himalayas and he told her about Yogini Chakreswari and suggested that she go and see her. This she did, and she knew from the moment of her arrival that at last she had found the place where she could take up the holy life under her true guru.

"During those years when I was searching for my guru I did not spend all my time in ashrams," she said. "I sometimes returned to my parents' home in Lucknow and I listened to the news on the wireless and I read the daily papers like everyone else. I came to realise more strongly each day the chaotic state the world was in, including my own country. Wars, corruption, riots—almost everywhere seemed to be in a state of upheaval and acute tension.

I became very much aware that any peace and calm I found would have to be found within; I could not expect to find it in the world."

"But up here things are very peaceful," I said.

"Yes, up here a spirit of calm still reigns as it has done for untold centuries. But it may be broken at any time. Look at Tibet. An outer peace, even the deep peace which one finds up here, is too precarious to rely on, although one accepts it gratefully when one finds it somewhere, as a passing boon, as it were. The only true peace is what one discovers within and that is particularly so these days when the world is passing from one age to another.

"Not everyone likes being in the Sacred Range," she continued, "particularly in a lonely region such as this. A primitive man or a worldly man would find such a place 'cold'. But many people, and we who live up here, use a different word to describe this great range and that is the word 'pure'."

She pointed to a far-off range, the peaks all mantled in snow and ice, and said, "White has always been a symbol, both in the East and the West, for purity, wisdom and truth. Here these qualities have been made manifest. Nature is at her most sublime, and since the distant past down to the present many of the most spiritual men and women that Bharat has produced have chosen to live here. These white peaks also symbolise abstract thought, something which a developed human being can meditate upon but which a primitive man cannot do. Even the idea of the abstract strikes him as 'cold', for he is very materialistic and the abstract is ideal and non-material."

That night I sat for some time with my sleeping-bag wrapped around me. When the sun had sunk, an icy chill filled the atmosphere.

I thought of what the yogini had said about the chaotic state of the world in this era, a chaos which is matched very often by the equally chaotic state of men's minds, the inner and the outer being equally confused.

During past ages in civilised lands the external world has always been recognised as a source of dissatisfaction and suffering. To find a way out of this suffering which living with his hopes and aims centred on the outside world entailed, man would turn about and seek a refuge within his innermost self, which in previous ages had always been a place of calm and silence and, at the best, enlightenment.

But this is far from being the case nowadays. Man rushes out to the world to escape from the chaos within, to be greeted by an equal chaos outside. He runs back into himself again but the fears and tumult have not lessened. His inner self today has become unbearable, not to say unlivable, so he hurries back into the world again to be met with wars, upheavals, disturbance, the outward signs of the chronic inner unbalance. Despairing, he asks himself where he can turn for refuge. The old religions and the old ways have lost much of their meaning for him. The psychiatrist's probing questions, the couch, do not really help. The psychiatrist is often as neurotic and unbalanced as his patients. Where can he go, then? And the answer is nowhere. Man has lost his age-long refuge, the inner shrine where he could commune with his soul in peace. Chaos reigns within and without. Moreover, there are many today who have lost the art of being able to retreat within themselves into the disordered interior. These persons can only live in the outer world and the outer world mercilessly grinds them down. Unable to reach even a disordered world within, they have ceased to believe in the interior realm. They are the complete extroverts. They cannot bear to be alone in a silent room even for a few minutes and so they turn the wireless on or ring up a friend or flip through the pages of a magazine. Silence and solitude must be avoided at all costs.

Where lies the glimmer of an answer which will lead modern man, those who still believe in the ancient refuge, out of his spiritual crisis? The sage says that it lies in courage and daring: the courage to venture within again in spite of the chaos of whirling thoughts and fears, and to sit there until the pace slackens and silence begins to seep back. And, he would remark, a little housework is necessary too, a cleaning up and a throwing out of the debris.

The night sky shone with a thousand stars, so brilliant and appearing so close that it seemed I had only to put out a hand to touch one. The white peaks shone with an unearthly light and the silence was so profound that it was like a living force. But the cold cut me to the bone.

When I woke next morning I felt stiff all over. With cramped fingers I lit a fire and drank a mug of tea under the airy branches of the pines while the sun warmed my frozen limbs.

The morning was one of breath-taking beauty, with white clouds hanging like wreaths over the mountain ranges.

Later that morning I saw in the distance the tiny figures of four men, three on horseback and the fourth walking beside a laden pony. They were approaching the mountain from the direction of Nandaprayag and were heading northwards in the direction of Trisul. I decided I would try and go along with them. I thanked the three women ascetics for having me and Yogini Chakreswari said that I could stay again in the cave on the way back if I liked, for which offer I was grateful. Then I hurried down the mountain.

By the time I reached the lower slopes, the men and their ponies were ahead of me across the plain. I waved and shouted and finally caught their attention. To my relief, they stopped and waited for me to catch up with them.

The party consisted of three men and a boy. Two of the men spoke English and they told me that they were returning to their village, which was in a valley by the slopes of Mount Trisul, after having made a trip to Nandaprayag to sell goods and buy supplies. I was welcome to go along with them to the mountain.

They naturally wanted to know why I wished to go there and why I was travelling by myself. I told them that I was on a pilgrimage and that I had heard that Trisul was a sacred mountain, an abode of the gods, a very beautiful mountain, moreover, and so I had decided to visit it. This satisfied them.

By the evening we reached a stone dharmasala where we were to stop for the night. Also staying at the small building was a Tibetan monk and his wife, refugees from their homeland. One sect of Tibetan monks are allowed to marry, but the other sect, which is headed by the Dalai Lama, imposes a vow of celibacy on its members.

Whatever doubts I had had about setting off with the two yogis from Nandaprayag vanished that evening. At the very least now I had seen some superb Himalayan scenery, had met some interesting people and would soon see Mount Trisul, one of the giants of Himachal. I had no regrets about coming. How I would get back to Nandaprayag, or when, ceased to be a matter of concern.

The next morning after a breakfast of tea and chapatties we were off early.

The weather was overcast. As we made our way down into a valley a storm broke and we had to take shelter under some rocks. But by mid-day the clouds started to clear and I had my first sight of the Trisul massif. The villagers pointed out to me the snowy peaks of Nandaghunti and Mount Trisul. Only the upper reaches of the massif were visible, as the Chananiyakot Range lay in front. These mountains before us under the rain-washed sky were a vivid blue and their slopes were covered by the darker blue of huge pine forests, while shining in the distance lay the long white upper reaches of the Trisul Range, the peak itself, which is 23,380 feet high, standing out clearly.

That night we stopped at another small stone building which was situated on the Chananiyakot Range. We arrived there under the bluest of blue skies. One of the men told me that in winter up here there are often snowdrifts lying fifty feet deep. They and the rest of the villagers have to be completely self-contained during the winter months, with sufficient stores to last till spring. If I had come here a few weeks ago, he said, we would have been able to take a quicker route by crossing snow bridges which lay across certain ravines, but these had now melted.

Next day the trail seemed to be heading for the clouds. It climbed higher and higher in ever more twisting spirals. We took it in turns to ride the ponies. Those without a mount held on to a pony's tail and in this way got a little help up the steep and winding track.

High above us, soaring over the snow peaks, was that noblest of birds, the golden eagle. To the ancient Egyptians this bird was a semi-god and was known as the bird of the sun, the lion of the heavens. To the ancient Greeks it was likewise a sun bird of royal lineage, a messenger of the god Zeus. The English named it golden eagle, not so much because of the dark golden colour of its plumage, but because of its connection with the sun. In both Asia and Europe it was trained to hunt, and the golden raptor would sit on the wrists of emperors and kings in the intervals between the chase.

The men had suggested that I stay in their village for a while. I could rent a room in one of their houses and spend some weeks among the mountains. This seemed to me quite a good idea and I told them I would think it over.

"Tomorrow," one of them said, "we reach the village."

We spent that night high up in the mountains, still in the Chananiyakot Range, with wonderful views all around us. The hut was the usual stone building of the sort which are spaced at roughly a day's journey along the trail. The evening was very clear and after supper had been eaten the men treated me to some songs. Under the glittering stars they sang Garhwali jagars, ballads which had been passed down to them by word of mouth through countless generations.

From their village, I felt, with a roof over my head, it would be an easier matter to make inquiries about the ascetic I was looking for. My quest struck me as being very much like the proverbial hunt for the needle in the haystack. Nevertheless, having got this far, I was now hopeful that I would eventually achieve my goal.

We were greeted next morning with clear skies. The Garhwalis pointed out a row of blue hills lying far below us and said that their homes were hidden among those hills in a valley to the far side of them.

Just as we had started off, two yogis appeared walking up the track towards the hut. One was wearing only a loin-cloth, the other had a length of saffron-coloured material wrapped around his shoulders which hung to his knees.

They were friendly and asked me what I was doing up here. I told them that it had long been an ambition of mine to travel in the Himalayas and now my wish was being achieved. They then told us that they had been spending the last few days with a very holy sannyasi who lived in a cave higher up on one of the nearby peaks, a cave well above the tree line.

I immediately felt that perhaps this ascetic might be able to help me. Anyway, I would like to meet him, and I asked the two yogis if they would give me directions as to how I could reach his cave.

A heated argument broke out. The Garhwalis told me that I would be utterly foolish to go higher up the range by myself; I would be lost in no time. But I felt very strongly that I should go and I told them that I would find my way to their village later.

The yogi wearing the saffron-coloured cloth seemed to approve of my wish to visit the sannyasi and he told the Garhwalis that it was all to the good that I wanted to see this holy man. He thereupon gave me instructions as to how to proceed to the cave.

"The ascetic's name is Shri Satischandra. When you get there tell him that Yogi Prasannamukh gave you directions as to how to reach his abode."

We parted, the two yogis going on up to the hut while we went down. The Garhwalis now refused to speak to me and kept a morose silence. But when we reached a fork in the trail where I was to leave them, they became friendly again. I bought a few supplies from them and they gave me detailed instructions as to how to reach their village later.

I was on my own now but that did not trouble me. I kept a careful check of my bearings so that I could be sure of finding my way back again. The track was often covered with large patches of thin ice, and carpets of snow lay on the slopes and the ridges. The scenery was glorious but there was more to it than a superb beauty. The very atmosphere was charged with powerful currents which could be sensed in the stillness and solitude of these mountains. They have been set in motion by the rishis and yogis who have meditated in the Great Snow Range for untold centuries, and who can say, except perhaps the ascetics themselves, how far beyond these mountains the currents extend. Indians say that the rishis can be compared to an iceberg, in that it is believed that in all eras only a small percentage of them, like the tip of an iceberg which shows above the waters, live in and are known to the outside world. The majority, something like three-quarters, remain hidden. They live secluded lives in the high mountain ranges or deep in the jungles, alone or with a few disciples, and few persons in the outside world know of their existence or their whereabouts. But the effect of these highly advanced men on the world beyond their isolated dwelling places is said to be far from negligible.

A modern sage who spent the latter part of his life largely in solitary retirement within his own ashram was Sri Aurobindo. During a period when he emerged temporarily from his isolation, he was asked by a Western journalist why he did not go out and about in the world doing some good. Replied the sage briefly, "How do you know that I don't?"

High above me on a ridge was a landmark the yogi had told me to look out for: a ruined Buddhist stupa. When I reached it, I scrambled up an incline to inspect it. Although most of the top had gone, the base was still intact and round it there was a design composed of that Aryan symbol, the swastika. These were evolutionary ones; that is, the top arms of the centre prongs were facing right. When the symbol is reversed, that is, when the top arm faces left, then it is a symbol for everything that is retrograde and evil, a symbol of black magic. Hitler and his Nazis used the reversed symbol.

Soon after leaving the stupa I came upon a near invisible track leading off the one I was following. It zigzagged up the stony mountainside and in some places disappeared altogether because of drifts of snow which covered it. I came round some rocks to see the yogi's cave lying a short distance above me.

Over the dark entrance to it hung several large icicles like monstrous crystal teeth, while in front lay a sheet of ice with a carpet of snow and stones extending out on either side. Hardly a cosy dwelling place, but cosiness is not something that interests a true ascetic.

The place seemed deserted. There was an iron cooking pot at the side of the entrance and I could just make out a carved ceiling in the dim interior and what appeared to be a small picture hanging on a wall. I stooped under the icicles to get a better look and see whether anyone was in. But the cave appeared to be empty.

As I straightened up and turned round I was confronted by the owner of the cave, who had no doubt been silently watching me peer into his chilly dwelling place.

He was near skeletal in appearance. Wild white hair surrounded an emaciated face but an extraordinary inner strength was revealed in a pair of gleaming eyes. Their glance probed me and almost sent me flying down the mountain. I quickly told him that Yogi Prasannamukh had given me directions as to how to reach the cave. Could I, please, have a few words with him?

His burning eyes never left my face and I was beginning to feel uncomfortable. After a long pause he said, "Have you come to question me about spiritual matters?"

"No—well, not exactly, I—"

He snapped out, "Then we'll not waste each other's time," and indicated that I should leave.

The meeting had not got off to a good start and already seemed to have grounded. I said I wanted to talk to him because I hoped he might be able to tell me the whereabouts of a certain ascetic. He said nothing, but hurried into the cave like a wiry mountain goat while I stood outside wondering what to do. I would no more have ventured to take another look inside now than I would if I had known a tiger was in there. But I called out presently, asking him if I could possibly have a few words with him and he rapped out, "Wait where you are."

I waited. The minutes passed and I looked around for somewhere to sit down but there was nowhere and so I stood. I must have stood for twenty minutes or so before he re-emerged. The only thing he wore was a dun-coloured piece of cloth which years ago might have been orange.

As though realising my frailty in not wanting to sit on the ice and scorning such weakness, he promptly sat down on it and gestured that I was to be seated also. I sat. A bed of nails would perforce have been more comfortable than this freezing sheet of glass.

"Yes?"

That was my cue and I started off nervously telling him why I had come and my hope that I would eventually be able to find my way to this ascetic. He stopped me after I had been talking a short while and told me to recount every direction that Yogi Rishabhdeva had given me. Every so often he would stop me again and ask a question. The longer I spoke, the more my feeling increased that he knew several of the places I mentioned and the various landmarks I was to look for and that he might even know who the ascetic might be.

When I had finished speaking, he got up and started to walk further up the mountain, I following behind him. The mountain flattened out at the top and we walked across a narrow plateau with jagged rocks sticking up out of the arid soil and the patches of snow. And clearly visible in all its majestic beauty lay the Trisul massif to the north, perhaps five or six miles distant.

We came to a tall solitary rock which towered upwards like an obelisk in the barren landscape. Below it was a curiously shaped pool and as I looked at it I exclaimed, "A lotus leaf!"

And I remembered the words spoken to me by Yogi Rishabhdeva which I had related to the ancient ascetic standing beside me: "Look out for a pool which lies at the top of a high mountain close to the Trisul range and which is shaped like a lotus leaf and is guarded by a tall rock like a finger which points up to the sky."

The old ascetic walked to the edge of the plateau and showed me the route that I must follow down the mountain and across the wide valley which separated it from Mount Trisul.

I just had time to thank him for his help before he had set off back to his cave. I watched his incredibly thin figure with its thatch of white hair hurrying along the mountain top and then disappearing down a stony ridge; then I started to walk down over the far end of the plateau, following the route the old hermit had indicated.

CHAPTER TWENTY-TWO

AN UNKNOWN LAND

I CROSSED THE plain and reached the lower slopes of Mount Trisul at a place the old hermit had pointed out to me. The knowledge that I was now actually on the mountain, its peak hidden behind clouds, was a wonderful feeling. I decided to spend the first night under a group of deodars. Camp number one. A scent of resin filled the air like the fragrance of incense sticks. The sun shone. White clouds sailed like ships across the blue expanse of sky.

Shri Satischandra had pointed out a waterfall falling like a silver ribbon over some high rocks. It was not far from the deodars. I went there and collected a pan of water and washed. As I was walking back to the deodars I noticed a landmark that he had told me to look out for. High above me, perhaps two miles up the mountainside, was a tall rock, and perched on top of it was a pine tree. The rock and tree stood out like a signpost on that barren stretch of ground and I knew now that I was going the right way, for it was one of the signs that the forest sage of Mount Abu had told me about too.

When I started off next morning on the day's climb I felt well rested and braced for the trek ahead. I walked steadily towards the rock. It was further away than it had appeared to be. Beyond it the ground swept upwards towards a distant valley bordered by rocky walls. When I reached the end of this valley I could see a bare hill lying ahead and it was topped by two jagged peaks, the nearer one curving 'like a breaking wave'. All I had to go by were these various 'signposts', yet I realised now that they were as exact in their way as any map. As I caught sight of each one and passed it, my eyes watchful for the one somewhere ahead, I was filled with a growing confidence. By the time I reached the hill, the sun was directly above me. I stretched out on a patch of grass shaded by some rocks. I had made up my mind to reach an escarpment of rock further up the mountain and spend the night there. Reaching it would probably take another two hours or so of climbing.

As I was idly looking at the shale-covered ground leading up to it, I saw a leopard walk from behind a boulder and make for the escarpment, where it disappeared, perhaps into a cave. I thought again about spending the night there. But I had not walked far enough that day to stop where I was and make camp two. So I got up, having decided to increase my pace a little, pass the escarpment, giving it a fairly wide berth, and spend the night at whatever likely site I could find some distance above it.

It was after I had passed it and was walking slowly up a steep stretch that the sky suddenly darkened and there was a fierce spatter of hailstones. The temperature dropped and the hail changed to an icy rain. I made for the shelter of the nearest rocks and sat huddled in a small hollow. The sky became black and I did not know when day ended and night began. A gale started to blow and sheets of icy rain poured down the mountain. I was still dry, thanks to my rock shelter, but I felt nearly frozen with cold. I was much too cold to try and sleep. I sat there, my chin on my knees, thinking that if the weather did not improve soon I would surely die from exposure. I gave up looking at the weather. Each time I had glanced at it, hoping for some sign of improvement, the sky was the same stygian black. An eternity went by.

When I finally forced myself to raise my head and look out, only a few heavy drops of rain were falling. The sky was still dark but here and there were patches of light and I could actually see for a few yards beyond my hiding-hole.

A pallid sun appeared high up in the sky and I reckoned that the time must be around noon. My watch had stopped and no winding or shaking would make it go again. It had obviously died of the cold.

I crawled outside and sat against a rock to thaw. The patches of yellowish light increased and I knew I must make the effort to move on while the weather was moderately good, if only to find a better shelter.

Staff in hand, I began to walk slowly up the mountain, forcing myself to put one foot in front of the other. It never occurred to me to go back. I had come so far and things had gone so well up to yesterday that I did not doubt that conditions would soon start to improve again.

The ascent became much steeper and my progress ever more slow. That evening I again took shelter under some rocks. The night was so bitterly cold that once again I thought I would surely die from exposure, but my memories of that night are vague. I had eaten only a few apple rings and my fatigue was such that in spite of the cold I dropped off to sleep intermittently during the long icy hours. In the morning everything was blotted out by a thick freezing mist. Towards mid-day, when the sun revealed itself as a faint yellow blur overhead, the mist grew less dense and I left the shelter of the rocks and started once more on my climb.

The scene was something out of this world. Here and there were tufts of green grass and patches of snow, but most of the ground was covered by shale which was frozen to the earth. Rocks of all shapes and sizes loomed ahead, some as large as galleons, and off them the mist curled in strange patterns and streamed from them like smoke pouring from a cauldron. At one moment it blotted out part of the landscape and then parted to reveal towering cliffs and deep gullies. I took advantage of any stretch of ground that was visible for some yards ahead. I progressed as if in a dream, only half aware of my surroundings, yet keeping a watchful eye on what lay before me.

I was brought out of this dreamy state when I suddenly realised that I had ceased to climb and was walking across flat ground. From what I could see about me, I had reached a huge plateau. Wreaths of mist condensed and dispersed and were blown upwards by the wind. Every now and then I thought I glimpsed through the whirling veils what appeared to be a small fire burning in the distance. A fire—that meant human beings and warmth! I set off towards it, stopping when the mist blotted it out and starting when I saw it again. I strained my eyes keeping it in view. I dared not lose sight of it for long. It was a beacon of hope shining in the mist-shrouded landscape, beckoning me forwards. But it never seemed to get much nearer and I began to wonder whether the flickering point of flame was a deceptive bog light. I stumbled over the rough ground and then halted a while, leaning on my staff, waiting for the light to reappear.

I have no idea how long I continued like this—one hour, three hours. I lost all sense of time. There were moments when I felt that I had been walking up here through the mist for days and would go on walking through it for days to come, the flickering point of light ahead of me but never growing any nearer. I felt no anxiety and I had ceased to feel the cold.

Presently I looked ahead, after resting on my staff, and the flame suddenly appeared to be much closer. I could see now that it was a burning log fire and that seated beside it were two figures. Every so often a thick veil of mist would sweep across them, momentarily hiding them from my sight, but I could still see the glow from the fire behind the mist.

As I approached, I saw that the two seated figures were ascetics. One was a boy and the other was an older man whose hair was piled in coils on top of his head. The smoke from the log fire mingled with the veils of mist which blew about them.

I greeted them in the traditional manner, with my palms pressed together. They returned my greeting and then the boy got up and asked me to follow him.

He led me to a cave, where he left me. The cave was shrouded in darkness but I could feel the skin of an animal on the floor. I lay down on it, too tired to even unroll my bedding, and fell into a deep sleep.

When I woke next day the sun was high in the sky. I went outside and found an earthenware jar of water by the cave's mouth and a bowl of food consisting of tubers and some kind of grain. When I had eaten and drank, I took a look at the cave's interior. It was quite large. I was able to stand up in it. A deerskin was stretched out on the floor. There was a smaller cave leading from the main one and it was in semi-darkness. I decided that in the future I would sleep in the small cave and spend the daylight hours in the outer cavern. I had known when I had reached the two ascetics seated by the log fire that I had reached my destination, but how long I would be staying here I did not know.

My cave faced on to a huge amphitheatre which was surrounded by snow peaks. Waterfalls fell from high cliffs. The splendour of the scene was breathtaking. But where were the two yogis? There was no sign of them. I walked along beside the escarpment of rock in which my cave was situated and presently I saw the boy yogi. He was sitting on the grass and appeared to be threading some berries on to a cord. When he saw me he got up and came towards me.

"Are you all right now? Did you sleep well?" he asked.

"Yes, thank you."

"I want to take you to see someone. Will you come now?"

I said I was ready to go along at any time.

"It's across this plain," he said. "Not very far."

We set off. The boy was dressed only in a narrow loin-cloth. His black hair hung well past his shoulders. He had fine sensitive features and looked as though he came from a high-caste family, but I did not ask him any questions about his past and he asked me nothing about mine.

We walked across the plain. It was covered with rough grass, flowers, and stretches of bare stony ground. There were no trees to be seen, only a few clumps of the dwarf rhododendron which grows above the snow line. After crossing this flat expanse, the boy led the way through a wild and hidden valley lying between two peaks. Sometimes the way was half blocked by boulders. Presently the young yogi began to climb up a steep incline, half walking and half running around the rocks like some light-footed deer and then waiting for me to catch up with him.

We reached a cave situated in a cliff-face and hidden among towering boulders. Sitting just inside the entrance on an antelope skin was a man briefly clad in a loin-cloth and with long black hair falling past his shoulders.

Suddenly I knew without any words being spoken that this was the man who Yogi Rishabhdeva had spoken about to me, the man whom I had come to seek on Mount Trisul. Now my search was over.

I pressed my palms together in greeting and sat down in front of him. There was a force, a stillness that radiated from him. I did not want to ask any questions, only to sit in silence before him. The sound of the wind faded, the cry of a bird no longer impressed itself on my consciousness. It was as though I were suspended in silence and that an inner link had formed between this man and myself.

Presently he said, "Call me Ajana. You can come here again tomorrow if you wish."

He spoke in a pleasant, well-modulated voice but there was in it, as there was about the man himself, a sense of effortless power.

The boy and I left the valley and crossed the plain.

"My name is Yogi Sivajaparakh," he told me.

"And what is the name of the other yogi?" I asked.

"His name is Yogi Chennakesavaswami."

I spent the evening sitting outside my cave and looking at the changing colours of the peaks: rose and violet, purple and a dazzling white. I might have been alone on these heights; there was no sign of the other two yogis.

My supper was stark, to say the least. I finished the remainder of the apple rings and cooked a little rice. During the rest of my stay on Trisul the only food I ate was what could be found in the vicinity—roots, herbs, a kind of wild grain, a few berries—no more. All I had to drink was water.

Evening merged swiftly into night. The stars blazed down and the moon rolled across the blue-black sky which was pierced by the glittering snow-capped peaks.

The next day I returned to Ajana's cave, guided there by the young Yogi Sivajaparakh.

Ajana was sitting as I had seen him the day before, on his antelope skin, still and concentrated. His eyes were half closed, as though he were oblivious of the outside world.

I looked at the calm figure before me. He had almost classical features, with a wide sensitive mouth and a perfectly shaped nose and a strong well-formed body. But his physical form apart, his presence seemed to have an aura of radiance about it.

Presently he opened his eyes, raised his right hand, the thumb and forefinger touching, the other fingers upright, and said to me, "When you return to your cave sit down inside it and then enter the cave of your own mind and see what you can discover. Don't come out of it because you feel bored or cold or for any other reason. Stay there for an hour or so—don't condemn or praise—just listen and watch."

He walked along the valley with us and filled a copper loshta with water from a stream which cascaded down a rockface. His whole manner was simple and natural, yet neither then nor later did I cease to be aware for a moment while in his presence that this man was an unique being. He was one of the very few persons I have met who had nothing of the conqueror about him and he was in no way submissive. He might bend and I do not doubt that in the past he had conquered. It was as though he lived in the centre of his being and had thereby acquired an equipose and a harmonious uniting of the strong and the gentle elements in his nature. There is a North Indian adage relating to the sages and rishis that often came to my mind when I was with him or thinking of him. It is: As strong as a thunderbolt and as tender as a flower.

Late that evening I sat down in the inner cave and retired, as it were, within my own mind. I felt that here, undisturbed in the stillness and silence of the cave, I had a better chance than ever before to penetrate deeply within myself and thereby acquire a deeper self-knowledge.

But as I sat there in the darkness and bitter cold of the night, immured within my own mind, I became ever more oppressed by a sense of confinement and a darkness that was deeper than the darkness of the cavern. I watched my thoughts appear and disappear and that night they seemed to be of a particularly mundane and trivial nature. The bony confines of my skull began to feel more and more like a prison, while I, the prisoner, became increasingly aware of a feeling of utter loneliness. I thought it strange that when I set off on my own up the Chananiyakot Range to meet the old recluse and later on Trisul, I had not felt at all lonely or concerned, although I was all by myself in the wilds of the Himalayas. But now, alone and centred within the cave of my own mind, I was lonely as I had never been before. An absolute solitude wrapped me about and it brought no peace or a calming of the thoughts that whirled in my mind. And all the while the darkness seemed to deepen and I was ever more oppressed with a sense of being a prisoner within my own skull. Oh, that Pisces, under whose sign I was born, should transform the two fish into an axe so that I could hew a cleft in the roof of my prison and let in some light! But I had no axe and presently I slumped on to the floor defeated and fell into an uneasy sleep.

When I went to Ajana's cave in the morning he asked me, "Well, what did you discover?"

"Nothing," I said.

"Nothing?"

"Only how trivial are most of my thoughts and how narrow are the limits of my own mind. I felt like a prisoner inside it."

"We must become aware that we are prisoners before we can strive for release. Continue to spend some time each morning and evening 'within yourself'." And he added, "I'll help you."

As the days passed I began to experience a gradual slowing down. My thoughts became fewer, my mind more serene and I lived in the present. When I sat in my cave and shut out the outer world, I still experienced a sense of confinement but I also felt now a certain stillness within. I ceased to struggle against the walls of my skull; I waited and listened.

Then one night I heard the sound of the flute. It was very faint but quite distinct and seemed to come from within the depths of myself. As I listened to the music I had a deep yearning—for what? The music faded and I felt I had received a half-forgotten call.

During the nights which followed I began to hear the call of the flute more clearly.

I asked Ajana, "Who is it who plays the flute?"

And he said, "Ishvara or one of his messengers. Ishvara is the manifestation of the Divine, the Archetype. He is everywhere, within and without, but we only hear the sounds of his flute when our minds are calm and we listen intently."

"What does the sound of his flute mean?"

"The music of his flute reminds us of our true home and calls us back to the source."

Not long after I had begun hearing the sounds of the flute, I had a deeply significant experience. I was sitting in the cave, immersed within myself, when it was as though a sudden gleam of light pierced my mind, like a shaft of sunlight breaking across a darkened landscape. It was a pathway leading me, through the *far side* of the mind, to an unknown land, an invisible and boundless realm which I had been seeking, sometimes consciously, sometimes unconsciously, for the greater part of my life. And paradoxically, although I travelled outwards towards it along a path of light, I also travelled inwards, deeper into myself.

This liberating experience only lasted briefly and then I returned to the confines of myself, but an ambience remained and I knew that, come what may in the future, that brief timeless experience would remain with me like a light shining through the clouds of everyday worldly experience.

When one lives almost continuously in the present, one gives little thought to the future. Simple though the life up here was, I had become completely absorbed in it.

Summer had arrived and most of the days were very hot but the nights were always bitterly cold. When the sun shone, the sky was a pellucid blue and the clouds and the snow peaks were of a purer white than any I had seen elsewhere.

Most of the day I spent by myself. I meditated in my cave, went for long walks and sometimes in the evenings I talked with the two yogis.

It was Yogi Chennakesavaswami who told me one evening as we were sitting by a fire that they were going to spend the night in meditation with Ajana by his cave and that I could go along with them if I wished.

I put on everything I had in the way of clothes and set off with the two. They were dressed in nothing more than their usual loin-cloths.

Ajana was immersed in meditation outside his cave, a living centre of stillness, and the two yogis, after prostrating themselves before him, were likewise soon sunk in meditation.

For some time I gazed at the motionless figure of Ajana before me. Although it was night there was a clarity under the starry skies and those objects not hidden in the velvety shadows were plainly visible. I felt that the veil between the visible world and the invisible was very thin and transparent.

The night hours flowed by. An incomparable silence filled the atmosphere, a silence which spoke.

In the early hours of the dawn the two yogis emerged from their meditations, prostrated themselves once more before Ajana, and then walked away down into the valley. I glanced once more at the utterly still figure before following them.

Sometimes on this great mountain with its numerous snow peaks, its unexplored gullies and secret ravines, its windswept plains and its caves where the ascetics meditate, I used to think about Fo on that other much smaller mountain in Lantao. I knew something of Fo's life before he went to live on the mountain for good. I had questioned him about it and he himself had been quite willing to talk about himself. But of Ajana I knew nothing. He proffered no information about himself nor did he once ask me anything of a personal nature about myself. Whereas I had not hesitated to question Fo about his boyhood and so forth, I would never have dreamed of asking Ajana similar questions. I sensed, although nothing was ever said, a barrier against any such questioning. A kind of invisible fiery fence surrounded him which effectively barred such intrusions, as questions of a personal nature would have been in his case.

Although I knew nothing of the facts of his life I was well aware, nevertheless, that he was a being of a transcendent quality. One was somehow aware that emotions such as fear, anxiety and hatred never touched him and that his consciousness had reached heights of which I had no knowledge. A deep and perpetual calm surrounded him.

I sometimes wondered whether Ajana was his real name or whether he had a name at all, but I was never to know.

However, one day I did learn something concerning him and this by a direct question, though not of course put to Ajana himself.

It was blazing hot. I had climbed high up the steep slope above my cave and I was gazing out across the ampitheatre towards the peaks and valleys opposite when I saw Yogi Sivajaparakh coming up towards me swinging a string of beads.

I had seen him carving these beads from a piece of sandalwood and now he had threaded them on a yellow cord. I did not ask him how he had acquired the sandalwood or the cord but I had watched him chip away at the beads with a sharp knife, getting them rounded and all to the same size.

Now he handed the necklace to me, saying, "It's for you."

And he went on to tell me that it had a hundred and eight beads, that was a sacred number and that sandalwood was a sacred tree. Then he suggested that I perform a japa each morning, pronouncing the sacred syllable 'Om' one hundred and eight times and passing a bead through my fingers each time I pronounced it to keep a check on the number.

Quite spontaneously he suddenly burst into a song which began, "Na me bhaktah pranasyati . . ."

"That means," he said, 'No! God never deserts a true devotee.'"

He took the necklace from me and began tightening a knot, an intent expression on his face. As he was doing this I asked him directly, "Tell me, who is Ajana?"

He looked at me with his clear eyes and said, "He is a liberated being, a Jivanmukta."

Presently I asked him, "Why is it that so many yogis, like yourself and Yogi Chennakesavaswami, live in the solitude of the mountains?"

"God speaks more clearly in deserts and on mountain tops," he replied.

This boy was a strange mixture of youthfulness and maturity.

When I went for walks I did not go up the valley in which Ajana's cave was situated, as I did not wish to invade his privacy. The only times I went there was when I received a message from one of the yogis saying that it would be alright for me to go along.

At the time that Sivajaparakh gave me the necklace—and 'events' up here were so infrequent that I could remember each one very clearly—I had not seen Ajana for days. Several times I was on the point of asking one or other of the yogis whether I might go along to the cave but something always stopped me from making this request.

Then one afternoon when I was sitting just inside my cave Ajana's face appeared at the entrance. He was bent over and he gestured that I was to come outside.

We walked up a nearby slope, from the top of which could be seen a sweeping panorama of the surrounding countryside. Although the magnificence of the scenery never ceased to stir me, on this occasion it was not the snow peaks and the distant ranges of purple mountains which held my attention, but Ajana. This was the first time I had seen him away from his cave in the valley. He stood on the barren rocks staring up at the sky, his long hair blowing out behind him. He looked about thirty-five but he might well have been older. But whatever his actual age, there was a quality of agelessness about him.

The only sound for some minutes was the grass stirring in the wind, and then he said quietly, "The unknown land is really the land of the spirit. After our long wanderings in time and space we are called back to the eternal source of our being. Fix your consciousness within and not on this transitory external world and then the trackless path leading to the invisible realm of the spirit will become ever clearer to you," and he gave one of his rare but beautiful smiles.

Something of the ambience and power of his presence remained with me when I got back to my cave. Since I had met this man I had come to feel ever more strongly that inner links had been formed that, come what may to me in the future, could never be broken.

His enlightened and liberated state was something that one was intensely aware of. The young yogi had said that Ajana was a Jivanmukta, and yet, I thought, although he has soared far beyond the flight of birds, he is still a man.

I stood outside the cave looking across the expanse of grass and stones to the distant slopes opposite, where the entrance to the valley was just discernible in the violet light of dusk.

"He is still a man," I thought, "a human being..."

Some words stirred in my brain, words once spoken by Fo on an island in the South China Sea. He had said, when I had remarked to him that Lantao seemed to me to be different in some way to the other islands, as though it had undergone a transformation, "Let's be practical. Lantao is composed of earth and rock and is surrounded by the ocean just like all the other islands. So if there is a difference, it can't lie in the basic ingredients. The difference must lie elsewhere." And I had been left with an unsolved question.

Then I saw in my mind's eye two white eagles—messengers of God—alighting on a hill in southern India. They were different from other birds of their species; the predatory instinct had vanished or died in them. Yet, as the yogini had reminded me, they were still eagles.

Now I had met a man on Mount Trisul whose consciousness had transcended the narrow limits of the mind and who was forever free. It was as though the basic ingredients of his being had been purified and transmuted, the dross metals transformed into gold, thus enabling him to dwell in the pure land of the spirit even though he might live on this mountain. Yet Ajana was still a human being, and the very fact of his humanity offered the sure hope that others too would one day also achieve the great accomplishment.

I had solved the question which had been at the back of my mind ever since I had left Lantao. The human being must transform himself, transmute the dross of his nature into gold, before he can become a dweller in the pure and immaterial realm of the spirit, for the pure and immaterial do not mix with the impure and material. No sooner had I resolved the question than it was as if a hand came out of a cloud, its forefinger pointed directly at me. And I realised that the most enlightened of human beings, the most inspired of teachings, could do little or nothing for me unless I myself strove with heart and mind for this inner synthesis and transmutation and kept the goal constantly in mind. I had seen transformations of various kinds and degrees in my journey through the East, the most sublime of which had taken place in a man. But these encounters along the way and my meeting with Ajana would be of hardly any significance unless I realised clearly the need for a transformation here, within myself.

To live from day to day, from hour to hour and from moment to moment. Not to look behind or to dream of the future. The past is behind, and the future (which may never arrive) is in front, while the present is in the middle. By living here and not there one may more easily experience the timeless, and it is the timeless which is of the spirit, the bright central point of our beings.

I found myself living 'here' and I began to experience more frequently that state of living within the centre of myself. Fo's words to me in Lantao about keeping in the centre of oneself became a reality and not simply a theoretical concept, and thereby I achieved an equilibrium I had rarely known previously.

The days passed. I did not ask myself, How long have I been living here? When will I be leaving? And I began to feel Ajana's presence again when I was by myself in the cave or walking alone on the mountain. Helped by his presence, I found that I was sometimes able to reach the land beyond the rock of my own skull and live briefly in that realm for which I had so long been seeking.

One chilly evening when I was sitting by a fire with the two ascetics, Yogi Chennakesavaswami told me that Ajana had left the valley that day and so there would be no point in my going along to his cave any more.

Ajana had left without having said a word to me that he would be going. News of his departure would have caused me a sense of unbearable loss had I not come to realise that, although it was unlikely I would ever see him again, I could not lose him in any real sense. Wonderful though it was to have sat before him outside his cave, I knew that his physical presence or absence was of relative unimportance to me now. His true presence would never leave me wherever I might go. I *knew* there could be no real separation between us. It was he who had guided my footsteps up the mountainside and had brought me to his cave, and he had helped dispel something of the darkness within myself. Why should I feel a sense of loss when I had lost nothing except his physical presence?

The grass was turning yellow. Autumn was approaching. There was nothing to keep me any longer on the mountain now that Ajana had gone. Moreover, I could not possibly live here during the winter months. When I told Yogi Chennakesavaswami that it was time I left, he said that he would come with me down the mountain.

"In the spring and summer," he said, "we yogis share the Sacred Range with pilgrims and visitors. When winter approaches, they leave the remote places and the shrines and Himachal belongs to us. We alone remain here among the snows and the icy winds."

I asked what he wore then and he pointed to his cotton loincloth—"Just this."

I do not profess to know how ascetics living in the Himalayas in the freezing winter temperatures amid the snow and ice manage to survive.

Next day I started off with the two yogis down the mountainside. They knew of caves along the way where we could spend the nights.

Two days later we reached the base of Trisul and stood looking across the valley at the Chananiyakot Range opposite. I thanked the two for all the help they had given me while I was living on Trisul and said that I would often think of them in the days to come.

"Separation is Maya," were the last words Yogi Chennakesavaswami said to me before we parted.

When I reached Shri Satischandra's cave on the Chananiyakot Range there was no one there. Perhaps he had moved on to some other place. I should have liked to have told him that I had eventually found the way to my destination.

I waited two days at the resthouse on Chananiyakot until a party of villagers arrived who were on their way to Nandaprayag. From Nandaprayag I caught a bus back to Rishikesh and from there I journeyed to Bombay, where I boarded a ship to England.

Before leaving Britain for Hong Kong, I had left my affairs in what I believed to be good and safe hands. I had been very wrong. During the months which followed my return to Britain I went through a harrowing period while I was regaining control of my affairs. I have never been able to save much money; a few hundred pounds in the bank is the most I have ever had. I have never had nor wanted more than a few necessary possessions. During this time I lost, not just everything I possessed in the way of money and belongings, but more than everything. I found myself stripped of everything except a few clothes and my own life. I had to start again, not from scratch, but from less than scratch, building up the bare minimum on which to live. Had I not learnt to bend before the wind and to have gained a certain amount of inner balance, I would have been in danger of being knocked down on discovering what had happened to my affairs during my absence. I thought of my great-grandfather, the actor, and the battles he had fought and won during his lifetime, and somehow I pulled through. Although I was reduced to penury, I could at least still call myself an artist. But what sustained me most during this time was the knowledge that the innermost core of my being was and would be forever untouched and immune from all worldly disasters.

More recently, when I have read a paper or listened to the news, I have learnt that the once peaceful Colony I knew is no longer so; there have been riots and unrest in both Hong Kong and Kowloon. And Lantao? I never hear about Lantao. I wrote to Mr. Chan but got no reply. Perhaps he has become a hermit over there. The few friends I still have living in Hong Kong never go to Lantao. And so, never having heard anything to the contrary, I think of that island as I knew it, a place of peace and quiet where you can listen to the silence.

And I think, too, of the many people I met passing through

Hong Kong, people who had left the countries of their birth because they had to or because they wanted to, all of them hoping to find a better life in a new land, and many of them will. Yet we are so vulnerable if we rely overmuch in finding our happiness there, in any particular country. It is here —not there— that we must look for our true fulfilment and set off on the long inner journey to the centre of our innermost selves. Within and transcending the self lies an undiscovered country, an invisible, boundless and nameless realm which is not subject to change.

There is a call. The traveller listens and turns within. He has taken the first step towards that bright land, in comparison to which the countries of this world appear as fleeting shadows.

DATE DUE

IL 62989616			
sent 100224			
due 100406			

PRINTED IN U.S.A.